THE GIRL WITH NO NAME

The Girl with No Name

The Incredible True Story of a Child Raised by Monkeys

MARINA CHAPMAN WITH VANESSA JAMES
AND LYNNE BARRETT-LEE

MAINSTREAM
PUBLISHING

EDINBURGH AND LONDON

First published in Great Britain in 2013 by
MAINSTREAM PUBLISHING COMPANY
(EDINBURGH) LTD
7 Albany Street
Edinburgh EH1 3UG

ISBN 9781780575797

This book is a work of non-fiction based on the life, experiences and
recollections of the author. In some limited cases, names of people have
been changed to protect the privacy of others.

A catalogue record for this book is available
from the British Library

Printed and bound by
CPI Group (UK) Ltd, Croydon, CR0 4YY

3 5 7 9 10 8 6 4

This book is dedicated to Maria Nelly & Amadeo (Forero)
And in memory of loving Maruja

Foreword

'Stop the car, John. I want to get out!'

Hearing my mother's words, my father glanced in the rear-view mirror and skidded to a halt without saying a word. It was as if they had a secret arrangement, though no one knew what she was about to do. The sun was gradually retiring from the sky as dusk approached, and the quiet Yorkshire country lane where we stopped was framed by dark hedges. They stood tall, like a domineering army barrier, protecting the miles of open space beyond.

My mother rushed from the car excitedly, jumped over the hedge and disappeared from view. My fertile young imagination went into overdrive with possibilities. What was going on?

My eyes were fixed on the dense shrubbery as I eagerly watched for her return. After some time, I saw a flash of messy black hair. Mum climbed carefully back over the hedge, holding something in both hands. I watched her petite feet as they dangled over the edge before she jumped nimbly back onto the roadside. She bounced back into the car, panting from her exertions and grinning at my older sister and me with her wide Latino smile. In her lap, firmly clasped, was a large, unhappy wild rabbit. 'I got you a pet, girls!' she announced in delight.

That is the earliest memory I have of my mother, and of my first pet, 'Mopsy'. I wasn't surprised at my mother's actions; when you've been brought up around her quirky and unpredictable performances, this was just another ordinary day.

My mother has often said, 'A life like mine isn't extraordinary in Colombia. Ask any street child, and you'll have your story there.' She has never thought her own story special, as kidnappings, abductions, drugs, crime, murder and child abuse are a common theme in descriptions of Colombia in the 1950s and '60s.

You may be wondering why my mother is choosing to share her story now, after so many decades. Well, to be honest, she's never had the desire to do so. She's not one for chasing the neon lights of fame or gain, for she is simply besotted with having her own home and a family – her ultimate goal and dream.

This book began purely as a daughter writing down her mother's life story. It was my way of documenting our family heritage, as I realised Mum wasn't getting any younger and her memory might start to fade with each year. I also wanted to understand the struggle she had gone through, without which my sister Joanna and I would not even exist.

It's not been easy to piece together Mum's tangled memories, but after two years of chatting over many cups of coffee, delving deep into her past and making a research trip back to Colombia in April 2007, we then started to build a picture from her floating memories. And it soon became clear that we had a great book.

Although we hadn't started the project with this in mind, we began to see the potential benefits that releasing her story might bring, such as the chance of bringing forward Mum's real family. And in a world where millions of parents have lost their children in similar ways, we hoped that her story might bring some hope or comfort.

It also gives us the opportunity to shine a light upon certain charities that are dear to Mum's heart: SFAC (Substitute Families for Abandoned Children), a non-profit charity founded within our family, and the deserving monkey charity NPC (Neotropical Primate Conservation). In addition, we hope that to hear how a fellow human triumphed over adversity in so many ways will provide those in darkness with inspiration.

People often ask me how I learned about Mum's story. It's never been a case of her sitting us down to tell us about her past but more that almost every day something would remind her of her time in the jungle. A vanilla pod, for instance, would open up the paintbox for her to colour a whole magical world for me right there in the kitchen. I loved seeing her excitement

8

when she rediscovered something from her past – like finding a picture of a certain plant or tree, or visiting a market stall to find the variety of banana that was a certain monkey's favourite.

And the story didn't come out only through her words but also as a result of her actions. Being brought up by such a wild and spontaneous mother suggested to us that she herself had been raised by another breed. She has always been our own 'monkey mummy'. She was sometimes criticised for her unorthodox style of parenting, but her only example was from a troop of monkeys. So, from what we've seen, my sister and I are clear – they must be the most loving, fun, inventive, creative parents on the planet!

Typical adventures of a Chapman day out would involve us three girls scaling the trees while Dad studied the bark and lichen below (no doubt pulling out his pocket specimen bottles). At some point there might be an animal-rescue mission, then a spot of getting lost as a result of trying to discover a hidden back road or following something that sparked our curiosity, and the day would usually finish with Mum cooking up steaks on the portable BBQ (which would be brought out without fail in all seasons, even in snow). Thanks to my family, I am rarely able to have a 'normal' walk, simply following the path. Instead, I often return home with twigs in my hair.

Painting a picture of life at home involves revealing some embarrassing truths, although it's only since moving away that I have realised how unusual we were. We had an unconventional way of asking for food at times. As a game, Mum would sometimes sit with a bowl of sweet porridge and have my sister and me ask for it by doing our best monkey impressions. I'm glad social services never visited us!

After dinner, we would often spend what felt like hours grooming one another, by picking through each other's hair. It was a magnificently relaxing activity – the best way to pass the time – and the three of us would appear to be in an almost drugged state. I remember when a case of head lice plagued our school – I think that had to be the highest point of our grooming careers!

When it came to pets, she'd only allow us to have one if they were out of cages during the day. Caged animals upset her. So we had a number of rabbits who hopped around our garden and those of our neighbours, although this didn't work so well with the birds, obviously . . .

As she couldn't read well, I don't remember Mum reading me a bedtime story. Instead, she would invent stories of her own. She would come up with the most magical tales and base them on one of my less admirable character traits (such as lateness or over-sleeping). It would unfold into a gripping story that ultimately taught me valuable lessons in life. She has never let her so-called deficiencies stop her from giving us the best upbringing. The one she never had for herself.

*

As far as Colombia is concerned, much has changed over forty years. Today, it is a vibrant, progressive and, in the main, safe place, but when my mother was growing up there in the 1950s and '60s certain parts were plagued by kidnapping, trafficking, corruption, drugs, crime and injustice. The country's response to attempted social reform by the liberals in the late 1940s brought forward a decade of rebellion and banditry. They call this era 'La Violencia'. Accounts of killings, torture, abduction and rape were common, and there was an atmosphere of insecurity and fear. Hundreds of thousands of deaths (including those of innocent children) came about because of this unrest. That Colombia is very much still in Mum's blood. When she had just given birth to my sister Joanna, she wouldn't let the nurses take her from her because, from what she knew, a hospital was a market place for swapping a handicapped child for a healthy one or stealing newborn babies to sell on.

In 1997, it was estimated that one in three of the world's abductions happened in Colombia. Sadly, kidnapping is still a regular occurrence. For the past few decades on a Saturday night, there has been a radio show called *Las Voces del Secuestro* (Voices of Kidnapping), and from midnight until 6 a.m. the phone lines ring continuously with family members wanting to send messages to their loved ones in captivity. It's heartbreaking.

For those children – for all children who have been affected by other people's greed, as my mother's life has – she is living proof that circumstances don't need to be the end of anyone's story. In fact, it is her upbringing that has made her into the strong, grateful, loving, generous, selfless, positive – and of course wild and unconventional – woman she is today.

While we were growing up, Mum would never allow us to sulk for too long. Instead, she would inspire us, saying something like, 'Pick yourself up, stand up tall, invent something with what you do have, be grateful in the little, and get moving!'

Mum sees the value in everything – for the breath in our lungs, for a new day and for the greatest joy in her life, of being a mother, a grandmother, a wife and a friend. So allow me to introduce to you an extraordinary woman with an extraordinary tale to tell. Marina – my mother and my hero.

Vanessa James

Prologue

I have a story to tell you. The story of my life. And I had thought that this bit, where I introduce myself to you, would be the easiest thing in the world. I was wrong. In fact, it is the hardest.

When meeting someone for the first time, it's customary to tell them your name. It's the first thing that we all do and gives others a way to identify us. I do this. I tell people that my name is Marina. But rather than it being a name given to me by my parents at birth, this is a name I chose for myself at the age of around fourteen. My birth name, like everything else from my early childhood, has been lost over time.

The things that matter, you see – the early memories that help us to establish our identity and which most people take for granted – have, for me, long been forgotten. Who were my parents? What were their names and what were they like? I don't know. I have no picture in my head of them at all, no hazy memories. I have no idea what they even looked like. I have so many questions that will never be answered. What was my home like and how did we live? Did I get on with my family? Do I have any siblings who remember their sister, and if so, who and where are they now? What did I enjoy doing? Was I loved? Was I happy? When is my birthday? Who am I?

For now, this is everything I know about myself: I was born sometime around 1950, somewhere in the north of South America. It is most likely to have been Venezuela or Colombia. I'm not sure which. But as most of my later life was spent in Colombia, that is where I tell people I am from.

The only real memories I have – that I can remember with sufficient clarity to be able to share them with you – are very faint and not particularly insightful. My black dolly, for instance. I do remember her. I still remember the detailing of her black frilly rah-rah skirt and the red-satin ribbons that were threaded down her blouse. Her skin was soft to touch and her hair was black and straggly; I remember how it framed her delicate, dark face.

I also remember a sewing machine. It was black with gold squiggles on the side and beside it there was a chair, on which would often be piles of fabric. Were they unfinished dresses? Perhaps my mother liked sewing? I will never know. What I do know is that my home was a humble one – our toilet was a hole in the ground. I also have a strong sense of activity going on. Of there always being lots of people around. Of the village being alive with the constant noise of children.

I recall the outside of my small world rather better. A redbrick path is very clear. I remember it ran from the house into a garden, and then on to a kind of allotment, where I am sure I spent many hours picking vegetables. I remember that place well, and alongside that memory there's one of being called for, of being shouted at by someone to come back, to return home. Which I would mostly disobey. When this memory comes to me, it's as if I am on the point of remembering my real name, as of course that's what they would have been shouting. It tantalises me, remaining just outside my reach.

And what else? What other things are still clear to me? There's an image of adults walking down a long winding hill and then toiling back up again, carrying containers full of water. I remember cars. They were very rare. No more than three or four a day came. Today, when I see mountains, something stirs in me, so I have the feeling I might have lived up in the mountains.

And that's all I can tell you, for I know nothing more. Because one day everything changed for ever.

PART 1

1

There was something about pea pods that mesmerised me. I didn't know why, but there was something magical about the way the bloated pods burst so cleanly in my hand when I squeezed them. So the corner of the allotment where the peas grew was special, and I would spend hours there, engrossed in my own little world.

The vegetable patch was a piece of land at the end of our garden. On that day, as with many others when there was nothing else happening, I had sneaked off down the brick path that led from our back doorstep, down the garden and through the back gate. I was aware of other children being around. I could hear them but had no desire to find out the cause of their excited chatter. I just wanted to sit in the cool, leafy shade, cocooned from the glare of the sunlight.

I was four, almost five – I recall waiting impatiently for my fifth birthday – and from my diminutive vantage point, the vegetable plants were like giants. They grew in raised beds, forming bushy green bowers as well as tall vines that seemed to clamber across the fence. First there was the cabbage patch and lettuces, then the ranks of tall, straggly runner beans, then the place where the peas grew, the plants dense and bushy, a mass of tendrils and leaves and heavy pods.

I knelt down and plucked the nearest pod, marvelling at the satisfying *crack*! it made as I burst it open between my fingers. Inside the fat jacket were the glossy emerald globes I was after, and I popped the tiny sweet ones into my mouth.

Very soon I had a small pile of spent pods all around me and a growing pile of discarded peas neatly heaped by my side. Lost in my activity, I was oblivious to the fact that I was not the only person in the allotment that day.

It happened so quickly, it's only a brief snippet of a memory. One minute I was squatting on the bare earth, preoccupied. The next, I saw the flash of a black hand and white cloth, and before I even had a chance to cry out it had sailed towards my face and completely covered it.

I think I probably tried to scream. It would have been instinctive to do so. Perhaps I even managed to. But away in my special place, who would have heard me? And as I jerked in surprise and terror, there was the sharp smell of some sort of chemical that had already shot into my lungs. The hand was huge and rough around my face, and the strength of whoever held me was overpowering. My last thought as I began to slip into unconsciousness was a simple one: I was obviously going to die.

*

I had no idea of how much time had passed when I slowly began to rouse from my drug-induced slumber, but I was aware that everything felt strange. I started to tune in to faint noises around me, willing my ears to catch something that might reassure me. Where was I? What had happened?

I tried pulling my body out from its intense sleep, but my eyelids felt too heavy. I couldn't muster the strength to open them to see, so I continued to listen and try to make sense of things, attempting to paint a picture in my mind.

Soon, I was able to identify the sounds of farm animals – I was sure I could hear hens. Pigs too, perhaps. Ducks. I could also hear another sound I thought I recognised. It was an engine. And soon after came the realisation that the noise of the engine was all around me and that I was jerking in time to its tune. The noise rose and fell and juddered, and I juddered with it. I was in a car! Or – no, that might be it! – a truck.

What was definite was that we were travelling over an uneven, rocky surface – a fact confirmed when I finally managed to find the strength to open my eyes. Bright daylight almost blinded me, and colours blurred into stripes as they rushed past me. I had no idea where I was, much less where I was being taken, but the vehicle I was in seemed to be travelling at great speed and I kept sliding around.

Next, I realised I wasn't alone in the back of the truck. Though I couldn't focus my vision on the other passengers around me, I could hear crying and whimpering and anguished sobs of 'Let me go!' There were other children in the truck – terrified children, just like me.

I don't know if it was the fear, or just the effect of whatever they'd given me, but the voices and images then began to fade into a blur of sound and colour, and I drifted once again into unconsciousness.

*

When I woke next, once again I had no sense of how much time might have passed. I was focused on just one thing: the slap of irregular wet splashes to my face. The ground around me seemed to be shaking, and I realised I was being carried by an adult. My body was being thrown around in time with hurried footsteps, and I was facing the moving earth, my hair swinging over my eyes. I was getting tangled and slapped with leaves and twigs as I travelled. Thorns snagged my legs and feet, tearing my skin painfully.

I was being carried on the shoulder of a man who was running through dense forest, and, though I couldn't see him, I was aware of another man running with us. I could hear snaps and crackles, and the thud of both sets of feet. But that was all – where had the other children gone? There seemed to be an increased urgency with every stride the men took and I wondered if they were running away from something, frightened, just like I was. An animal? A monster? I knew from stories that scary monsters lived in the forests. And the men's breathing, which I could hear was heavy with panic and perhaps exhaustion, seemed to suggest we were being chased by something dangerous.

Every so often the man who carried me would lurch alarmingly, his knees buckling. I had no idea how far we'd run, or where we were running to, but I could sense we'd come far. The man was staggering, almost falling, and as I was too terrified to think beyond the instinct to cling on to him, I could only hope that soon we'd have outrun whatever it was that was after us.

Finally, he stopped, and my whole body jerked violently. I then felt myself being whirled around, as if the man was unsure in which direction to go next. But then we were moving again, plunging onwards into deeper and denser undergrowth, before stopping again, this time even more abruptly. I tightened my grip but, aware of the aggressive way he'd grabbed me, I let my hands go as he hauled me roughly off his shoulder and dumped me onto the ground.

Dazed, I tried to scramble up and see who it was that had carried me, but by the time I had pulled myself up onto all fours and turned around, all I could see were two pairs of long legs running away. One pair of brown legs and one pair of white legs, both of which were soon lost in the gloom. I tried shouting at them, screaming at them, begging them not to leave me. Even though instinct told me that these were not good men, I was much more frightened of being left in the jungle all alone. But just like in a dream, no sound seemed to come out of my mouth, and soon even their blurred outlines began to fade, melting away into the shadows of the trees and the bushes that were all I could see. I knelt there for a long time, hardly daring to move, just peering into the dark and willing them to return, or at least hoping to hear the cry of one of those other children. I felt helpless, abandoned and so frightened of being alone. Why didn't they come back? Why had they run away from me? Where was my mummy? How was I going to get home?

The darkness deepened and now that the men had gone away the eerie night sounds of the jungle were terrifying. I had no idea where I was, why I was there or when someone would come back for me. I had nothing on but the cotton dress and knickers my mother had dressed me in that morning, and I felt the heat of the earth on which I lay seeping into me as I curled myself into the tightest ball I could.

The sense of desolation and loneliness was gut-wrenching and I ached with it. All I could hope was that if I closed my eyes it would all go away. If I squeezed them tightly enough, perhaps the dark wouldn't be so scary, and soon – please let it be soon – my mummy would come and find me. Perhaps if I slept, when I next woke I would be safely home in bed and would realise all this had all been just a nightmare . . .

2

It was the heat of the sun that first woke me. Beneath my left cheek I could feel only a warm, pungent softness but against my right there was a sensation of great heat. It was a strong, searing heat, and as I opened my eyes the light was so blinding I immediately squeezed them shut again.

I rolled onto my back, still halfway between sleeping and consciousness, aware of a new assault now. This time it was on my ears, the air as full of sound as the light was full of sparkles. There were frightening screeches and strange whoops that I couldn't identify.

As I carefully allowed my eyelids to part again, I found myself looking straight up into a big shard of blue. Bright, bright blue, surrounded on all sides by dappled darkness, and as I looked, trying to shade my eyes from the dazzle with my fingers, I gradually realised what it was that I was seeing. It was a patch of sky encircled within a ring of leafy treetops, so high above me that they were just a raggedy black blur.

At last it became clear where I was. In the jungle! The realisation shot through me, and with it came panic, as the memories of the last evening came rushing to greet me. I had been snatched from my home by men who had then dumped me here.

I brushed dark earth from my palms and pulled myself up to my knees. Then I scrambled to my feet and began searching for a way to escape. All I could think of was to find the men who left me. To catch up with them and beg them to take me home. I wanted my mummy. Where was she? Why hadn't she come to find me?

I had no sense of how much time had passed since I'd been abandoned here by my kidnappers. I strained my ears, hoping

21

to hear any sort of sound that would reassure me. The laughter of children, a shout of greeting, the clatter of a cart rolling by. I cried out for my mother, sobbing as I called for her and called for her. My throat rasped with lack of moisture, but at this point I had no thought of finding something to drink or eat. I just desperately wanted to find a way home, so I tried to thrash my way out of all the undergrowth and the tangled hairy vines that looped down from the tree trunks. The gnarled branches and boughs seemed to cut off every exit, and the leaves – leaves so big and so strange and so different from one another – seemed intent on enclosing me in this frightening green hell.

But where to go? There didn't seem to be any kind of path and I didn't recognise anything. I couldn't make out where I'd come from.

As I spun around, every vista seemed the same as the one before it. Trees, trees and more trees, as far as the eye could see. Now and then, as I tripped and blundered my way over and under and around all the tangled obstacles, I would get a glimpse of something brighter beyond. A distant hill, perhaps? But all too soon the plaited walls of my green prison would close in again, and the further I travelled the more a trembling panic surged inside me. This was stupid! Why was I doing this? I should go back, shouldn't I? What if my mummy came to find me? What if she came for me but found I wasn't there?

I turned straight around, choking on the sobs that kept coming, and tried to make my way back to where I'd just been. But it soon became obvious that I had completely lost my way. There was no trace of my passing, no clue to lead me back.

I cried freely now. I couldn't stop the tears streaming from my eyes. And as I stumbled along, intermittently being scratched and snared by vicious branches, I kept trying to make some sense of how I came to be here. Had my parents planned it? Was that it? Had they wanted to get rid of me? I tried to think what I might have done to make them so cross with me. Was it the pea pods? Were they cross because I'd picked so many of them? Had my mummy or daddy asked those horrible men to come and take me?

I tried to remember the man who had taken me from the allotment. The black man, the one who'd covered my mouth with his hand. Who was he? An uncle? I tried to recall his features. He had been tall and very strong. Was he someone who knew me? One of my most treasured possessions back at home was my beautiful black dolly and for some reason this fact kept returning to me. We were a white-skinned family and yet I had a black dolly. Why was that? Did it mean something I didn't understand?

Too drained and upset now to thrash furiously through the endless waist-high undergrowth, my pace slowed, my shoulders drooped and my spirits plummeted. Yet what else could I do but keep trudging on? So I did. It was barely a conscious decision. I just kept going because perhaps I would find a way out or someone who would help me. Or just some sign that meant I might be a step closer to going home.

But as time went on, and my limbs became criss-crossed with scratches, the fear grew in me that this was not going to happen. And when the light began to dim I felt my hope disappear with the sun. It was night-time. It was bedtime. The day was all done. A whole day had passed and I was still trapped in the jungle. I would have to spend another night alone.

The night was blacker than any other I had ever seen. Hard as I strained to see, there was not even the tiniest pinpoint of light apart from the far-away glimmer of stars. The sky itself, though, felt oddly close – almost as if it had fallen down on top of me, settling like an enormous black bedspread all around me and trapping me beneath it with the creatures of the night. Without chemicals to blur the edges of my awareness, my terror now took on an even more desperate quality than the night before. It was the noise again, the incredible volume and range of noises, which I knew, because I'd heard grown-ups talking about them, must come from the jungle beasts that came out at night. And they did that, I knew, because hidden by the dark it would be easier for them to catch their prey.

I had searched around as the blackness had swooped down to claim me and found a small patch of bare soil, unadorned by plant life, that sat within the base of a wide-trunked tree. Here I sat, and as the air grew thicker and murkier I curled myself once again into the tightest ball possible, my back against the reassuring solidity of the bark and my arms wrapped protectively around my bent knees.

I felt strongly that I needed to keep still and quiet. Like in a game, I told myself. A game of hide-and-seek. If I kept very still and didn't make a sound, then the creatures of the night wouldn't know I was there.

But their presence was terrifyingly obvious to me. I could hear so many different sounds, and many were close by. I could hear the same rustlings that I had made as I trampled through the foliage. Scurryings, too – the sound of small animals moving by. And then a crack. A loud crack, frighteningly close to where I cowered. The crunch of something crisp – dead twigs? – being trodden on. The noise moved around me. Whatever it was, it seemed to be circling me, waiting for the right moment to pounce. Could it make me out clearly with its big night-time eyes? And what were those swishing sounds that seemed to follow it? A tail? Was it a child-eating monster? Could it smell me?

I tried to make myself smaller. I wished so much for a cage that I could scuttle inside. A cage that would protect me from slashing claws and biting jaws. Or a light. How I longed for my mummy to bring a light that would scare the monster away.

But then something must have startled whatever it was that stalked me, for there was a rush of small sounds as it darted away, and I felt a blessed moment of relief. But it wasn't to last. As the night wore on and I lay in my tight ball inside the tree trunk, my lack of vision merely served to terrify me even more. Frightening though it may have been to see any jungle creatures close up, I decided that not being able to see them was even worse. As it was, I could do nothing but flinch and quake in terror as creeping things crawled up and down my limbs, tried to explore the contours of my face and crept inside my ears. I longed for sleep like I had never longed for anything before, because no nightmare, however scary, could possibly be worse than the nightmare I was trapped in right now.

*

The same sun, with the same strength, shining down from the same dazzling blue sky, greeted me again the next morning. It had taken time to convince myself that I should open my eyes.

In the comfort of semi-consciousness, I could almost believe that the warmth was that of the blanket on my bed and the sun was streaming in through my bedroom window. But the sounds of the waking jungle quickly dispelled that notion and dragged me cruelly back to reality.

I cried again inside my tree trunk, my throat sore and rasping, my belly aching to be filled with food. But I could only cry for so long. And who was going to hear me anyway? I rubbed the backs of my hands across the puffy surface of my tear-stained face, and as my eyes cleared I thought I saw a butterfly.

I looked again. No, not one butterfly. There were lots and lots of butterflies, in all sorts of different colours, all flitting just above my head. They were fussing around the petals of beautiful pink and white flowers hanging down on lengths of green stem that seemed to start high in the trees. They were mesmerising, and as the jungle floor steamed and made mist all around me, every scrap of my attention was held.

But the pain in my stomach wouldn't let me rest for long. I was hungry and I needed to find something to eat. But what? There were pods on the ground that I carefully inspected. They smelled good and even made the air around me smell fragrant, but they were coal-black and wizened, and I had only to snap one to see that these pods were very different from peas. Did peas grow here? Or corn? Perhaps I could find some. I got up then and began to explore my surroundings, only this time in a very different way.

Being so young, I was unaware that I could be poisoned by any of the strange plants, berries and fruits I could see. I didn't want to eat them simply because they looked alien and unappetising. I could see nothing in the undergrowth that was familiar to me.

Once again my thoughts returned to my predicament. If I could find nothing to eat, then I would starve very quickly. And then, as I knew from stories I'd seen in picture books and the things I'd heard grown-ups say, I would die and get eaten by animals. But it seemed that there was nothing here for me to eat. And not wanting to die and be eaten by animals, once again I decided I could not stay where I was. Today I would walk. I would walk and keep walking. If help didn't want to find me, then I would have to find it. I resolved to continue for as long as my legs could support me, which would hopefully be long enough for me to find a human being who would give me food and take me back to my parents.

I set off once again through the impenetrable thickets, with no plan other than to get away from where I was. After all, the two men had run into the jungle with me, so if I walked for long enough then I must surely get out.

Most of the time I couldn't see further than the mesh of leaves in front of me and my skin was soon protesting at another round of scratches, as the branches I'd displaced sprang back viciously to punish me for disturbing them. It was hot and claustrophobic inside the eerie green bower, and it wasn't long before my quest for food was forgotten. As the trees dripped above me and the mists rose and vanished, a new sensation overtook my previous raging hunger. I realised I was incredibly thirsty.

But how would I find water? I had no idea. Though everything around me seemed glossy with moisture, finding water to drink seemed impossible. I began scanning my surroundings with a keener sense of purpose. Where would I find water to drink in such a place?

I looked for hollows in stones and crevices, and scoured the forest floor for puddles. Copying the insects that buzzed and whirred in every direction, I peered hopefully into every kind of flower until finally I came across a plant with coiled, almost cup-shaped green leaves, edged with hairs. If they looked like cups, I reasoned, they might act like cups too, and, sure enough, when I peered into the interior of one of them, I saw a small pool of liquid reflecting up at me.

Feeling almost as if I had discovered a secret treasure, I pulled the cone of the leaf towards me and leaned into it. I then let my parched lips touch the glimmering surface. It felt like heaven, and I'd soon tipped the leaf carefully up and deposited the rest into my mouth. The water tasted odd. It was like drinking soil. But I didn't care. My thirst was quenched for a moment.

And it wasn't long before I was able to satisfy it even more. I found a tiny stream, the water trickling and splashing over rocks, and this time when I drank, it was cold and clear and pleasant. But my stomach was not to be fooled. I soon felt it grumbling and complaining, and renewed my focus on finding something to eat as I walked.

What I found was not food, but a parrot. Weak as I was with hunger, I was still entranced by it. Blue and green and yellow, and around the size of a large squash, it sat on a low branch, chattering to itself. It was reassuring, the way it sat there so boldly, just watching me, and I instinctively wanted to get closer. I reached a hand out. Perhaps it would come and sit on my finger, as the confident village parrots sometimes did.

But I was wrong. No sooner had I got within touching distance than it leaned towards me, squawked loudly and sharply bit my thumb, before flapping off in what looked like great annoyance. I looked down at my thumb, which was now throbbing painfully, and at the sight of all the blood dripping across and off my palm I burst into hot, self-pitying tears again. In years to come – decades to come – that moment would be dear to me, because I would recognise it as being key to my survival. I'd been so shocked that a beautiful creature like this might want to harm me, but it was that same shock that would form the basis of what would perhaps be the greatest lesson I could learn. That this was not a man-made place, full of pretty domesticated animals. This was a wild place, and wild animals would kill to survive. As it was, I just traipsed on, dejected.

My spirits, however, soon lifted. It was shortly after the unfortunate encounter with the parrot that I noticed a change in my surroundings. The undergrowth seemed to be thinning a little. My thumb, which had been pulsating with discomfort, was forgotten, and I pushed back the ever-decreasing barricades of branches with a real sense that I might be about to escape. On and on I went, scrambling with ever more urgency as it became obvious I was reaching some sort of clearing. And the closer I got, the more my eyes seemed to confirm it. I was getting ever bigger glimpses of the jungle giving way to what looked like open space.

This must be it! So intent was I on reaching the edge now that I didn't care how many irritable boughs and saplings lashed out and whacked me. And it was with a sense of elation that I finally burst through, to find myself at one side of a small area of grass. But my joy was cruelly short-lived. No sooner had I escaped than I saw that on the other side of the scrubby, withered circle of grass was undergrowth just as impenetrable as that from which I'd just emerged. I'd come so far! I had walked for so long! I was exhausted, still starving, and there seemed no escape route. I had, I knew for certain, just walked further into the jungle.

Why? I thought. Why, why, why, why had this happened? Why hadn't my mother come to find me? What had I done to deserve this? And if this was a punishment for something I'd done wrong, then what was it? I looked down at my dress, which had once been pure white with pink flowers and was now a ragged grey thing, stained with soil and blood. I had no shoes and my bare feet were worn, cut and filthy, and both my stomach and mind cried out hopelessly. I slumped down into a pitiful heap on the ground, smelling the grass in my nostrils and the ever-present tang of soil. I could think of nothing else to do but just lie there and weep. I wanted home, I wanted my mother, I wanted to be comforted and cuddled. But I had nothing and no one to cling on to.

I curled up there, on my side, for what seemed an eternity, and I might even have fallen asleep for a bit. Certainly, it seemed I was experiencing nightmares. Strange jungle sounds made me jump, and loud whoops and calls seemed to taunt me. I could hear the sound of branches thwacking, grasses moving, sharp snaps and thumps.

All I wanted was to die. But eventually my hopelessness and fear turned to hunger, and the sheer physical ache from deep down in my stomach made me accept that I wasn't going to die any time soon.

I opened one eye, just a little bit. The sunlight still bathed me. I opened it a bit more, my sightline tracking straight along the ground. And what I saw almost stopped me from opening it any further. So I closed it and, as gently and noiselessly as I could, turned my head to face the other way.

A tiny peek from the other eye confirmed I hadn't dreamt it. I had company. In fact, I was surrounded.

3

All trace of sleep had gone now, and as I opened my eyes fully I realised I wasn't just surrounded, I was being watched. All around me, at a distance of several paces, were monkeys. Motionless and afraid again, I tried to count them. Now I was nearly five, I could count up to ten, and it seemed there were lots more than that number ranged around me, and perhaps more behind me, out of sight, which scared me even more.

But as I watched them, and they watched me, I felt my fear ebb a little. They looked like a family. Though they were all different sizes, they looked related. Big ones and little ones. Old ones and young ones. All with the same chocolate-coloured fur and paler belly, and ranging from what looked like the size of a small dog to no bigger than the parrot who'd bitten me. I knew they were wild animals and, after my experience with that parrot, I couldn't trust them, but some sense made me feel they wouldn't hurt me.

That feeling didn't last. After a short time, one of the monkeys left the circle and began to approach me. He was one of the biggest, with a coat that was greyer than the others, and there was something about the way he loped towards me so boldly that made me think he was the one who ran the family. Afraid again now, because I didn't know what he might decide to do to me, I shrank back into a ball, trying to make myself as tiny as possible, tucking my head tight to my chest and hugging my arms around my knees.

I was just about to squeeze my eyes shut when I saw him reach out a wrinkly brown hand and, to my surprise, with one firm push, knock me over onto my side. I quivered on the soil, tensed for the second blow that was surely coming. But it didn't, and after some seconds I dared open one eye again, only to find that the monkey had lost interest. He'd now returned to the circle, squatted back on his hind legs and resumed watching me, along with all the others.

It wasn't long, however, before a second monkey – another of the bigger ones – began walking towards me. It approached slowly on all fours but without a trace of uncertainty. This time I instinctively scrabbled to my feet, but as soon as the monkey got to me it reached out, grabbed one of my legs and yanked it from under me, causing me to fall back on the soil again with a thump. I curled into a ball again but felt the animal begin to dig around in my hair and move its leathery fingers over my face. Now I was frightened and wriggling, trying to free myself from its questing fingers, but, like the other monkey, it seemed to have decided I was a plaything; once again, I was firmly pushed over.

This action seemed to give the other, smaller monkeys confidence. Having decided I posed no danger to them, they all seemed to want to inspect me. They had been chattering to one another – using sounds that almost seemed like they were goading each other and laughing – and in no time at all some had come to check me over. Once upon me they began to prod and push me, grabbing at my filthy dress and digging around in my hair.

'Stop it!' I pleaded, sobbing. 'Get off me! Go away!!' But they took no notice and I had to wait, cowering and whimpering, until they'd finished their inspection. I could feel myself relax just a little, however, because if they'd wanted to hurt me then surely they would have done so by now. They hadn't and now they seemed to lose interest altogether, returning to whatever it was that they had been doing in the dense undergrowth from which I presumed they'd come.

Having nowhere to go, and still fearful of running, in case they chased me, I sat in the clearing and watched them. They climbed the surrounding trees, they played and dug around in one another's coats, they picked up things and popped them in their mouths. Nuts and berries? Grubs and insects? Small lizards? It was difficult to see at a distance. And, I quickly noticed, they copied one another. A big one would do something and a smaller one would copy it. As I watched this, something my mother often said popped into my head: monkey see, monkey do.

I sat and watched them for a long time. I was mesmerised and felt somehow reluctant to leave them. There was something about the way they seemed to enjoy one another's company that made them feel like a family. While close to them, I felt like I wasn't alone any more.

They were so pretty too, with their milk-chocolate fur and camel-coloured bellies, their tufty grey ears and their dark, bushy tails. I was especially enthralled by their hands, which intrigued and bewildered me because, though they weren't human, they looked just like mine. They were the same colour and size as my own, with four fingers, a thumb and hard fingernails.

And they were constantly active, leaping high and low, chattering and chasing one another round the trees and shrubs. They seemed to love playing and, in the case of what looked like the young ones, play-fighting and squabbling as well. They were watched over by the bigger monkeys, who would shriek and pull faces as if they were telling them off when things got too rough. This was just what the grown-ups in my world would do, and somehow this sense of order and family made me feel better.

4

After a while, I was distracted again by the gnawing pain in my stomach. It was my third day in the jungle and I badly needed food. As I continued to watch the monkeys, I became fixated on how much they were eating. Whatever else they were doing, they seemed to be constantly feeding. I needed to do that too, I knew, or I would die of the pain.

Startled by a siren shriek from above me, I looked up to see a small monkey swinging above me, swooping from one tree to another smaller one close by. The leaves of the tree were dark and shaped like slender teardrops, deep green and glossy, and about the size of a man's shoe. The tree also bore flowers – pretty purple flowers that seemed to transform themselves into banana-like bunches, except that the fruits pointed up rather than down. The fruits looked unripe, as they were still tiny – about the size of my finger – and were also an unappetising shade of green. Bananas at home were yellow, but these little ones definitely looked similar, and as the monkey dropped a bunch in his haste to grab a handful, I quickly darted over and snatched them up from the forest floor.

I had already watched the monkeys eat them, which they did differently from the way my mother had taught me: peeling the skin off in strips from the top end. The monkeys would either just break them in half or, starting at the bottom, peel the skin up from there, sometimes using their teeth to help, too. I watched a nearby monkey who was feasting on the contents and, with my mouth watering, copied him.

The flesh was delicious. Soft and sticky and so incredibly sweet: better than any banana I had ever eaten. It was my first taste of jungle food, and I wolfed it down greedily. But no sooner had I done so and picked up a second, than another monkey, who had clearly been waiting for its moment, swung over on a vine and, in a deft, practised fashion, stole the rest of the precious bunch from right under my nose.

Ah, I remember thinking, so this is how the game works. But it didn't matter. I looked around to find a stick and had soon snagged another small bunch of the delicious fruits for myself. I had found company – a family of sorts, even – and something that I knew I could eat till my mummy came to find me and take me home. As I dived into my second bunch of tiny bananas, I felt my spirits lifting just a little.

*

Though I had worried all day that my new companions might scamper away and desert me, they didn't. This patch of forest seemed to be their home. And for the moment, I decided, it would be mine as well, so I spent my third night in the jungle with the monkeys. Though they seemed to prefer to sleep high up in the canopy, I had to be content with curling up on the bare earth far beneath them, in a tight space between two shrubs. Part of me was desperate to return to the safety of the hollowed-out tree, and I later would. But that night, I was so frightened of losing the monkeys that I chose to stay and take my chances. Just knowing they were there made me feel a little safer. And as the night came rushing down to cloak everything in inky blackness, the sound of them calling to one another gave me comfort.

But I still lay there quivering with fear. The jungle was once again full of murderous shrieks and howls, and the bushes around me kept shaking and rustling. I was filled with a cold, intense terror. What was out there?

Then I held my breath as I felt movement: a steady pressure from behind me. A gentle, slow shove that pressed into my back. I had no idea what it might be, only that it was smooth and warm and felt frighteningly big. It also seemed to slither.

Was I imagining it or had a snake come and found me? Was it slithering alongside me, intent on making me its dinner? My imagination ran wild. Unable to see what was behind me – even if I'd dared to open my eyes – the picture in my mind grew steadily more terrifying. I could hardly dare to breathe, let alone roll over to try to see it, so I just lay there, my heart pounding, my ears straining as the sound it made – a kind of truffling, groaning, creaking – seemed to begin to move above me and the pressure lessened. It was a giant snake, I was sure. One that was now ascending back to wherever it had come from.

Knowing the creature was up there made it impossible to sleep. It didn't seem to matter how exhausted I felt, I was simply much too afraid of being eaten. Yet eventually I must have drifted off, because the next thing I remember was waking up to see the sky bright once again. To see the sunshine-dappled ground and feel the heat on my limbs was a huge relief, and all thoughts of the snake vanished. But with the sun and the rising mists came thoughts of home. Why had my mother still not come for me? Surely she should have been able to find me by now? But my only companions, now as yesterday, were the monkeys, who whooped and chattered and swung among the branches up above me, as playful and carefree as I was dispirited and scared.

Now they were used to me, the troop didn't take a lot of notice of me. Apart from the older ones, who acted as the parents and who seemed to want to keep an eye on me, most of the monkeys ignored me. There were more of them than I'd first seen – looking back now, perhaps thirty – and though they seemed happy enough with my constant presence, they didn't include me. They had no idea that to me they were lifesavers, friends. They just allowed me to stay close, and I was grateful.

I was also able to watch them and learn about my surroundings. Where food was concerned, I made a habit of copying. I assumed that the seeds, nuts and fruit they favoured would all be acceptable for me to eat too. Some things were spiny, some were bitter and unpleasant, but I generally just copied, trying things I saw them relish.

Not that I ate everything the monkeys did – far from it. At no point did I ever even think about trying to catch and eat a lizard. The idea made me gag. I also found out by trial and error that I didn't like the taste of flowers, grass or insects, and that fruit, nuts and berries were the best things to go for. But not all of them. Almost immediately, I learned my first crucial rule: that brightly coloured berries, however enticing they looked, were, without exception, to be left alone.

Figs seemed to be prized over any other foodstuff, and a monkey with figs was a monkey who was hounded. Most of the thieving seemed playful, but where figs were concerned, no one was left alone. And I shared their love. Those first days in the jungle gave me one lifelong passion. To this day, prepared in traditional Colombian style, figs are still among my favourite fruits.

Not all foods gave themselves up easily, and watching the monkeys made me realise another truth: that you had to work for some of the tastiest morsels on offer. There were many different kinds of nuts in our patch of the rainforest, and though I could see from a distance that the monkeys could obviously find their way into the shells, it wasn't clear to me how they went about it.

But there was one monkey who always seemed to let me get a little closer than the others. It could have been a boy or a girl – I had no idea how to tell the difference – but in my mind, he was a boy monkey, a medium-sized animal who stood out to me because of a spot of grey fur on his belly. He was playful and bold, but most important for my purpose he seemed very good at breaking into nuts. I would watch him for ages, trying to see what he was doing, and then hit upon the idea of leaving nuts for him to 'steal' from me, in the hope that I could work out how he did it.

Sure enough, he obliged, snatching up the nut I had 'dropped', putting it to his ear and shaking it, presumably to check if it was ripe. I didn't know what sound would tell him this but whatever it was, it was the right one because, as I trailed him, he then seemed to cast around the forest floor, looking for something hard on which to crack the nut. Finally he found a rock that seemed to serve his purpose, because it had a dimple – a small hole in it – in which the nut could be placed, enabling him to whack it open with a piece of branch, without it rolling away as he struck it.

I watched this simple yet clever process several times. It would vary: sometimes the resting hole would be in the fallen trunk of a tree, other times the tool in his hand would be a piece of rock. But every time the result would be the same. The nut would split, and the monkey would pop a tasty prize into his mouth. *Monkey see, monkey do*! I remember thinking to myself as I searched for a tool with which to crack my own nuts.

Those first couple of days with the troop saw me spending almost all of my time trying to satisfy my hunger. The jungle was generous in her offerings, and as well as the bananas, figs and nuts there were all sorts of different fruits to try.

Once again, I learned from the monkeys. They loved uchuva, guanabana and guava unreservedly, but with other fruits they were clearly more picky. One particular fruit, the lulo, they would always seem to test first: shaking and sniffing the big orange globes before deciding whether to pick them from their bushes. I would come to learn there was a good reason for this. The unripe fruits were incredibly sour. It was the same with the curuba (which looks a little like a fat gherkin). They would only touch the yellowish-brown ones, leaving the green ones well alone. The monkeys also ate leaves, which I found I couldn't stomach, and a variety of insects and grubs.

But life in the jungle in those first days wasn't just about feeding. Or playing and grooming and chattering, come to that. For the monkeys, it was also about survival. To my new family, this meant having territory, and, crucially, protecting it from intrusion by other monkey troops. And this, I soon came to learn, meant fighting.

The first time I saw the monkeys fight with intruders, I was terrified. I simply couldn't understand what was going on. One minute they were all playing, above and around me, and the next there was the clatter and crash of breaking branches as they massed in the canopy and fought. On this occasion it was with monkeys that looked different from the ones I knew. They had reddish fur and had come from I knew not where. The sound of the violence above me was petrifying, the noise of their screams as they fought so intense and horrific that I scrambled to escape it, hiding under a bush and clamping my hands over my ears. And when they came down again, the intruders presumably having being beaten, I was shocked by the sight of the blood around many of their mouths. Had they eaten the other monkeys? Or had they just wounded them to frighten them? And if I displeased them in some way, might they decide to turn on me?

It was a stark reminder that I was in a dangerous place, with dangerous animals, but when I thought about how the monkeys had treated me since stumbling upon me, I decided they must have accepted that I posed no threat. Why else had they not driven me away with screams and bloody violence? Why else had they let me stay so close to them?

Ever anxious for reassurance, I decided that perhaps they had seen me being abandoned. Perhaps they had seen how the men had so callously dumped me, and, understanding my plight, had taken pity. It was comforting to think that they seemed to accept that I wished them no harm and only wanted to be their friend. And, as I watched them start cleaning the blood from their mouths, I could only hope they didn't change their minds.

5

No one came.

The day passed, as did the next day, and the one after that, and still there was no sign of my parents. There was no sign of anyone. No one human, at any rate. My hope of rescue, which had been at the front of my mind since I'd been abandoned, was fading as fast as the flower pattern on my dress.

It perhaps wasn't surprising then that slowly, over a period of time I can only guess at, I began to stop hoping to be rescued. Instead I found myself blocking out all thoughts of home and concentrating on my strange new jungle life.

Each new day turned out to be exactly like the last one. The jungle would wake at the hot insistence of the sunlight, the steam rising in fragrant clouds as the light shafted down through the branches. I would watch the monkeys – being careful not to annoy them – and follow them to find food, then watch them some more. This would continue till the sun disappeared beneath the trees and the night suddenly dropped its curtain of blackness. I'd then find shelter where I could and crave sleep.

The only break in this routine in the early days was when one day (without warning, as I was so sheltered by the canopy) the heavens opened and my world was full of rain. I'd seen rain before, of course, but now it took on a whole new significance. It danced on the leaf tops, made the forest floor jump and jive, and created enough noise to drown out almost every other sound. It provided a ready source of water for me, creating a small pool from which I could drink, and soaked through my heavy matted hair and ran in urgent streams down my limbs. It felt almost magical: a fierce and cleansing force.

But apart from that marker, I really was losing all sense of time – of the hours and the days and the weeks and how to measure them. What I remember most clearly from that period is the feeling of incredible loneliness, the like of which I never hope to feel again. As the monkeys were the only jungle animals that didn't scare me, it was perhaps natural that I felt drawn to them. They seemed so like me that I felt a need to try to understand them better.

Doing so didn't just involve watching them. It involved listening as well. They communicated with one another using a great number of different noises and, starved of human contact (particularly the comfort of human voices), I would sit and listen avidly to these sounds.

I was also starved of the opportunity to speak and somehow communicating through my voice was a powerful and instinctive need. At first I imitated the noises the monkeys made for my own amusement, though probably also for the comfort of hearing the sound of my own voice. But I soon realised that sometimes a monkey – or several monkeys – would respond, as if we were having a conversation. This galvanised me. It felt like I had been taken notice of, finally. So I practised and practised the sounds that they made, always desperate to get a reaction.

It's impossible to represent monkey-speech using letters, and it's extremely difficult to reproduce, too. Even with my high-pitched little girl's voice, there were some sounds I wasn't physically able to copy. I do, however, remember the first sound I seemed to be able to imitate was one they made often – a warning call. It was a kind of guttural scream – a loud, urgent noise. Which it needed to be – it had to alert the whole troop. And it soon became clear that they made this call often. They were constantly alert, constantly on the lookout, vigilant all the time in case of anything abnormal, and reporting almost anything that moved or entered their territory. They had a particular stance that went with this as well. They'd pull a face – a sort of open–mouthed stare – before they did it and would rise up on their hind legs, almost on tiptoes. Then they'd start by making low sounds, presumably while assessing the level of threat. Then, once they'd identified an intruder and deemed it threatening, they'd move on to screeching, often swinging their heads from side to side. They were no different from children – or any human, really – in that, the scarier the threat was, the louder they'd scream at all the others.

If the danger was immediate, the call would be even higher – a sharp, high-pitched scream, which was usually accompanied by them slapping their hands on the ground. When this happened, the rest of the monkeys would join in, and they'd all scamper up to the safety of the canopy, leaving me (now I'd learned what the calls were about) scared and panicky as I rushed about trying to find a place of safety on the ground.

But I quickly learned that I didn't always need to be frightened. Perhaps because I was such a small child myself, I soon picked up on the fact that the little ones in the family would make the 'immediate danger' call just for the fun of it, and that the adults seemed to know when to ignore them. That too was a comfort in those early days.

Less comforting would have been to know that I would be there so long that I would have time to learn the meaning of almost every monkey sound. If I had known that then, perhaps I would have died of despair. But thankfully I didn't. Every day dawned with at least a thread of hope to cling to, and, fragile as it was, that was enough to keep me going.

*

After my first night-time brush with what I'd thought might be a snake, I was terrified of encountering another. But my fear very quickly abated. Snakes were actually among the most timid of the jungle creatures. They liked to do what they did without anyone noticing them. Though I had always been afraid of them, thinking they wanted nothing more than to bite me, I soon realised they didn't even like to be seen. Most of them had markings that made them blend into the background – looking like the leaf litter on the forest floor, or the bark of the trees – and they seemed altogether more scared than I was. The smallest noise would send them anxiously slithering away for cover, and, watching the monkeys, I learned to whistle whenever I saw one, which would invariably send them on their way.

Timid too, were the spiders, which were almost all huge and hairy. If I'd seen one in my bedroom at home I would have been sobbing in terror, but in the jungle they were so different – so sweet and so shy. I found them fascinating and would watch them for ages, wanting to reach out and stroke their lovely silky legs. I'd watch how they'd scuttle into little hidey holes if you dared to come near them, then look out at you, their little black button eyes peeking out, as if pleading 'Please, please don't hurt me!' It wasn't long before I thought them really cute. I still do.

Not that they were completely defenceless. Within a very short period of time I learned that it was silly to tease them. I would sit for ages watching them go about their business, just as any small child with time on their hands would do. If you watched for long enough, you could begin to learn which spider lived where, and I soon got to know the location of all their little 'houses'.

They were very private, of course, and there were periods when they'd all be inside and nothing much would be happening. So after a time, anxious for action, I would get myself a stick and try to tease up the little 'lids' that formed the entrances. Understandably, this made them very cross. They'd come bustling out to see who was interfering with their front door, and I noticed they'd often stop and shake their furry bodies, much like a wet dog would do. One day I also noticed that after just such an episode of irritation, the spider in question, having shaken itself, seemed to have a little cloud of something rising from its body.

It wasn't water. It took the form of tiny particles that looked like dust and I soon realised this must have been the source of the painful stinging and itching that I suffered afterwards.

Not all the lessons I learned in those early days were about the world around me – some were about me, and the day-to-day business of taking care of myself. I was a little girl of not quite five. I was used to being looked after. Used to my mummy helping me to dress and undress, to wash myself, clean my teeth and brush my hair.

All these daily rituals were now gone. My pretty cotton dress was ripped and filthy, and within days I had no choice but to discard my white knickers, as the elastic around the waist had snapped and they kept falling down. And though not being made to wash or having a comb forced through my hair was no hardship, going to the toilet and cleaning myself afterwards became something quite distressing.

Again, I watched the monkeys for clues about what to do. They would go to the toilet whenever and wherever they felt the need. If they were high above me in the canopy, their poo would simply rain down onto the forest floor, or have its progress halted by the undergrowth. On one occasion I saw a dollop of it land on a fat, tufty fungus, which immediately responded by puffing out a big spore cloud, as if to let me know it was fed up.

If the monkeys were on the ground themselves, they would bury what they'd done by covering it with earth or moss and leaves. They would also, I noticed – but by no means that regularly – clean themselves by sitting on their bottoms on a grassy area and sliding themselves along the ground. Alternatively they'd rub their backsides against a moss-covered tree trunk. That done, they would simply finish the job by contorting themselves and licking themselves clean.

This last part was obviously a physical impossibility for me, but I was desperate to feel clean and not smelly. On the first few occasions I had to go to the toilet, I remember I wiped my bottom on my dress. Once my pants had to go, I then used the material as a rag. But once that was no longer usable, I copied the monkeys or took to wiping myself with unfurled dry leaves. I soon realised, however, that if I grabbed myself handfuls of moss, its softness and moistness did the job all the better because it didn't tear my poor bottom to shreds.

The rest of my body, on the other hand, grew filthier and filthier, and as the days passed I found myself scratching more and more. Like the monkeys, I became home for all manner of little creatures. Not only was my skin growing drier and scalier, I was also soon crawling with fleas. As beautiful as the jungle was, it was also very dirty. Flies buzzed unceasingly, clouds of them – all green-blue and jewel-like, and feasting excitedly on the many piles of animal poo. They buzzed around me too, which I found upsetting; was I as smelly as the poo all around me? I was certainly gathering more dirt and fleas daily, as well as crawling lice, beetles and strange, silvery-white insects that seemed to shimmer as they teemed on my skin.

Sometimes, initially, this would drive me to a frenzy.

Scratching frantically all over, I'd weep with frustration, unable to work out how to stop it happening. It only took the briefest of looks around me to realise that I could not. If I sat down, I just became another part of the landscape – another piece of ground over which the relentless tide of insects could scuttle. *Escarabajo* (scarab beetles) and *cucarron* (small brown cockroaches) simply ranged over my limbs as if they had every right to do so, nibbling at my increasingly gnarly flesh as they saw fit. This was frightening. How could I stop it happening before they began to eat me all up?

The monkey's solution was, again, to lick themselves clean. And if I physically couldn't – and definitely wouldn't – lick the poo from my own bottom, I thought that at least I could lick some of the skin on my filthy, crusted, bitten limbs. But my first lick was destined to also be my last. I had never before tasted anything quite so vile. I was so foul and bitter that I simply couldn't fathom how the monkeys managed to do this all day.

My hair, of course, was faring even worse. Unwashed for so long now, and playing host to even more scuttling insects, it was literally alive with jungle animals. I knew from the itching that it played host to even more crawling wildlife with every passing day, as it matted and wound itself into lumpy black dreadlocks.

I would sit and watch the monkeys carefully grooming one another, desperately wishing they would include me. But for now they didn't. I was allowed to be close, but not that close, and I would look up enviously as they sat in the cool of the upper branches, picking the nasties that they dug out of one another's chocolate coats.

*

Wanting to be up in the trees with my adopted monkey family fast became a preoccupation for me – even more of a preoccupation, over time, than thinking about my lost human family. I was sleeping each night now in the hollowed-out trunk of an old tree, and though it felt safer, there were periods – long periods, sometimes – during the days when the whole troop would ascend to the top of the canopy. A place where I simply couldn't follow.

I wanted to get up there so badly, yet the idea seemed

impossible. The trees were almost as big a problem to master as the Brazil nuts they unwittingly flung down for me to eat. With the latter, I could only even attempt to break into those fruits whose outer pods had split open from the fall. The intact ones were just impossible. Even the nuts inside didn't yield without putting up a fight; it would take an awful lot of bashes, using my cranny-and-rock system, before I could make so much as a single crack in their armour.

Similarly, the trunks of these trees seemed to spite me. About six to eight feet in diameter, they towered upwards to the sky – an almost smooth vertical corridor. If I looked up, it made me dizzy to see how impossibly high they grew, disappearing up through the steamy air before seeming to almost come to a point, and only then graced with any branches I could climb on.

But there were smaller trees too, striving upwards between these colossal kings of the jungle; the friendly trees that provided the delicious little bananas, and others, jewelled with the hanging waxy flowers I would later learn were orchids. These would also be draped with graceful looping vines and fronds of dark, spongy mosses, and, between them, the curls and arches of delicate green ferns.

Perhaps, I wondered one day, when the monkeys had again deserted me, I could find a way to join them by making my way up the smaller trees, in the hope of somehow gaining access to the upper reaches of the Brazil trees. My plan was doomed to failure – it would be many months before I mastered that particular monkey talent – but it was to provide me with an unexpected discovery.

It had just rained, I remember – perhaps not the best time to try being an acrobat, because as ever the whole jungle ran with water and dripped. The boughs and vines were slippery, but, perhaps invigorated and energised by the cooling, cleansing downpour, I decided I would give it a try; if I didn't try, as my mother used to say to me, how did I know what I could or couldn't do?

At first, it wasn't too difficult. I made my way upwards about six or seven feet, using a tangle of roots and vines and low boughs, and finding plentiful foot- and handholds. But no sooner had I ascended to the top of a small tree than I was faced with a difficult horizontal clamber across a bough, to have any hope of getting higher.

I tried anyway (now I was this far, I could hardly bear to look down, much less climb down), but the slippery, slimy branch was my undoing. As soon as I put all my weight on it, I immediately lost purchase and crashed down, screaming loudly and frantically, terrified and sure I was about to die.

But the undergrowth was kind to me. While buffeting me and winding me, the tangle of massed foliage and latticework of stems, stalks and branches also broke my fall. And as I lay there getting my breath back, feeling tears of self-pity spring to my eyes, I realised I was looking straight at something I'd never seen before. It was a tunnel – the entrance to which was just about big enough to crawl through, and which disappeared into blackness around a bend.

I looked more closely. It seemed to be fashioned out of the same tangle of tree roots and undergrowth that had just been obliging enough to break my fall. It looked like it had been hollowed out some time ago as well, as its inner edges – the same latticework of branches and roots, mainly – were quite smooth of snags and spikes.

I pulled myself up and crawled across to it. It was a bit of a tight fit, but I could just about wriggle into it and venture in. I still remember that I didn't feel too frightened. Sufficient light filtered through so that, although gloomy, it wasn't pitch-black, and as I crawled along it opened out – it was a whole network of tunnels! – with branches heading off in several directions.

I began to wonder what kind of animal would have made such a tunnel, but curiosity triumphed over anxiety and I decided to crawl a little bit further. It was then, rounding a bend, that I made my next big discovery. There was a monkey up ahead of me – one of my monkeys – and it was scampering towards me with a nut in its hand. No sooner did it see me than it veered off down a side tunnel, with another monkey (they were both young and playing chase, it was obvious) scrambling along and screeching playfully in hot pursuit.

Seeing this made everything fall into place. They had created this network of tunnels on the floor of their territory to enable them to get around on the ground just as easily as they traversed the tops of the trees. And I realised that I would also be able to use it to get about the jungle floor speedily and safely. My disappointment about my lack of climbing skills now all but forgotten, I crawled after the monkeys and finally emerged in a small, familiar clearing, feeling as uplifted as at any point since I'd been abandoned in the jungle. Making this new discovery felt – and I remember the feeling to this day – almost as if Christmas had arrived. It really was as thrilling to me as that. A mark, perhaps, of just how feral I'd become.

I was certainly beginning to feel I'd learned all the skills I would need to keep me safe in this wild and remote place. But it was an assumption that turned out to be very wrong.

6

I was going to die soon, I was sure of it.

I had no idea why, only that the sense that I was dying was one that was diffusing through the whole of my body, causing me to clutch my stomach and whimper in pain.

I tried to think back, through the fog of pain, to what I'd eaten that might have done this thing to me.

Tamarind! It suddenly came to me. The day before, I'd eaten tamarind. It was one of my favourite things to feed on. Similar in shape to the bean pods that used to grow on our allotment, the tamarind pod was dark brown and furry, and, when spilt open, the insides were sweet and sticky, with the texture of figs.

But even as I'd tasted it, I'd known it wasn't like the usual tamarind. This variety – doubtless one of many others to be found – had lots of small fruits inside, similar in size to peas, and, if anything, tasted even sweeter, like dates.

I couldn't stand. I couldn't sit. Trying to work my muscles defeated me. But through my dizziness I felt a grim certainty form inside me. I had eaten delicious tamarind's deadly twin. If there was one thing I'd learned from my time with the monkeys, I thought wretchedly, it was that things can look almost identical in every detail, but just a couple of tiny differences could have a seriously large impact – the difference, perhaps, between life and death.

But as I writhed, I saw that sympathy, if nothing else, might be at hand. Though my vision swam, I could just about see Grandpa monkey. I'd called him that simply because that's what he looked like. He was older than the others, moved differently from the young ones and had the same sprinklings of white fur that triggered a clear if distant memory of the few old people I'd encountered in my former life. I recalled one clearly – not someone related, so perhaps a neighbour or friend. A white-haired woman who had no front teeth. Grandpa monkey had lots of teeth, but he was similarly white-haired in places and grey in others, especially on his face. He also walked slowly, just as the old woman in my mind's eye had done, and had an old injury to his arm or shoulder, I thought, because he didn't range around the treetops like the others.

Grandpa monkey had kept a very close eye on me from a very early stage. But I didn't think it was because he was concerned about my welfare. There had never been any warmth in the way he behaved when he was around me, so I decided it must be because he was very protective of his family. Perhaps he hadn't quite decided if he liked me or not.

I watched him jump down from the tree he most liked to sit in and then approach me. What was he about to do? I had no idea but couldn't care less, in any case. I was much too busy crying from the horrible gripping pain.

Grandpa monkey drew level, squeezed my arm firmly, then began shaking me slightly, shoving me, as if determined to herd me somewhere else.

He was purposeful and determined, and I wasn't about to resist him. Scrabbling to get a purchase, I half-crawled, half-stumbled into the foliage, in the direction his repeated shovings seemed to suggest he wanted me to go.

It was out of the question to disobey, but I was still very fearful as I edged my way deeper into a patch of thorny bushes. And once in them, at least I had the pain of repeated stings and scratches to divert my mind from the pain inside me. Where we were going, however, I didn't have a clue.

It was mere seconds before I found out. One minute I'd been scrabbling through a tangle of branches, now I was falling – tumbling over and over down a mossy, rocky bank, which was running with cool water and which eventually deposited me into a little basin below.

I looked around, panting as I tried to catch my breath. The basin was around eight feet wide, surrounded by rock and earth and tree roots, and looked almost like an open-topped cave.

A tight collection of black rocks had created a lip to one side, over which a steady stream of water formed a waterfall. The water I had landed in wasn't deep, not enough to submerge me, but right away I could see that Grandpa monkey had come too. Was he going to take advantage of my weakened state and try to drown me?

It seemed I had my answer, for almost immediately he began shoving me again, trying to direct me towards the stream of water. I sobbed. All the worst things that could happen to me seemed to be happening all at once. I was terrified and in agony, and I hated the water – it was something I'd been afraid of all my life. Apart from drinking small quantities and being hammered by rainfall, I'd not seen water – water that could drown you – for a long time, and I hated to see it again now.

But Grandpa monkey was relentless and, though we were of similar size, he was also very strong. He seemed intent on putting my head under, keeping a tight grip on my hair. Was he trying to drown me? Or was he trying to make me drink the water? Or maybe he knew I was going to die anyway and was just trying to help me on my way.

Whatever his intentions, I struggled, heaving myself away from him and slapping the surface of the pool, splashing him, and as I did so he yanked my face up and looked me straight in the eyes.

As I looked back at him, I could see something I hadn't before. His expression was completely calm. It wasn't angry, or agitated, or hostile. Perhaps I'd been wrong, I thought, as I coughed and spluttered and tried to catch my breath again. Perhaps he was trying to tell me something.

I didn't know what it was, but in that instant I trusted him. The look in his eyes and the calmness in his movements made me realise he was trying to help me. Accordingly, this time I did as he seemed to want. I went under and drank in great mouthfuls of muddy water, swallowing as much as I could and feeling it force its way up my nose.

At this point, Grandpa monkey let go of me. I wasted no time in scrambling out and up onto the rocky bank, where, completely spent, I just collapsed on the ground, face down.

I began coughing again and soon the coughing turned to

vomiting – first the water and then behind it great heaving gouts of acid liquid that burned my throat and washed painfully over the skin of my scratched limbs.

But Grandpa monkey wasn't done yet. No sooner had I stopped vomiting than he began chivvying me all over again to get back into the pool, this time to the other edge where the water was much shallower and where a second smaller waterfall dripped steadily.

I needed no urging. I drank from the waterfall thirstily and was happy to remain there, even as leeches clamoured to attach themselves to my legs, just to feel the flowing water cooling me and healing me, and the tortuous spasms inside me subside.

I have no idea how long I sat there, semi-conscious, trance-like, but at some point I felt restored enough to clamber back up again. Grandpa monkey had been sitting at the pool's edge, immobile all this time, just watching and waiting. As I moved, so did he, rising up to his feet, then, seemingly satisfied with his efforts, turning and scuttling off ahead of me, back to his tree.

I will never know for sure what it was that had poisoned me, just as I'll never know how Grandpa monkey knew how to save me. But he did. I am convinced of it.

And the encounter didn't just teach me yet another survival lesson. It also marked a point when my life with the monkeys changed. Because, from that day on, Grandpa monkey's attitude towards my continued presence changed completely. Where once he'd been indifferent and then obviously wary, he now felt like both my protector and my friend.

Now he seemed happy both to share food with me and groom me, and would often feast upon the wealth of bugs that lived in my mat of hair. And, bit by bit, my sense of loneliness and abandonment began to fade. Though there would still be nights when I'd be overcome by what I'd lost and weep for hours, these instances of grief were getting fewer. Curled up in my little ball, in my hollowed-out piece of tree trunk, with the comforting, familiar sound of the monkeys up above me, I was gradually turning into one of them.

7

The incident of my being poisoned and 'saved' by Grandpa monkey proved to be a turning point in how the monkeys responded to me. Taking their lead from their elder, more and more of them seemed happier to approach me and groom me. No longer was I just a tolerated outsider; it felt as if I was becoming a real part of the troop, which made the ache lodged in my heart that tiny bit more bearable.

Though I had by now become aware that my new family sometimes changed – some animals disappearing and returning with tiny babies, others disappearing and never being seen again – I began to get to know some of the monkeys quite well. There was Grandpa, of course, who was a constant during my time there. But also energetic Spot, gentle, loving Brownie and timid White-Tip, one of the little ones, who seemed to really love me and who would often jump onto my back, throw her arms around my neck and enjoy being carried wherever I went.

Of course, I hadn't actually given any of the monkeys names at the time. By now I had no use for human speech at all – only my crude version of monkey language. I don't think I even thought in human language any more. So I'd no longer consciously 'think up' something as abstract as a name. I had simply begun identifying each animal by some distinguishing attribute or physical characteristic. My life had become all about sounds and emotions. And 'missions'. All of life was now broken into missions. Missions to find food. Missions to find company. Missions to find a safe place to hide if there was danger. I had only two concerns: to satisfy my basic needs and to satisfy my curiosity – the same simple life that the monkeys had.

*

Now I felt more accepted, I became even more determined to learn how to climb to the top of the canopy. I was beginning to hate that I had to spend such long solitary periods on the ground, from where I could hear the joyous whoops and shrieks of the games going on high above me but was not able to get up there and join in. Getting up there, from then on, became my new mission.

I had not stopped practising my climbing since my first failed attempt. It would be so wonderful to be able to escape the dampness of the forest floor and to feel the sun on my back – the whole might of the sun – instead of having to make do with the long shafts that angled down from between the branches, where I could only linger in the patchy spotlights they created. Despite the colours of the jungle, it sometimes seemed to me that I was living in a black and white world. Some parts of the undergrowth, even at the brightest part of the day, were so dark as to seem shrouded in perpetual night, pierced by arrows of light so white and blinding it hurt my eyes.

I was also desperate to have some respite from the heavy, stagnant air and the endless irritation of all the creepy crawlies. I was used to bugs, but never had I seen so many different kinds in one place. The jungle teemed with them: flying things, scuttling things, jumping things and biting things. There were flying beetles that looked like tiny machines – today I'd liken them to helicopters – which had whirring wings that made a special sound as they landed. There were blue bugs and green bugs, bugs that looked like sparkly treasure, and bugs that thrilled me because they would light up at night. There were big black beetles that seemed to have pairs of scissors on their noses, and any number of different squirmy, wormy, wibbly, wobbly grubs. It sometimes felt as if I saw something new every day.

There were also lots of different kinds of brightly coloured frogs, toads and lizards. They also made their homes in the shelter of the undergrowth, so the air would hum with all manner of buzzes, croaks and hisses. And it was a home that suited all of them. So rich with food, so hot and humid, it was a glorious earthly paradise for them all. But not so much for me! How I craved the chance to leave them to their baser insect pleasures – being stirred by stinking breezes, heavy with the stench of rotten plant life, and massing in excited clouds on any dead or dying thing.

Day after day, for what might well have been several months, I would try to climb the shorter, slimmer trees. I fell often – sometimes many times a day, and often far and painfully – but I didn't let my failures deter me. I had already learned by now that the one thing I could be sure of in this spongy, tangled world, was that I'd be guaranteed a reasonably soft landing, even if I did amass lots of bruises, cuts and scratches along the way.

I didn't just climb randomly, either. I didn't have the advantages the monkeys had – their incredibly long, springy limbs, their sense of balance, their usefully curling tails – but I laboured hard to find the best technique. With so little in the way of hand- and footholds on the masters of the canopy – the majestic Brazil nut trees – they were still beyond me. The only way I could make upward progress from the forest floor was if I happened to be locked in the embrace of strangling vines. But with the slimmer trees, the most efficient way turned out to be one in which I employed my whole body, using my knees and elbows to grip the trunks. Then, while using my outwardly turned feet to push, I could employ my upper body strength and hands to pull me upwards.

After a time, my body seemed to adapt to this new form of daily exercise. I grew stronger, the muscles in my arms and legs developing and becoming sinewy, while the skin on my hands and feet, elbows, knees and ankles grew progressively more dry and leathery and so was better able to grip the bark.

There was also another plus. Dry skin was always flaking, and picking at the flakes was one of my favourite things to do. I would sit and worry away at it for hours.

And I needed my rest, too, because strength, of course, was vital. With the first boughs of the Brazil nut trees being so high up, I needed to be strong enough to cling on vertically for some considerable time, with only meagre hand- and footholds, which was extremely tiring. Some trees were a little easier to manage than others, because they'd acquired a thick covering of the stringy, strangling vines. But these trees were always dying, so their usefulness would be temporary. Not long after, they'd be nothing but hollow dead shells and would sink back down into the soil from which they'd sprung.

Coming down was much quicker and a great deal more straightforward. Once my palms and the soles of my feet had become sufficiently hard and leathery, it was simply a question of letting them do the work, allowing me to slide back down to a soft landing on the composty floor. After which, of course, I'd often climb straight back up again. For up was where I wanted to be.

*

The day I reached the canopy will be another of those days that I will remember for the rest of my life. You might find it simple to imagine what sort of sight greeted me, but then, as a very young child, I had never seen anything quite like it. I had no store of television images to prepare me, no past experience to compare. I was seeing what I was seeing for the very first time, and I couldn't quite believe the evidence of my eyes.

The view was breathtaking – literally. The rush of cool air up there was such a shock to me that it made me gasp. And in my disbelief and awe, I think I probably did forget to breathe. There was just so much sky above the green giants that had formed the ceiling of my world for so long that I found it difficult to adjust to the fierce light. And when I did manage to open my eyes fully, I still couldn't take it in. It seemed there were only trees and clear sky for as far as I could see. And I could see for what looked like many miles.

I had no idea how high up I was. A hundred feet? Two hundred? I have no idea. Just so high up in the sky that I felt dizzy looking down, particularly when the trees began swaying. So high that it was as if I was in a strange and different world now; one where nothing existed but the colours and shapes I was squinting at – the dazzling blue of the sky up above me, the lush green of the broccoli treetops below. There was nothing else to see whatsoever.

The monkey troop, of course, was indifferent. The monkeys seemed to be going about their usual business with no apparent interest in the fact that I was suddenly up here with them. But I couldn't have been more excited. So here was where they most liked to be, I thought, as I tentatively began to explore this new territory. And I could see why. What a wonderful place it seemed to be. All around me, the pillowy surface of the canopy rose and fell as it faded into the far and hazy distance, the treetops undulating and in some cases rising in steps: cushiony emerald terraces that looked so soft and beguiling compared to the thorny tangled mass of vegetation below.

Sufficiently confident that the vast web of branches below would support me, I began to clamber across the springy boughs, with little White-Tip close behind me, and could see that the canopy in the near distance seemed more yellow-green than green. I wondered if the trees were all covered in flowers, tilting their happy faces to the unbroken sky. It was a bright, intense yellow that seemed to reflect the sunshine and made everything seem even more dazzling.

It was no less hot up here, but drier – the breeze a constant welcome friend, as if it had hurried along specifically to counteract the relentless rays of the sun. And the monkeys clearly loved it, for they had even set up little homes here with what looked like beds, or seating areas – some of the troop were certainly sitting in them – where they could bask and groom each other far from the damp and steamy forest floor. Closer inspection revealed that they seemed to have made these by collecting bits of branches they'd snapped off while playing 'look who's the strongest' (which was something they did often) and had brought up to the canopy to use. These had then been laid crosswise over bigger branches that were still attached to the trees.

For softness, Mother Nature had helped them out, it seemed, because the 'nests' would naturally collect any fallen or drifting leaves. They had also added strips of bark – something that was always in plentiful supply, because one of their favourite things to do was to pull off long strips of tree bark in order to get to the tastiest, juiciest bugs.

I sat and watched my monkey family for some time, contentedly taking in the excitement of it all. Compared to what was below, it just felt like such a lovely place to be. And I soon realised that they didn't just use the structures they'd made for sitting and sleeping on. They also seemed to use them as places to play: jumping up and down on them, whooping and shrieking, making a great deal of noise and giving off bursts of an intense odour, the air becoming even more hazy than it usually did with the sharp, acrid smell of their excrement.

Not that I minded. By now I was immune to such odours. I was just so happy to be up there and joining in. It felt as if I'd at last escaped my prison and properly become one of them, which, physically, was happening, even though I probably wasn't consciously aware of it. I was growing a new, muscular body, strong in ways a child's body normally isn't. I had harder heels and palms, and an appetite for strange jungle foods. I was also beginning to move around like a monkey, and one of the reasons, perhaps, that I wasn't aware of how I was growing, was that I almost always walked on all fours now. There was just the one skill I lacked and that I'd struggled to master – flying. How I longed now to sail through the treetops as they did, via their expressway, à la Tarzan, on the vines.

As the vines were thick and plentiful, especially high in the treetops, it seemed that it was yet another skill I could master if I tried. So, after the first few days of being able to climb to the canopy, I would spend time trying to do what my monkey family did: get from tree to tree, bough to bough, by means of these stringy curtains, feeling the euphoria and wind-rush, the giddy sensation of being airborne, and then landing – in my case, mostly messily and indecorously – on whichever bed of branches had been my goal.

But again and again, something was telling me I shouldn't. No sooner would I launch myself than I'd feel a sudden crunch and the unmistakeable sinking feeling that the vine I was holding onto was coming loose from its anchor. I'd then be sure of one thing only. That I was about to get my back, arms and legs thoroughly grated. The first couple of times this happened, my fall was mercifully short, because the vine tangled in another and I jerked to a stop. I also had the consolation, once I'd got over the painful bit, of a fresh crop of scabs to sit and pick.

But one day my run of luck ran out. I had clung on and launched myself on what had seemed a sturdy line, when only a second later I felt the snap of the vine breaking free. This was closely followed, inevitably, by a stomach-churning plunge and the feeling of pure terror that only the sight of the ground rushing up to meet you can provoke. Thankfully, I was spared by the embrace of a spray of branches which slowed my fall sufficiently that I was able to grab them as I hit them and get enough purchase to stop me plunging straight on down to my death.

Hanging there with the forest floor dizzyingly far below me, I perhaps should have felt some sort of powerful instinct. That I wasn't like my simian family. That I wasn't a monkey. That I was simply not built to be swinging through the trees.

I didn't. I was much too busy clinging on for dear life. But I would learn, as it turned out. And very soon.

8

With my existence now contained within the all-encircling vastness of the jungle, it was perhaps natural that at some point I stopped thinking about the life I'd lived before and began feeling part of my new monkey family. Now that I had access to what I realised was their main home, up in the canopy, I could be with them all of the time, which made my life all the fuller and richer.

The monkeys were incredibly intelligent. They were so inventive, so sensitive to their surroundings and so inquisitive, and, most of all, they were very quick learners. As well as being my friends, the monkeys were now my school class and my tutors, though the knowledge I was acquiring bore no relation to what I might have been taught in school. I was a child, and like all children I wanted to play. And though the young monkeys would always beat me at tree climbing, there was no longer much else they could do that I couldn't.

But they had incredible energy. They would often tire me out with their games of rough and tumble, and I soon learned that sometimes it was best if I just sat still on the ground as a way to signal that I had no strength left to play any more. Similarly, when they became too rough, I learned how to make the right kinds of noises to show my irritation and send them on their way.

But they seemed to have as much emotional intelligence as they had energy, and if I got cross with them they'd sometimes lie down on the ground beside me, tongue lolling, and make a soft, melancholic sound. It was almost as if they felt guilty for upsetting me, or perhaps it was their way of apologising.

Such nuances of emotion felt every bit as real to me as human feelings, for my monkey family were sensitive and complex. All shades of emotion seemed to exist here: humility and pride, surrender and protection, jealousy and celebration, anger and happiness. I was now finely attuned to their relationships; I could readily see if one of them felt lonely or isolated, or if another craved affection and was hoping for a cuddle, or if another felt aggressive or possessive.

I also became continuously more aware of the diversity of their language, from their strident warning shrieks and howls to expressions of annoyance or joy, to the gentle fluting sounds of their everyday conversations. They were social beings, who lived within a hierarchy of relationships. There were few moments, day or night, that they didn't spend together, whether grooming or playing or communicating in some other way, and I was just happy to be one of them – to feel included. I felt that I belonged where I was now.

*

For all that I loved to be with the monkeys, one thing I never did was sleep up in the canopy. Not after the first time I tried it, anyway. Reassuring though the idea had seemed in the daytime – I would no longer have to sleep alone – being so high up in the dark was a very different matter. For one thing, the treetops would sway, which was frightening and made it very difficult to fall asleep. If I did, I'd then begin to toss and turn, which was equally unnerving, because I could so easily tip off the edge of my perch. And, of course, eventually, I did.

I wasn't at the very top of the canopy the night I fell to what could so easily have been my death, but, even so, the fall was terrifying. It was also a great shock, as I had been fast asleep and I hit my head and hurt myself badly. Badly enough that it was something I knew with some certainty that I had absolutely no intention of repeating.

Instead, I returned to sleeping in my hollow tree trunk, though, following the monkeys' example perhaps, I began to make it cosier. I collected moss to line the base to make my bed. I also hung some on the walls, along with flowers that I thought particularly pretty. I have a strong memory that I would also talk to the moss, after a fashion, using my new simian language. I have no idea why; I only know that it made me feel better, perhaps in the same way a child would cuddle and converse with a teddy bear.

I did have company in my tree trunk, though it took the form of bugs rather than teddies, and in time I grew not to mind their various scuttlings and whirrings. I always took care, though, to cover my ears with my hair before sleeping, in case they found them too inviting to resist. And though I would have dreams in which I was being chased by hungry animals, I also grew less afraid of the real predators that I would hear passing by my tree from time to time at night. Perhaps it was because I knew I was well hidden, or perhaps just because I knew I had no choice in the matter. It was certainly preferable to feel a little anxious than to plunge from the boughs of a very tall tree.

But as dawn broke each day and the sun showed its face, my confidence rose along with it. During daylight hours, I would now spend the majority of my time in the canopy. And like the monkeys, I would often have a siesta up there, away from the cloying humidity down below, enjoying the caress of the cooling breeze instead.

It was afternoon – the sun was burning low in the sky – and I had just woken up from one such dreamless slumber when, looking down, I saw something glinting up at me. The forest floor was way, way below me, the air full of dewy mist, as ever, but whatever it was, it was brilliant enough to cut through this and catch my eye. The jungle had just been through a period of heavy rain that morning, so my first thought was that whatever it was down below me was simply glistening as a consequence of its drenching, but as I continued to look I could see that this wasn't the case – it shone far brighter than anything else I could see.

I was still drowsy, but whatever it was had sufficiently caught my interest to prompt me to make my way back down to the undergrowth to investigate. I climbed down carefully, keeping my eyes fixed on the spot where I'd seen the diamond shimmer of brightness, and, once back on the ground, I set off to investigate. What I found when I reached it was unfamiliar. It was a wedge-shaped piece of some hard, shiny material, the like of which I didn't think I'd ever seen before. It was sharp at its apex and curved at the other end, and was tiny enough to fit easily into the palm of my hand.

I played with it for a moment, inspecting it carefully, intrigued by the way it seemed to flash and glimmer in the sunshine, how its edges felt rough but its surface was so smooth. One side was dark, while the other, though scratched, seemed (at least to me) almost to be made of light itself.

I drew it closer, to better see how this light effect worked, and it was then that I got the shock of my young life. Two eyes were staring back at me – the eyes of some wild animal? I dropped the thing in terror and stared ahead of me again. The eyes had vanished. What was there? What had been looking at me? And where was it now?

But there was nothing, and, eventually, though I still felt quite frightened, I crawled across to where I'd thrown my treasure, rummaged around till I found it, and, heart racing with anticipation, picked it up again. This time I drew it more slowly to my eye line, and once again I saw two eyes staring back at me. It was then that some long-buried memory must have surfaced, because I realised what I was staring at wasn't a vision of a wild animal. I was looking into a mirror that was reflecting a face.

I was transfixed. In all this time I had never once seen my reflection. Perhaps I might have, had my fear of water not been so profound. Perhaps, had it occurred to me to seek out my reflection, I might have made a point of investigating it every time my little pond re-filled with rain. But I had never done so.

It was barely bigger than a thumbprint, but my little mirror enthralled me. I could see so little, but enough that I could tell it was me. Though I didn't know my face, I could immediately see the relationship between what I made it do and what happened in the mirror. I blinked my eyes, I moved my mouth – the shard of mirror obligingly did likewise. I changed my expression and the face in the mirror changed hers too.

Shocked and thrilled, I remember I let out a hoot of great excitement and bounced around, looking for someone who could share in my discovery. I can't really describe just how it felt to have made it. My best attempt would be to say that it was both scary and exciting. To discover you have a face – it felt amazing! But at the same time I was frightened to see myself in it, because I had begun to believe that I looked just like the monkeys. I knew my body was a little different, but for some complicated reason – perhaps a human need to belong? – I felt my face would be exactly the same as theirs.

I was astonished to find that this wasn't the case, and I clutched the tiny piece of glass to me as if I'd found something magical. And as I carried it around, looking for a safe place in which to keep it, I wondered quite how it had found its way into the jungle, because it was like nothing I had ever seen in there before.

But my feelings of euphoria weren't to last, because with the coming of the evening came a subtle change in me. Is it a necessary evil, I wonder, that, with the darkness, comes a shift in the way everything emotional feels? I have no idea, but what I do know was that as day turned into evening, my earlier ebullience was replaced by anxiety. The more I looked at my cracked image, the more obvious it became to me that I was mistaken in my belief about who and what I was. I wasn't one of my monkey family, I was different – a different animal. One with wide eyes, smooth skin and a tangle of long, matted hair. And as soon as those thoughts had taken shape in my mind, it was as if a door had been forced open inside my head. It was a door that had been shut for as long as I could remember and which led me back to feelings I'd either forgotten or suppressed. I had been in denial – that had been my protection. But now, all at once, I felt horribly alone again. I was lost here, completely isolated from a world I could barely recall but which at the same time I now remembered I had been ripped from.

Once again I was a creature without an identity. I didn't want that. It shook me and chilled me, made me feel hollow to the core. I had forgotten I was human and now I'd been reminded.

And very soon I'd receive an even stronger reminder.

9

My little shard of mirror was the first and only thing I 'owned' for the whole of my time in the jungle, and over the coming days, I guarded it carefully. Initially the monkeys were very inquisitive about it and would clamour to see what I had found that took up so much of my attention. They would fuss round me, anxious to get it off me, but once they had all worked out that, as I hadn't eaten it, it probably wasn't edible, they lost interest and stopped trying to pull it from my grasp.

I had a home for it, tucked safely beneath my soft, mossy bed, and would bring it out often and just carry it around with me, wanting only to keep it for ever.

And then one day, perhaps predictably, I lost it. I dropped it during a fall from a low-ish tree bough and it skittered away down into the undergrowth. The feeling of distress was a powerful one, as I had become obsessively attached to my treasure. I spent many, many hours trying to find it again and covered every single inch of ground in that area. I only gave up when it seemed that the mirror must have fallen into the depths of the pond, from where I knew I would never be able to retrieve it. And though I harboured hope that perhaps the water would one day dry up and I would see that magical glint once again, it never happened, and eventually I accepted its loss, even though it stayed on my mind.

I was bereft for a long time without my tiny talisman. It was like I'd lost a friend and, even more than that, a protector. Now the genie was out of the bottle and I could sense my difference from my loving family, having the fragment of mirror had made me feel less alone. It was almost as if someone was looking out for me, somehow. Just looking into it made me feel safer.

*

That there was a world beyond the boundary of what I now thought of as 'our' territory had never been in doubt. Not the world outside the jungle – I had long since ceased to be aware of that – but the world of other territories, other monkeys, other animals. I was reminded of this every time another troop of monkeys came to fight us, or when, while playing up high in the canopy, the breeze would carry strange, distant sounds. And as I grew in confidence and inquisitiveness to match my growing body, so I felt brave enough to explore further afield.

Initially, I didn't wander far. I had come to realise that the jungle seemed to be divided into territories, each one home to different kinds of animals. And they didn't tend to mix; each type of creature seemed to stay in its own region, which I realised was the reason there was always such a big fight when a different kind of monkey troop strayed into ours. There seemed to be any number of these territories. As well as our 'monkey land', and others nearby which were like it, there seemed to be a land mostly inhabited by toucans, another by parrots, and, I think, one ruled by big cats of some kind, though I had only once fleetingly seen a big, scary feline, as I was too frightened to venture further to find out.

There was also a river, I'd discovered since I'd managed to reach the canopy: a wide silver snake that coiled between the pillowy green forests, which I could only see from one part of our territory. I would sit high in my eyrie and watch it for long periods. I was scared of it yet also mesmerised, my fear of water accompanied by a compelling fascination for something so different from the enclosed emerald world I already knew.

The animals that seemed to rule the river-land were caimans. I didn't know the name for them at the time, but I would crouch safely up in the canopy and watch them slithering off the riverbank, and instinctively knew that these were creatures I didn't wish to meet. They would slip so silently into the water, had such a cold, unfriendly look to them, and, even at a distance of many, many feet, I could see just how many pointed teeth they had in their gaping mouths.

And they were teeth I saw them use to good effect. I soon realised that when any animals ventured to the riverbank to drink, the action – which, frustratingly, I couldn't always see – seemed to be done in groups, with much splashing. I also noticed how the caimans would lie and watch what was going on, sometimes slipping into the water and causing even more noise, as the animals would splash around in terror.

It was a big bird, however, that I first saw killed by a caiman. A big, ugly grey bird, which I suspect might have been a vulture and which took its last drink oblivious of the silent devil that watched it from beneath the surface. I had never seen anything so dreadful or so bloody. The bird was gobbled up in three enormous bites.

But although I was sensible enough to keep away from the river, my curiosity about the world beyond our territory grew. It was to be rewarded by the discovery of a territory that belonged to a whole other species, one that I had never seen before in the jungle and perhaps the last that I would ever have expected.

Wishing to discover something exciting was a big part of my day. I was curious about the world and had an instinctive need to see and do new things. I was always looking for a new tree to climb, a new vista, or a chance to observe my surroundings from a different vantage point. Perhaps it might lead me to a new piece of treasure, to replace my last one, or perhaps to the discovery of an abundant patch of exotic fruit.

Sometimes I would turn back because the ground changed for the worse, the fallen leaves spikier. On other occasions I would simply run out of courage and run scared back to the safety of the territory I knew. But the pull of the new called to me, tempting me, always. So off I'd set in yet another direction.

On this day I had wandered for most of the morning, far enough to begin to explore places I'd not yet seen but not so far that I couldn't hear the calls of my monkey family, and certainly not far enough that should I lose my bearings I would be unable to find my way home again.

Eventually I came to a new and enticing area, where one particular tree – proud and tall and bearing wide, inviting arms – seemed to call to me to climb it, so I did. It was a quick and easy climb, and in no time at all I had reached the topmost branches and had a clear view of the jungle below. I perched there for a moment, breathing in the cooler air, while, still and silent, I surveyed this new territory. Tropical birds circled, flashing blue and green and scarlet, and the wind played its whispering song on the swaying boughs.

I ranged around for a while, exploring different treetops and different vistas, before settling in the comfortable apex of two branches, happy to spend time just observing the activity around me – the birds and insects flying above me – and the land down below.

It was from up here, idly watching, that I was to make a discovery that was to change my life completely. Initially, however, I didn't know it. All I knew was that the legs that I could see moving far below me were unlike the legs of any monkey I had ever seen before. They were long and straight, and they looked to be hairless, though, at this distance and with a mass of branches blocking my vision it was obviously difficult to be sure.

Intrigued, I changed position slightly so I could get a better view. The animal was walking, and now I could see it more clearly I could get a better appreciation of its size. It was a big animal, certainly much bigger than the monkeys – bigger, too, than the wild boar I would sometimes catch sight of and mostly took care to avoid. It also, I realised with something of a start, seemed to be walking on two legs.

I changed position again, feeling the strangest of sensations: that this creature reminded me of myself. I studied it, enthralled at our similarities. It had long, straight black hair, not so different from my own, and moved in a way that I knew my own legs could if being on all fours were not now so natural. It also seemed to be on a quest to find something. It kept stopping and peering into various bushes then, apparently dissatisfied, walking on again. It also looked tired, with a weariness about it that put me in mind of how Grandpa monkey often behaved. Though this creature, unlike Grandpa, didn't look at all old.

It did look sick, though, I decided, and as if it was in pain. It had a strangely distended belly, which it clutched with one arm and seemed to find a great burden to carry around. Had it been poisoned as I had? Was it soon going to die?

I kept looking, transfixed now, keen to see what it would do. It was just such a strange sight. Terrifically exciting. But also one that left me unsettled. My eyes kept coming back to its odd gait, its weary manner, the cloth (though I barely registered the idea of clothes now) that hung from its middle, tied with what looked like vine. I was also confounded by what hung around its neck: a string of something that, from where I was, looked like berries.

All too soon, however, it walked out of my sight line, so I quickly and carefully shimmied back down the tree to a vantage point that would give me a clearer view of the animal but one not too dangerously close to the ground. Once there, now terrified that it would hear me and so look up and see me, I crouched motionless, my breath held, till it moved further away.

But it didn't move far. It was still inspecting bushes and finally seemed to see one it liked. Or at least that's how it seemed because now it crouched on the ground and began awkwardly crawling inside it. All of a sudden the air was full of the clamour of angry birds that had been shaken from the bush by this intruder. But I had no interest in their noise, because beneath the frantic cawing came a new sound that demanded my attention.

I'd never heard a noise in my life like the one that was coming from the animal that day. It seemed to groan, it seemed to hoot, it seemed to scream and sob and roar. These were nothing like the sounds I would hear from the monkeys; no attack shriek could compare to the intensity of this.

I had no idea what to do. What on earth was going on here? I was torn between the urge to climb down and so see better, and the fear of whatever was going on.

As the noises ceased – which they seemed to do with unexpected abruptness – I began, after a time, to wonder if the creature had left the bush. But how could it have? I had not taken my eyes off it for an instant. I would have seen it happen. So where could it be?

I have no idea how long it was before I got my answer. It could have been moments, or it could have been hours, because what I saw was such a shock to me that it filled my mind completely, causing all other thoughts in there to take flight. And as soon as I realised what I was seeing, it was obvious.

This wasn't an animal – an 'it' – it was a female! A mother! A mother who'd just had a baby!

Eyes almost out on stalks now, I watched as she emerged from the bush, carrying the tiny mewling infant in her arms, wrapped up in some sort of material. I remember the material well: it was hard-looking, off-white, and all I could see of the baby wrapped in it was the nut-brown dome of a tiny wrinkled head.

I could barely comprehend what I had witnessed. My thoughts were a maelstrom of emotion at that moment. This was a mother who'd just given birth to a baby, and I could see from her expression and the tenderness of her movements that she would love it and take care of its needs. I was captivated. And, at the same time, I felt bereft. I don't think I've ever felt such a longing to be wanted as I did at that moment. That was the kind of bush baby I wanted to be.

Her baby born, the new mother began walking back from the direction she'd come, her gait now completely different and her body straighter. And now that I'd found her, I was terrified of losing her, so I leapt from my perch and shimmied the rest of the way down the tree trunk, going so fast that I badly scratched the skin on my stomach and created a great cloud of bark-dust.

When I reached the ground, however, she was disappearing back into the undergrowth and the bush she'd been in was now empty. But was it? Might there be more babies in there? Torn between following her and answering the question that had just occurred to me, I decided to quickly wriggle inside the abandoned bush. It was dark, but I could see there were no babies, only a sticky and strange-smelling pool of what looked like blood. This shocked me. I still had no real idea how this baby had come about, even though I knew that such things did happen. Since I'd been with them, the monkeys had produced tiny babies from time to time, though I had never seen any of them give birth. They would simply disappear then reappear with a newborn, which would cling to its mother till it was big enough to play and so become of interest to the troop. But this animal wasn't a monkey. It was a creature like me. Which made what I'd witnessed today different.

I sometimes think back to that precious shard of mirrored

glass and wonder at the timing of my finding it. Would I have appreciated the significance of what I saw that day had I not been reacquainted with such a powerful sense of self? I don't know, but I was as determined as I had ever been about anything that I must find that mother, follow her and meet her.

I turned back to where I'd seen her heading and saw a sudden glimpse of movement. And did I hear something too? The unfamiliar mewl of an infant crying? It had to be. I set off in pursuit.

10

Trailing the mother and her baby wasn't as difficult as it might once have been. I was agile now and swift, and so familiar with the monkey tunnel networks that I could save time by using these rather than following her exact path. I was in new territory, obviously, but the principle was the same. And though my view was restricted, and the tunnels often veered me away from her route, I made sure to check regularly that she was still in my sight, even scampering up tree trunks to get a better view.

I was getting further from my home with every step, but my excitement and determination were powerful forces that lured me out of my normal comfort zone. I just followed her, and followed blindly, as I had only one goal: to go to wherever she was going.

As time passed, the whole look of the landscape began to change. It became clearer, less choked with the usual dense vegetation, and bit by bit I was beginning to see wide open spaces where the ground was no longer earthy but sandy.

By now, the woman and her baby were only a short distance ahead of me, and I felt a powerful urge to call out to her. I wanted to draw attention to myself, let her see me, make some sort of connection before it was too late. Something long dormant had definitely been awakened in me. I didn't know what – I just had this need for her to acknowledge me and want to meet me. And though it might now seem fanciful, my recollection is clear: I craved the opportunity for her to want me like she did that baby. I had no idea why this sensation was so strong in me. I had learned to be afraid now, to treat the new and strange with caution, yet I felt so drawn to the woman that my fear couldn't compete.

But I was too late. No sooner had I resolved to catch up with her than she suddenly disappeared from sight, having slipped through a gap in an unnatural-looking hedge that seemed to be made out of rows of forest sticks. I increased my speed, scrabbling across what was left of the undergrowth, but as much as I was committed to finding out where she'd gone, instinct stopped me from crossing the exposed open ground.

What I found, when I drew closer to the hedge the woman had gone through, drove all other thoughts from my mind. I crouched low, hidden among the vegetation, and slipped my fingers into the dense mesh of leaves so I could see. I had travelled far, so I was obviously in a new and different territory, but this was a territory the like of which I had never seen before.

As with my first sighting of the woman it took a few minutes before I could even begin to understand what I was seeing. But some tucked-away memory in my brain must have roused itself, because I definitely remember the sensation of it seeming strange but at the same time almost painfully familiar. And it set up a sort of yearning in my heart.

I don't know how old I was by now, or how long I'd been living with the monkeys, but my hunch is that it couldn't have been more than three years or so because memories from my life before the jungle must have come flooding back to me. Though I have very few left in my head now, several long decades later, I still have a strong sense that at that time I did still have them. I certainly had a conviction that the species beyond the fence were my species and that they lived in homes just as I had, even if they didn't look the same as the home I remembered.

In this case, they were huts, and there were three of them beyond the fence. They were very large and circular, with roofs made of lengths of long grass, and each had a single opening for a door. They seemed to be built from long wooden canes or boughs, which were tied together with strands of twisted vine, similar to the string the woman had been wearing round her waist.

There were also lengths of cloth slung from vines between trees, and after puzzling for a moment I recognised them too – they were called hammocks! I knew of hammocks! People used them to rest in, in just the same way as the monkeys would doze in their nests high in the trees. One of them held a man who seemed to be sleeping, the hammock which cradled him gently swaying.

Some of the men, to my unaccustomed eyes, seemed huge: well built, imposing and very scary. I was used to my monkey family now, where I dwarfed even the largest of the males. If I had been startled at the height of the woman I'd scampered after, I was in awe of these powerful-looking men. But once again, my fear was tempered – even if only a little – by the odd sensation that they were still the same as me.

There were several women around, too, wearing less than the new mother I had seen but with the same strings of berries around their necks. Only now another memory surfaced and nudged me. They weren't berries. They were necklaces: long strings of coloured beads. I remembered those, too. But where did they get them? There was so much to see and too much to take in. So many unfamiliar sights and smells and sounds.

Of the woman with the baby, however, there was no longer any sign, and I imagined she must have gone into one of the huts. But there were several other humans, of all shapes and sizes, and as I looked around from my hidden perch on top of a fallen log, I could also see that beyond the huts there was a riverbank. The water beyond it was flowing brown and slow, and I wondered if it was the same river I could see from the canopy. If so, weren't the people afraid of the caimans that might come up the bank and snap at their heels?

There seemed to be lots of activity by the river, however, so perhaps the scary caimans didn't go there. And at the water's edge there were two long, upturned structures made from tree trunks, which were glistening and obviously wet. They had been carved into a shape that initially made no sense but at the same time was frustratingly familiar, and it suddenly came to me that they must be boats.

So these people must travel on the river, for whatever reason. To get fish? To find new territories? Even to leave the jungle? I was transfixed as a new thought came to join the others. Did the river hold the key to finding my way back to my old home? The feeling came over me with startling intensity. I had barely thought of my old home in such a long time, and it shook me to be ambushed by the memory of it. I had forgotten so much, and now it all came clamouring back. These people were a family. A human family. And I was human, too.

I stayed close to the camp for the rest of the day. First I spied on them from my hidden viewpoint by the fence, and as the day wore on from a number of other locations, moving stealthily through the clumps of sparse vegetation that circled the camp on all but its riverbank edge. I just couldn't seem to drag myself away. But I was cautious. I was still very fearful of discovery – not by the women or the children but by one of the scary-looking men. The memory of the men who had brought me to the jungle had now been rekindled just as strongly as any other.

Watching these people going about their daily business was like being transported to a completely different world. Why did they have coloured marks on their faces? What was the purpose of rubbing lengths of material against stones? What were the strange green containers full of water for? Why was it that only the little ones seemed to have teeth? Just as it had been when I'd first come to the jungle, I was again learning about what seemed a completely different species, even as I accepted that it was probably my own.

I was particularly mesmerised by the children. Just like the monkeys, whose behaviour I was now so attuned to, the little ones, who were browner than I was and also cleaner, played and fought and frolicked and made happy sounds. The sound stirred up memories both from a life I'd forgotten and more recent experience. I had heard these shrill noises before when sitting in the canopy and had always assumed they were just a different kind of monkey sound. But they weren't. They'd been the sounds of these children!

Where the adults seemed strangely silent – unlike the monkeys, they didn't seem to want to interact with one another – the infants felt much more like me. Not just in their playfulness but also in their play – the way they used their hands and arms and bodies. And a part of me, naturally, wanted to show myself to them. To go and join in with their games and feel welcomed.

But it was my stomach that eventually dragged me away. It

was cross and grumbling because I hadn't filled it since morning. What did these people eat, I wondered, as I stretched limbs stiff from crouching. I had seen fruit that I recognised, piled in containers, but had seen no one eating it. So what did they eat? Fish from the river, perhaps? There had certainly been odd smells. The light was fading, but I decided to make one further foray, to the far edge of the fence, where I'd not yet been.

It was while doing this that I found a well-trodden path, close to the perimeter. It led away from the camp and, though I couldn't see the end of it, I became aware of a cloud rising up from the trees. Again I had a moment of complete incomprehension, watching the stone-coloured billows puff up into the sky. But then I realised. It was smoke! It was smoke from a fire! So that had been the source of the strange smell.

I edged hesitantly along the path, fearful that I might meet one of the scary adult humans. But it seemed I was alone. I neither saw nor heard anyone or anything. The path eventually opened out into another small clearing, which had the same dry, beaten ground as the camp itself. In the middle of this, two campfires burned. I had not seen a fire for so long that I barely recognised what it was. But somehow, seeing the smoke and the flames, I knew to be wary. More instinct than memory, I think. It served me well.

The closest of the fires was topped by a thin sheet of a shiny hard material. I didn't know it then, but this was a piece of metal and on top of it sat a large round container that seemed to have been made from the same material. Feeling the heat lick at my skin as I approached, I peered into it. It was full of bubbling water in which some large white root-like substance was immersed. My nose wrinkled as the mist from it swirled round my face. This was food for these people? I could hardly imagine eating it. It smelled so foul it immediately made me gag.

I moved across to the other fire, which was burning but empty apart from some sort of criss-cross of sticks. I placed my hands above the surface, marvelling at the heat I could feel on them. It was like the heat of the sun, only coming upwards. Incredible.

But there was nothing to eat, so I might well have slipped

away at that point except for the realisation that I could hear faint human sounds. The noise, which was low, was coming from just beyond the clearing, so I carefully made my way across the dusty ground to the source of it, thankful for the absence of twigs, leaves and branches that might unwittingly betray my presence to them.

Once close enough to hear them clearly, I poked my nose carefully through the undergrowth and was rewarded by the sight of two of the male humans, both squatting on their haunches by the base of a large, wide-trunked tree. They had set what I assumed must be some sort of trap. It was a container, made of sticks that had been criss-crossed and tied together. Threaded through it and coming out through the opening on the front of it was a length of a kind of string made of vine. The string was clearly there to lure something out – something they could eat – because they kept jiggling the end of it near the base of the tree. I waited to see whatever they were after, while the sun slunk even lower and the night took its place. Even in the gloom, I could see well enough. And what I eventually saw emerge was the biggest, hairiest spider I had ever seen.

I was used to spiders, even if these days I didn't tease them like I used to, but this was like no spider I'd ever seen in our territory. It was enormous – easily bigger than either of the men's hands – but sadly not much longer for this world. Almost as soon as it had emerged from its little home to chase after the end of the string, it was in the trap and stone dead – skewered in a heartbeat by one of the men's daggers, which had flashed by so fast I'd barely registered it.

The spider's body was transferred to a cloth bag by the men's side (which I could tell from its bulk probably contained other ill-fated spiders). As it was almost fully dark now, this was clearly their last catch of the day. They both stood up and made their way back to the clearing with the cooking-fires, and, fascinated – even if a little sad for the poor spiders – I wriggled out of my hiding place and followed.

It was here that I was to get my first ever cookery lesson. Once back by the empty fire, the men set to work. They removed several spiders from the cloth bag they'd brought, all of similar size to the one I'd watched them catch, and began fiddling carefully with each one. I would later learn that what they'd been doing was extracting the venom, which was clearly something useful, as they carefully squeezed it out into a small container that looked to be made from half a coconut shell.

It was difficult to see the detail, but once they'd dealt with every spider – as well as a couple of snakes that had been in the bag too – they wrapped them one by one in what looked like banana leaves, folding each leaf to make a parcel. These were then pierced with thin sticks to hold them together and popped onto the grid above the fire.

I had watched intently as they'd done this, my limbs again protesting but my stomach a great deal happier now it was anticipating food. And it seemed I was in luck because as soon as they'd prepared the parcels the two men got up again and walked out of the clearing. To hunt another kind of food? To tell the others? I had no idea. All I knew was that I wanted one of those parcels for myself.

I waited for some time, as I was frightened they might return, but once my ears had convinced me it was safe to go back, I quickly ran across to the grill and plucked out one of the parcels.

The heat was a shock. It was so hot I nearly dropped it and had to keep transferring it from hand to hand. I turned around then, to run with it back into the forest, but was stopped dead as I did so by the sight of three children, who had appeared as if from nowhere and now stood before me, staring with their huge black button eyes.

They said nothing, did nothing, seemed curious yet immobile, so I simply plunged back into the undergrowth and ran. They didn't follow. They didn't seem to care that I'd stolen their dinner. In fact, as I paused to take a breath before continuing, I could hear sounds that seemed unmistakeably like giggles.

I decided to stop then and get the first taste of my weirdly warm spider. I was ravenous and it seemed cool enough to eat now. I pulled the stick from the parcel and unfolded the charred leaf. The smell that wafted up made my stomach even happier, but as soon as I saw what was inside I felt sick. It just looked so horrible that I'd need to be much hungrier before I could bring myself to put anything so grim into my mouth.

My first taste of hot campfire food would have to wait. Perhaps they cooked other things, things that I could eat. I began the long trudge back to my own territory still hungry.

And hungry to see more. I would be back.

11

Once I knew where the human camp was, I couldn't keep away.

It was like a drug to me. So much so that, day after day, I would make the long journey, the route etched on my consciousness, and spend hours just sitting silently close by, taking it all in. No small child hankering after a special toy could have been more entranced than I was by what I'd found. And no student, however diligent, could have soaked up more information.

Food was a big preoccupation in those early days. After the excitement of finding – and stealing from – the tribe's barbecues, it had been a big disappointment to open that spider parcel and feel unable to eat what was inside it. But something kept calling me back, which I suspect might have been the hunch that other things would be cooked on those campfires that I *would* like to eat. And I was not to be disappointed.

Over the coming weeks and months, I was rewarded by a wide range of jungle food. I tried ant's bottoms, which were crunchy and delicious, and some huge shiny brown bugs that I couldn't identify, and which were not. They looked appealing on the outside, swollen and glossy with a pointed end, but inside they were raw and disgusting. I tried a tasty skinless meat that was reminiscent of sausage – looking back, it was a little like gamey chicken or maybe pheasant, but of course then all I knew was that I liked it. Sometimes the meat I tried had lots of tiny little bones in, and it occurs to me now that it was probably lumps of snake. I also ate fish and later on did try spiders, and when much later I found these tribes would routinely kill and eat monkeys, I had to concede – with great sadness and feelings of betrayal – that I probably ate monkey meat as well.

But at the time, I didn't know. I was hungry, and their food filled my tummy like nothing I could forage for ever would.

Not that I needed to forage much now. There was always fruit in abundance at the human camp. Why climb to get it myself when it was there for the taking? Helping myself now became a way of life.

I also, I now know, discovered alcohol! I have no idea what it was made from, or any idea of how they made it – all I know is that one day, on my way back to the monkey tunnels and my own territory, I came upon a container with a long narrow neck that was probably made from clay and which was covered in woven banana leaves. I tentatively sniffed it. The smell was pungent and made the inside of my nose prickle but at the same time was strangely appealing. Being very parched, I took a couple of big, thirst-quenching gulps. But as soon as I did I got a bit of a shock. Although the smell was enticing, when the liquid hit my throat, it was strong and incredibly bitter. It was also a taste that, after drinking nothing but water for so long, came as something of a surprise.

But it was as nothing to the shock of what would happen to me soon after. It was as if I'd suddenly forgotten how to work my arms and legs. I stumbled about a bit, enjoying the strange yet pleasant sensation that everything around was moving just as much as I was. So nice was the feeling that I even took a couple more swigs, which rendered me giggly and almost incapable.

It was a first and last experiment with underage drinking for me, as I felt strange and unsettled for the rest of that evening and far from bright eyed and bushy tailed the next day.

*

But it wasn't just food and drink that called me back to the Indians' camp. I continued to feel the strong sense of yearning I'd first experienced when I saw the new mother. I wanted to know everything about this human family and was keen to absorb all the minutiae of their everyday lives.

They wore little in the way of clothing – why would they, in the jungle heat? The men simply wore loincloths, as did the women. In fact, the only woman I had seen in something that covered most of her body was the woman who gave birth that first day. I wondered about the lack of teeth in the adults, as it looked so strange. In fact, it bewildered me. Had they fallen out? Been taken out? Was it a part of their grooming? There was so much to learn, and though some of what I saw stirred up memories of the life I'd lived before, most of it felt alien and strange.

But some things are universal across both animal and human kingdoms. I would watch the children play endlessly, loving how like me they seemed. They even did as I'd done when I'd first come into the jungle – found teasing the poor, long-suffering spiders a particularly pleasing way to pass the time. The women seemed busy every single second – they worked tirelessly. Unlike my monkey family, who spent much of their time sitting grooming one another and dozing, the women of this family seemed always to have so much to do. They would collect twigs to make the containers in which they stored their fruit and other things. They would lash together sticks of bamboo they had gathered before adding them to the already thickly covered hut roofs. They would also sew huge mats of bamboo and vine-string, which could be used both to lie on and also bent to make new walls to repair broken sections of their huts.

The men, too, were busy, and I soon came to understand how the work in the camp was divided. While the women kept the camp (and the children) neat and tidy, the men would go off in their wooden boats, down the river, or else spend time making poisoned darts, bows and arrows, and catapults. There seemed no end to the ways they had devised to kill things.

They had also made tree climbing much simpler than it was for me by tying a loose grassy rope between and around their ankles so that the rope tightened and gripped the tree trunk as they climbed. I could readily see how much pressure it took off their legs and feet, and they could scale a tree in no time, to get to the fruits above.

They also had a novel use for corncobs. Where I'd been dealing with my bodily functions both by using bits of moss and by doing as the monkeys did, I noticed one day, watching a child in the bushes, that they would use a hairy corn husk to do the job much more efficiently. It became a technique I adopted from then on.

*

So the days passed and the weeks passed, and my life became focused. Though I'd scamper back to my monkey troop every evening at around nightfall, most of my waking hours were now spent at the camp. I would carefully climb up into a tree close to the perimeter and spend hours, a silent wraith, just looking and listening. And the more I saw, the more I nursed a burgeoning belief that this was where I belonged, if only they would accept me.

Fear is a powerful emotion, and I was still very frightened. I had made a life with the animals and knew what to expect of them, and all I knew of humans, bar those fuzzy memories of home and mothering, was that two humans had stolen me and dumped me here. They had left me in the jungle not caring if I lived or died. Were these humans any different? I desperately wanted to believe they were. But what if they weren't? It would take courage to show my face here.

But as the time passed, the images of family here were so enticing. I would stare in at scenes that were tantalising and inviting: children playing, fires lit, all the family together. How wonderful it would be, I thought, from my viewpoint in the dark bushes, to be one of those cherished children, playing within the cosy confines of their cheerful camp.

I don't know now what made that particular day different from any other. I'm not sure if something triggered my sudden flash of boldness or whether I'd just had enough of being excluded from it all. Perhaps it was because there was so much going on that I thought I could slip in unnoticed.

It was around the middle of the day, and everyone seemed occupied. I'm not sure if anyone saw me, but if they did, they didn't make me aware of it. And perhaps I was oblivious to any attention anyway: I was completely focused on my mission to go inside. I had got it into my head that the pregnant woman who'd first led me here could be my route to being accepted by the camp.

I stepped out from the scrubby undergrowth and planted my feet on the beaten sandy earth beyond the fence. I didn't stand there for long, though. Open space was too frightening. Instead, I dashed to the nearest hut and peered cautiously inside it.

The interior was dark but every bit as enticing. There were

comfortable-looking beds made from grass and bamboo on the floor, as well as lots of mats, some plain and some patterned. The walls were hung prettily with bananas and other fruits – so many kinds of fruit, some of which I hadn't seen growing in the jungle. Where had they come from? There were a couple of hammocks slung from a pole in the centre and all around were items that the people had made: baskets and jugs, things made from raffia and branches, and clay.

The hut itself was empty, so I quickly turned my attention outside again. Just beyond it, and previously invisible to me, was a water butt. It looked like a giant version of the flask I'd drunk from. It was very wide at the bottom but quite narrow at the top and had a long neck – was this perhaps to keep bugs out? It was just wide enough at the lip to scoop water out of (for which they used some sort of half-shell), though this would have been difficult for a child if it was less than full.

The water, I had worked out, didn't come from the river – though I had no idea why, because it was fine for me to drink. Instead, it seemed to come to them in giant metal containers, which they would carry in pairs from some place I couldn't see. They would put holes in the top and fix two cans together by means of a long pole, which they would use to balance two of them on their shoulders. This triggered a memory, as I had seen adults carrying water in this way at my home.

Beside the water butt, and drinking from it, was a woman. And she was not just any woman, she was the woman who'd first drawn me here. My heart leapt at the sight of her. It was a sign, I felt sure, that I'd been right to approach. She was a mother and if she just looked in my eyes, then perhaps she'd love me the same way as she loved her baby.

What an intense thing it is – this human need to be loved. It's one of the most profound things that make social animals social. Just as the monkeys cared so much for one another, so I had learned that these human animals did too. And that was all I wanted: to be loved by them and cared for. And all it would take, or so I believed, was for a mother to see that need in my eyes.

But she didn't. As I stood there, not knowing quite when to reveal myself, she turned from the water butt and saw me. And her response was the opposite of what I'd expected. Yes, she looked into my eyes, but all I could see in hers was fear. She started skipping away immediately, keeping her eyes on me as she did so, as if I wasn't like her but some disgusting, filthy creature, utterly repellent to her.

Her fear didn't seem to diminish as she backed away from me. If anything, the more she looked at me, the more afraid she became. She began stumbling over stray objects in her panic, and all the while she kept shouting at me, over and over. I didn't know what she was saying, but it was clear that she wanted me to go away.

Whatever it was, the drama of her delivery drew attention from other people, and as I tried to make myself as small and submissive as I could, a well-built man came running from one of the nearby huts, obviously keen to find out what was happening. He wore a fabric headband into which were stuck a pair of feathers. One was a bright gorgeous blue, the other a deep green, and as well as these he wore other brightly coloured jewellery made of beads. He also had two stripes – one red and beneath it one black – daubed in some kind of paint, across his cheeks.

I instinctively knew he was the chief here. I knew about leaders from my monkey family, of course. In our troop, it wasn't Grandpa who ran things. For one thing, with his injured arm, he sat down too much and just raised an eyebrow at the things that went on. Our chief was younger, bigger and definitely stronger. He could snap big thick branches that others could not, and this made the whole troop respect him. He was forceful and pushy, and definitely not my favourite, but that was troop life. He was the one we trusted to lead us.

This man was like that monkey: confident and strong. And, having seen me and clearly not found me at all frightening, he approached me accordingly. I watched his eyes narrow as he appraised what he saw. Now it was my turn to be terrified again, because he immediately reached out and placed a strong hand on one of my shoulders, while his other hand grasped my face and pulled it forwards.

If he was shocked to see me there, or in the least bit confused by me, he didn't show it. And his inspection of me took no time. While my heart thumped in my chest and my limbs quaked in terror, he opened my mouth to inspect my teeth, pulled my head down to see the back of my neck and all the time mumbled some incomprehensible babble. The job done, he simply shooed me away.

As a gesture, it was unmistakeable. The monkeys would do it. It was the sort of gesture a bigger, stronger monkey would make if a smaller, weaker fellow monkey tried to steal their nuts. I was devastated. Couldn't he at least give me a chance? I tried begging to him, making gestures to convey my wish for food and shelter. But my voice and actions were those of a monkey, not a child, and he took not the slightest notice, just kept on shooing me.

Yet still I persisted. They had so much food and shelter! I needed so little and could help them so much, yet he was implacable and now began to push me. His hands were rough, his strength considerable, and he was determined to be rid of me, even making a gesture that I immediately understood – of a finger being dragged across his throat in great anger.

I needed no further encouragement to go then and ran back into the undergrowth before slinking away into the jungle, feeling wretched. I didn't stop till I was back in my own territory, with my dear, familiar monkeys, who seemed, if not exactly thrilled that I'd returned to them, at least happy, as they always were, to let me stay.

I learned a valuable lesson that day. And an enduring one, too, because it resonates with me still. Family is not just about who you appear to belong to, or what it says on your birth certificate, or who you look like, or even what they'd find if they studied your DNA. Family is found anywhere you are loved and cared for. That might mean friends or foster parents, a group or even a charity. What matters far more – so much more than chemistry or ancestry – is that precious bond, that reassurance that they won't let you down.

I thought hard over the coming days about what had happened to me and how to cope with it. A new feeling had now wormed its way into my consciousness. Somehow I knew that I really belonged in the human world, but I had been turned away. I felt raw and rejected, unwanted and hurt. Where did my future lie, now that my own kind had rejected me? But again and again I kept coming back to the same truth. That my family were the ones who had never let me down. Because the monkeys hadn't, had they? Even though I'd tried to replace them. Even though I'd been so dismissive and so disloyal to them. I realised I must put all thoughts of humans firmly out of my mind. The monkeys, not the humans, were my family.

12

Life, after a time, continued as it had always done, and as the days passed so my yearning for life at the camp faded. I did go back from time to time, but now it was for purely practical reasons. There was food there that I liked, and I was very adept at stealing it. So why wouldn't I? But that was where it ended.

Indeed, I immersed myself ever more joyfully into my jungle life. And life, in every form there, was abundant. It seemed that every single day I would see something different, be it a shimmering bird, the way the light danced around a puddle, a new path, a different vista, an unfamiliar call or song.

One of my most favourite of all the small creatures was a tiny pinky-beige lizard that, bizarrely, had a transparent belly. I could actually see the colours of the food in its stomach, which enthralled me. But I had to be patient to earn my pleasure. It was a shy little thing and would only come out if I sat and waited patiently for a very long time. Other lizards, in contrast, had no need to hide. They could lie and doze on a branch and just make themselves invisible by looking exactly like their surroundings.

The ants were real workers, as everyone knows – always busy, always rushing, and forming long trains of cargo, carrying leaves that were so much bigger than they were into the holes that led down to their colonies. They would never stop – not for a second – and if you planted a finger in their way, they just swerved around it. I recall spending many happy times just sitting in the dappled shade, playing traffic controller to those poor ants, sending them on all sorts of obstacle-avoiding detours.

I had also become less fearful around most of the birds there, many of whom seemed wonderfully wise and beautiful to me now. I was still wary around parrots, but other birds made me happy. There was a nosy toucan that would often sit a couple of branches above me and keep an eye on every single move I made. He had a dreadful call – the most annoying, rasping croak of a bird call – but he was so friendly I forgave him for his lack of musicality. His friendship was much more important.

My favourite singing bird was one I've later identified through pictures – the Mirla bird, a kind of everyday-looking blackbird with orange legs, who more than made up for his lack of fine plumage by having the most amazing song – one I often used to imitate, having discovered I had quite a pretty voice of my own.

Perhaps because I was older and more understanding of the jungle rhythms, the days now had a greater sense of order. The early mornings, when the sun began peeping shyly through the canopy, were mostly spent in what felt like a shared endeavour. It seemed every creature would rise and join in the universal chase to find food. But as the sun's heat increased with every inch it slid towards its zenith, so the middle of the day saw a common search for rest with a jungle-wide siesta. All the birds would quieten down, the general activity levels would slow, and, for those that could, there was a general move upwards into the canopy, in pursuit of cool air and an escape from the intense heat. In those quiet times I would often hear far-away sounds – including the distant roar of a waterfall that I hankered after finding but never did. I wonder if it still roars there today.

I had also developed a new interest in plants and flowers, and doing craft with them, for want of a better word. I would pick juicy green leaves and smash them with a rock, adding a little pond water too. The leaves were generous and would very soon reward my efforts by releasing a coloured liquid I could then use as paint. Trial and error soon taught me which leaves made the best colour, and, successful in this, I conducted further experiments. I could make orange using the seeds of a pomegranate-like fruit, the interior of which was the brightest shade of orange I ever saw. I could soon make a whole rainbow of pretty paint colours to play with, mixing the juices of seeds, nuts and flowers. I would then use the resulting liquids to decorate not only my skin but also bark, rocks and branches, not to mention any monkey who interfered with my art class.

And, like any other little girl, I made jewellery. My time watching the children in the human camp had opened my eyes to new diversions and one of my favourites was collecting orchids, other flowers and long stems to make chains I would drape on anything I fancied. I would hang them around my neck, as the Indians did, but also around the jungle, for no other reason than to make the place look even prettier, which I think must be an instinctive female need. My favourite form of necklace was made from a string of what I now know were vanilla pods, and the sweet scent would linger on me all day.

But for all the distractions, the best thing in my life was my beloved monkey family, who I knew so well by this time that I could distinguish every single one. I knew when one was born and I knew when another died. I knew which child belonged to which mother and what strengths, skills and traits each individual monkey had. I suppose at first glance they might have seemed like just a big group of similar animals, but to me they were as different from one another as would be any human family member.

In their company, I felt safe, and the jungle had become my home. But I was soon to have it spelled out to me, horribly and brutally, that danger was never far away.

*

It was an ordinary day in the jungle. Most were. It might have been as much as a year after I had left thoughts of the camp behind me: it's impossible to say. But given that I had once again lost interest in humans, I imagine that quite a lot of time must have passed.

Dawn arrived with its usual mad bustle of activity. The noise of the jungle traffic was never less than deafening as all the day creatures limbered up with the sunshine. But the regular cacophony was soon pierced by an immediate-danger call from one of the monkeys, which sent almost every jungle animal to seek shelter.

It was like a well-rehearsed fire drill. The birds were suddenly fewer, and those that remained airborne were now flying anxiously, high above us. The monkeys had disguised themselves as bulges of benign tree bark, and an eerie silence hovered over the suddenly stricken land.

Automatically, I followed the other animals in the dash to find a place of safety – in my case, this meant the hollow tree that had been my home for so long. Assuming I was close enough to get to it, it was always my chosen bolthole, and as I crouched there now, hidden from sight by some hastily grabbed fallen branches, I wondered what monstrous thing could saturate our land with so much fear.

I didn't have to wait long for the answer. I could just about see out, but it was the noise that came first. A loud and unsettling sound that was strangely methodical. Even rhythmical. It sounded as if the undergrowth nearby was being chopped down, viciously and violently ripped up and cut away.

My hearing didn't deceive me. That was exactly what was happening. First the noise grew. *Thwack*! *Rip*! *Slash*!, and *Thwack*! again. It was then accompanied, as the bushes terrifyingly close to me parted, by the sight of two white human men, both dressed in green clothing and carrying, as well as their fearsome glinting machetes, a variety of sacks, guns and nets. Had I not spent so long observing the Indian camp humans, these two creatures would have looked alien to me – a species of animal I might not have recognised immediately but one I'd instinctively have known to flee from. But knowing they were human gave me no reason to revise my opinion. They were monsters – everything about them looked monstrous – and the hair on my skin stood to horrified attention while my heart pumped a pulse through my head.

I held my breath as I watched them slash their way through the undergrowth, pushing my body as far back into the tree trunk as I could. I had no idea what they wanted or why they seemed so intent on destruction, but that question was soon answered. The nets, I realised as I watched them both, were for catching and stealing whatever creatures they fancied: first, a bright, unwary butterfly was scooped up in an instant, the net secured and slung over a shoulder.

Then their attention turned to birds. Again I watched mutely as they fired a different sort of net, this time to trap a parrot:

a beautiful bird I had already seen that morning and which they tethered by the legs, causing it to flap in a panic, its elegant feathers drifting to the forest floor.

I tried to still my breathing. Would I be the next prey they captured? It seemed they had the means to catch anything they wanted, from birdlife to insects, lizards and snakes. No wonder that monkey had been so insistent in his warning. We were clearly all in very great danger.

Though I was spared, that day marked the beginning of the end of my innocence and the start of a long period pockmarked by fear. I don't know if it was new – had our jungle land just been discovered? – or something that had been going on for many years, but from that day on I became used to the sound of a machete swishing through the nearby undergrowth and the feeling of terror it evoked.

And I was right to be frightened. One time, when I was quaking in fear in my tree hollow, one of the hunters came right up to my tree trunk. He stood so close to me that I could clearly see his black boots and the khaki of his trousers, and hear the click of his rifle trigger. In the silence he'd created, it was the worst sound imaginable, and it's one that has remained with me to this day. Then he lifted his rifle and BANG! I was almost deafened. I had no idea what he had aimed at, much less if he had shot it; all I could hear now was the wild thumping of my heart, while my hands began to shake uncontrollably.

I have been frightened many, many times in my life, but the fear I felt that day, being so small and helpless, was of a kind all its own. It's something I will never forget.

Sometimes the hunters came by day and sometimes by night. Other times they'd pounce just as dusk had begun falling, shining their torches into the eyes of tired, sleepy creatures whose shrieks of terror when caught or injured, or when dying, would rip through the darkness and wake us all. Worse than that, though, was that they sometimes came for monkeys.

In theory, the monkeys should have been too clever for them. With their early-warning calls and their strong sense of community, they had a system that should have kept them safe. But the hunters were too clever. They would pick off the youngsters. They knew there was a chance the young ones would be too distracted by their games to see and react to them until it was too late. They were still an easy target even when they'd heard their mothers' calls, a tranquilliser dart being too fast for them. They would simply be shot out of the trees like sitting ducks and then imprisoned in black sticky nets.

I don't think I can fully explain how much pain those hunters caused me, or how murderous my feelings were, and still are, towards them. But the image of a baby monkey taken from its screaming mother is one I shall remember for the rest of my life. The mothers with babies would often hide in hollow tree trunks, as I did, and to see a tiny infant snatched from the grip of its desperate mother feels as appalling to me as if it had been any human mother and child.

Worse still was to watch the mothers suffering in the weeks afterwards. Their pain and sense of loss were unbearable to witness, especially when nothing could be done to ease it. More than once I saw bereft monkey mothers simply lie down and die from the pain. The hunters took mothers too: shot them out of the trees and stuffed them into sacks. And, of course, their babies would then die as well, from starvation.

*

The spree of hunting ended as dramatically as it had arrived. Nature had obviously seen enough of the activities of these evil humans and decided to wash them away. I was used to rain by now, of course. Heavy, intense, hammering rain. The rain fell regularly, too: perhaps once a month, maybe twice. And once it had rained, the intense heat set about removing all trace of any downpour. The jungle floor almost never felt soggy or boggy; my overwhelming memory is of it being dry. But from time to time came a storm of such power and magnitude it was a very great event, one which impacted on every creature in the jungle.

This storm was one such, and it came without warning. Well, almost without warning. The monkeys seemed to know exactly what was coming. The day before had been particularly scorching. Was that a sign they'd already noticed? I didn't know. What I remember most clearly was that almost as soon as I woke I saw one of the adult monkeys performing an unusual dance. I assumed at first that it was just part of an early play session, but the reaction of the monkeys nearby suggested it had some meaning.

I knew then that something was about to break the normal routine, and as soon as I got a taste of the wind and saw the strange hue of the sky, I realised that this might have been some sort of rain dance. I had seen torrential rain before, but only once, perhaps twice. And I'd loved it. It had been a little terrifying at first, yes. But once the rain had started dancing on the forest floor, I realised how wonderful it was to suddenly feel so cool. I had danced, feeling the ground beneath my feet turn to mud, loving the way it squidged between my toes. Yes, my home in the tree had become a little boggy, but it was a small price to pay for the glory of mud on my scabby, itchy skin. I remember I had even rolled in it.

And here came another storm, I remember thinking with anticipation. I was half scared, half excited by the impending sense of danger. And it wasn't just me who felt the thrumming, swollen air. It wasn't long before all sense of normality had left the jungle. One by one all the animals, birds and insects slunk away, hiding in whichever places were best suited to their protection, while the leaves began to rustle as the wind started to whip through them. The whole jungle, it seemed, became one heaving, moaning mass, as if bracing itself for the coming ordeal.

Or adventure! Sudden whistles of wind seemed to fork and dance through whatever gaps were available, causing fruit, leaves and small branches to spear down to the ground. And then – in what seemed like a drum roll that began rising to a crescendo – Mother Nature unleashed her deluge upon us.

Strangely, I recall little of the period of the storm itself. I just waited it out, enjoying the maelstrom outside, from the comfy cocoon of my precious tree. I watched the needles of water drive their way into the undergrowth and the earth all around turn to a big slushy muddle. I remember the feeling of excitement about when the storm had passed and I could clamber out to investigate this sodden new world.

But perhaps the main reason the storm itself is a blur in my memory is because what happened as a consequence was of so much more importance: the hunters, unable to cope with such conditions, seemed to have disappeared as surely as the peace they'd destroyed. And, for a while at least, we gratefully grabbed it back.

13

Though I can't be sure of anything in terms of dates and times and details (my own age included), I remember that period after the hunters had moved on as being one of the happiest of my childhood. I had given up my yearnings to be part of the human village, and perhaps it was a good thing that we were stalked by the hunters, because this reminded me how cold and cruel my own species could be.

For a period, at least, I ceased to even see humans as my own species, because the older I got, the more I felt the love of my monkey family and learned to cherish them all as individuals. And, like anyone, I also had my favourites.

Of the younger monkeys – the ones I would naturally spend the most time with – my favourites were Rudy and Romeo and Mia. I didn't give them names then, as the concept of names was long lost to me, but whenever I think of them these days, it is with names attached to them, because long after I left them I would remember them so fondly and gave them names which reminded me of their characters – based on the personalities of people I encountered in my next life.

Rudy was distinctive because he had so much energy. He was always chasing other monkeys and invariably catching them, at which point he would pull their ears. This was his second-favourite pastime, his first, without question, being peek-a-boo.

He loved it if I hid behind a tree trunk, waited for his plaintive 'where have you gone?' call, then sprang out again and made him jump. He loved it so much he soon learned to do his own version, waiting in all sorts of places – high on branches, in deep cover – before leaping out and terrifying whichever dazed monkey was the target of his mischief on that occasion.

Rudy was always full of mischief. He was always the monkey making an awful lot of noise just for the sake of it, sounding the warning cry for no apparent reason and generally irritating the older monkeys in the troop. He could also be a bit of a drama queen; if he got cross, every other monkey had to know about it. He was affectionate, however, and I was always happy to let him groom me, even if, due to his ineptitude, it wasn't very useful – my hair always ended up knottier than it started.

Romeo, in contrast, was a very gentle animal and liked nothing better than to be physically attached. I don't know how he wangled it but, even though he had long since been too big for it, he could invariably be seen hitching a cheeky ride on someone's back. He was a peacemaker and a sweetheart, always wrapping his arms around your shoulders, and would chatter so beautifully that you were never in any doubt that he was delivering a sonnet that declared his undying love for the entire monkey community.

Perhaps my favourite – aside from Grandpa – was Mia. She is probably the character I missed – and still miss – the most. Like Romeo, she was affectionate, but unlike him she was also shy, and it took her a while to gain the courage to be near me. I first won her round – even though that wasn't particularly my intention – when I got cross and indignant about the way she was sometimes bullied and would use my size and strength to stop some of the more aggressive young monkeys from poking and shoving her and pushing her around. As she never stood up for herself, I felt I had to do it for her, and so began the closest of my friendships.

Mia liked to climb on my shoulders and was often with me as I went about doing whatever I was doing, both her arms wrapped tightly around my neck. Unusually for the monkeys, she also liked to lick me. And a lick on the cheek felt like a sure sign of her love.

But all the monkeys had their own endearing ways. Several would enjoy poking a finger up my nose or making a thorough inspection inside my ears. One in particular – a teenage male – just loved digging around in ears generally, and why not? After all, an ear was as likely a place as any other in which to find a nice juicy grub.

Again, I didn't mind. It was really quite relaxing – and it

also made me shiver! Neither did I mind any of them rooting behind my ears – if it was somewhere dirt collected, there were always rich pickings to be had.

Of course, I also saw the circle of life in action. I especially recall Lolita, an older female monkey, who in my time there gave birth to several babies. I never actually saw Lolita, or any other monkey, give birth in the jungle – they always seemed to disappear from sight to do that – but I think in general they might have done so approximately once a year. What remains, though, in terms of memories, was what a wonderful mother Lolita was: one who taught her children discipline and respect. A diplomat, she always made peace after their squabbles.

I miss Lolita, too. I learned such a lot from her. Though perhaps I learned the most of all from Grandpa. He'd saved my life that fateful day with the bad tamarind and had watched over me ever since. He was very wise and intelligent, and seemed to be the oldest of all the monkeys. He kept things in order and could often be seen prowling around the floor of our territory keeping watch, like a security guard. Sometimes, however, he just sat and watched, as grandpas do, while the youngsters – me included – larked about.

Every day seemed to bring opportunities for adventure and often some unexpected bounty. On this particular morning, I had woken up early and was down on the forest floor, foraging for fruit and nuts before the rest of the troop got up. After a while, a series of whoops and howls drew my attention upwards, and I noticed a small parade of them had decided to gather for a communal breakfast outing. The captain of the team – a monkey who behaved as if he always knew the best trees in the jungle – had amassed a school of several others for the tour.

I watched as they proceeded along the rooftop of the jungle, keeping in a single-file, tightly packed line. I followed their progress along a twisted branch that belonged to a large fruit tree, until the whole gang was on it, their fearless leader at the very tip. At this point he paused, as if deciding on the best cluster of fruit to go for, getting visibly irritated that the monkeys behind him kept shuffling up, each with their hands on the shoulders of the monkey in front and bobbing up and down for a better view.

The hesitation was his undoing. Perhaps more in the mood for mischief than breakfast, the last of the monkeys gave the line a firm shove, which sent their leader into free fall from the branch. Naturally, because monkeys like nothing better than to laugh, the whole jungle erupted with hilarity.

But it didn't last. Not once they'd seen their leader, who'd now regained his composure, climbing angrily back up the tree again. Wisely, they scattered, each now intent on hiding while I, keen to capitalise on this convenient development, took the opportunity to scamper across and collect as much fallen fruit as I could hold. A very satisfying way to get my breakfast!

The ends of the days too, I remember with great fondness. There would always be a big grooming party up in the canopy, and I loved the physical contact that meant. The little ones enjoyed digging around under my fingernails and opening my mouth to see if there might be something to eat hidden inside. I saw nothing revolting in any of this – it was normal and sociable, part of the bonding process that created such a close and happy family. But for all my immersion in, and love of, monkey life, my days in the jungle were numbered.

*

It was another day, another sunrise, another busy morning. It had been a busy period, one that happened every so often in the jungle, when a bounty of fruit had been shed.

Though there are no seasons in equatorial regions, as there are nearer the poles, there are still rhythms of life taking place. There were periods of intense growth, and periods of shedding of leaves, fruits and flowers, and though each species had its own plan, these often coincided, bringing a little novelty and excitement to our days. My favourite time was when we'd be treated to a mass shedding of flowers, and the whole jungle would be carpeted by showers of delicate petals that would cover the drabness of the dead leaves with beautiful, myriad, eye-popping colours.

The giant Brazil nut was kind too, if a little dangerous. When it chose to release its goodies, you could be killed in an instant, as the pods that held the nuts were as dense as they were big, and if one hit you on the head, it wouldn't just be the nut-case that was cleaved in two. They also fell from a very great height.

The Brazil nut trees being the mightiest in our jungle, the pods had a long way to travel and would fall at a terrifying speed. And they weren't the only danger; so forceful was their momentum that they would shear off old and weak branches as they passed, causing a shower of wood to rain down on you as well.

Sometimes when this happened, a patch of blue sky would be created, and smaller plants and saplings would race into overdrive, hoping to be the next to fill the precious sunny space. Absolutely no chance of light and life was wasted.

On this day, it was the sound that first alerted me. Perhaps because of the recent bounty of Brazil nuts I automatically decided what the source of the noise must be. You heard certain sounds and you knew you had to get out of harm's way. So my first thought, when I heard the snap of branches above me, was of nuts. Perhaps there were some pods coming down.

But then my brain caught up properly with what my ears had relayed to it – the sound was different from what I had first thought. It was more like the sound I'd expect to hear if a large animal trod heavily on a dead branch. I froze, straining to see what other sounds I could make out, attuning all my senses to receive them.

And then I heard it. A 'swoosh' sound. The sound of a machete! I had not heard that noise for a long time, but it was one that was as firmly engraved on my mind as any monkey warning call I'd ever heard.

Horrified, I made my own warning call – a panicked, fearful, loud one – and raced to the place that I now used as a hideout. I had never forgotten how close to me the hunter had been that day, and after it had happened I'd felt markedly less secure in my tree. Now I was bigger and more skilled at moving around the lower canopy, I could find somewhere higher, like the monkeys. My new hideout, accordingly, was high in a palm tree, behind a fan of dense spreading leaves.

Safely crouched, and with a good view of the forest floor below me, I now waited for whatever was going to emerge from the bushes that were now shivering and swinging unmistakeably. The next sound I heard was the distinctive cocking of a rifle, and moments later its metal nose poked through the undergrowth, followed by one hunter and then another.

Both were wearing the same khaki clothes I'd seen previously and had a look of concentration on their faces as they inched through the tangles and tried to spot things to shoot. They were both wearing strange cylindrical hats with sunshades and were by now getting close to the base of my tree. I glared down at them hatefully, as if just by doing so I could somehow prevent them from looking up and seeing me.

But then I realised there was something unusual here. One of the hunters looked different, and I realised with a gasp that she was female. I looked some more and once again a peculiar feeling overtook me. Though she was dressed like a hunter, her face told me something different. It just looked so kind, so compassionate and gentle, so much like a mother, like someone who might care. She immediately reminded me of the young woman I'd previously seen give birth, and I felt irresistibly drawn to her.

How can the head ever compete with the strength of the heart's feelings? In my case, not at all, because without thinking about what I was doing, let alone how dangerous it might be, I was climbing down my tree towards her. It was as if all my training and survival instincts had been neutralised by this woman, that something I didn't understand was drawing me to her. I felt compelled to show her my face – as if it was my biggest, deepest secret, something that could only be revealed to a very close friend. It made no sense – why would I offer myself up into the mouth of my greatest danger? Yet I did.

Within moments I stood behind the tree, feet on the ground now, and, with my head down (as if it didn't want to witness this stupidity), I stepped out in full view and stood before them both.

I braced myself for whatever was coming next, but nothing happened. What had I done? Such foolishness! Could they even see me? It was perhaps not surprising that when I did dare lift my eyes, all I could see in theirs was utter disbelief.

I don't know what they thought of me. I never will. But if I try to recall that day from their perspective instead of mine, I have a better sense of what they might have been thinking. My hair, thick and tangled, had by this time grown way past my bottom and covered much of my face and body. I was black – filthy black; I had not washed in years now – and I no longer stood on two legs. Crouched there, I suspect I must have looked like a primate. But like no monkey found in the jungles of the Americas. I was probably too big and too odd-looking. I imagine they must have thought that what they'd encountered was some undiscovered species of ape.

They were definitely frightened. The gun was once again lifted and aimed at my face. But I focused solely on the woman; it was she that I fixed my gaze on and, even knowing how much danger I was in, I moved slowly and submissively in her direction. I needed to touch her. In my monkey world, holding out a hand to another was a way of signifying that you wanted to start a friendship. And although my instincts were screaming 'No! Don't do this! They will kill you!', my rebellious feet seemed determined to ignore them. I needed to get close enough to touch her, to grip her finger.

Step after step I took, still aware of the gun trained on me, but as I got closer I could see that her expression was softening. That she'd decided she wasn't frightened. That she was instead intrigued. This was my cue. As I was now only touching distance from her, I slowly lifted my hand to touch hers. This seemed to charm her; she raised her hand to let me clasp one of her fingers and a moment of silent shock hovered between us all. It was a gesture so commonplace in my community of monkeys but my first human touch for many years.

My nerves disappeared at her touch. It really was as simple and as instant as that. All I wanted now was for her to choose to take me with her; that she would let me follow her to wherever she was going that day.

I knew the monkeys were watching me from high above, and for a fleeting moment I wondered what they were thinking. But my reverie was interrupted by the man with the rifle. Though I had no human language it was clear what he thought. Just as the chief in the Indian village had done, he was making it clear that I wouldn't be welcome.

Some sort of heated exchange began happening then, the man's rejection of me obvious, the woman's disagreement clear too. I squeezed her finger even more tightly, so she would know how much I wanted to go with her. I couldn't pick out anything from the weird babble that came out of their mouths, only the sense that everything now hung in the balance and that if the woman didn't get her way I would be left again, perhaps even shot.

But some sort of resolution was apparently reached, and when she looked at me again, I felt a surge of elation. Her expression was calm, her face friendly and, though I didn't understand her, I knew the things she was saying to me were what I wanted to hear.

She tugged my hand again then, clearly gesturing to me that I should follow. So that's exactly what I did. Without looking back at the watchful eyes of my family, which I knew were all trained down on me, I followed where the woman led – away from my home and into her life. My time in the jungle had come to its end now, and a new life, back with my own species, beckoned.

Little did I know that, for all my wild upbringing, an even wilder sort of life had just begun.

PART 2

14

As with the rings that mark the annual growth of a tree, so my hair has provided at least one kind of measurement to enable me to estimate how long I might have spent in the jungle. It's obviously not accurate to a scientific degree, but as its length when I left is one of my most certain memories, I suspect it's the best shot I have.

When my daughter Vanessa first suggested that we try to document my life, the question of dates was an important one. We therefore dabbled in a little science to see what we could find, and it's on this (among the other guesstimates – my size, my appearance and my clear pre-jungle memory of waiting impatiently for my fifth birthday) that my theory is based: that I was probably around ten when the hunters found me.

I am sure that when I was first abandoned, my hair was cut short. It would have been common for this to have been the case, as it would have been easier to manage, as well as cooler, in the tropical climate. When I left the jungle, of course, it had not seen a pair of scissors in a long time, and my chief memory is that it was something of a nuisance most of the time – always getting in my way. I had nothing to tie it back with – and perhaps wouldn't have even thought to – and when I squatted, as I often did, it trailed on the floor like a very badly measured pair of curtains. It certainly hung from my head like a curtain – a thick black one – and had grown, when I left, to my thighs.

So we measured. Using hair dye to mark it, I worked out my rate of hair growth, and my daughter Vanessa did the same. That way, we figured, with her being so much younger, we'd know if the rate of growth slowed down with age. And what we found was that both of us had similar growth rates. It seemed that one and half cm per month was the average, equating to eighteen cm per year.

But we wanted to be surer than that. So the next thing we did was go online and look at general hair-growth statistics, and only then, taking into account growth rates in different climates, did we feel we had something scientific. After that, it was straightforward to approximate the length of time spent in the jungle, based on there having been roughly eighty to ninety cm of growth in total, which would give an approximate time span of around four to six years.

Of course, it could have been longer. There were perhaps periods when growth was less rapid, just as is the case for other forms of life. And, given its condition, our reckoning might have been conservative anyway. My hair may have continued growing, but most hair reaches a limit. And perhaps its rate of growth was affected by breakage, due to the brittle and damaged state it was in. Above everything else, it was a dwelling place for wildlife – so much so that it's a miracle it managed to grow at all.

As well as my hair growth, we had one other marker: my physical development into adulthood. I had no sense of having grown – it was a concept that didn't occur to me – but one thing is a fact. When I left the jungle, I had definitely not entered puberty. I know because that happened several months later: an event no young girl is ever likely to forget! So, on balance, the age of ten seems the most accurate to plump for as the one where I returned to civilisation.

But the ten-year-old me had no notion of the word 'civilised'. All I could think of as I stood in that clearing with the hunters was the enormous step I was about to take. I was facing a possible new future – it was what had drawn me to them. But at the same time, I was also facing danger. And despite my earlier boldness – driven by my fascination with the woman – my fear was so great that I very nearly didn't go. I was, to all intents and purposes, a monkey. I had lost human posture and walked naked on all fours. I had forgotten whatever language I once spoke and had no idea of my name. I had no understanding of how to 'be human'. I had spent years as an animal and now thought like an animal, meaning that my focus was on only two things: food and how to find it, and survival.

They seemed determined to make me walk as they did. They kept hauling me up – the woman yanking on my arm every so often to try to make me walk on two legs. It seemed to anger them greatly that this was difficult for me: I could see it in their expressions with every step.

The man, especially, seemed angry that they'd brought me at all. Though I didn't know what he was saying, his tone was obvious. So I tried as hard as I could to do what they wanted, though it felt so unnatural and unsteady to use just my feet.

But it didn't matter how hard it was, I was now committed to going with them. Though I wrestled for a time with a desire to run back again, there was a stronger force inside me, compelling me on. We had also travelled some distance through the undergrowth by now, into territory that was becoming unfamiliar. The air was filled with the sounds made by other dominant animals, keen to warn their own colonies of our trespassing feet. All of which frightened me greatly, because hearing was perhaps my most attuned sense. The sounds I knew well were my map and compass. And suddenly, with new noises emerging all the time, I felt lost and disorientated.

But at least being with the hunters gave me some sense of security. For all my other anxieties, I felt safer with them than without them. No fierce boar, or big cat, or other scary animal would bother us, for I was travelling with the most powerful species in the jungle. I had seen enough of humans during my time here to be quite sure of that, even if the humans themselves didn't appear so confident, seeming more nervous and cautious than I'd expected.

I had fallen back from them now, keeping a fixed distance behind them, and held myself ready for anything that might happen. I wanted to be with them, certainly, but I knew I couldn't trust them, particularly the man, who seemed only to tolerate me. He took the lead, his machete slashing cleanly through the branches, forming a path into which the woman could then step, with me a few paces behind her.

We travelled far. My legs knew it and the sun above confirmed it. I had come across the hunters at some point in the morning, and I knew from the light and the lengthening of the shadows along the ground that the creatures of the night would be re-awakening. I thought of the monkeys then and what I knew they'd be doing. I knew all their routines: what they did at each part of every day. But I forced these images from my mind. Thinking of the monkeys was too hard on my emotions; I needed to block out all thoughts of regret and keep my mind fixed on what lay ahead.

I have no idea what drove me so relentlessly that day. Looking back at it, from a distance of many happy decades, it would be easy to imagine I was just following my destiny. But was I? Surely my conscious mind would have felt no such compulsion. I was leaving everything I knew and loved, a willing hostage to strangers. For the ten-year-old me it makes no sense at all. Yet it must have, for I remember no intense internal struggle. I followed the hunters because once I had set off down that path, going back just didn't seem to be an option.

And so I plodded on, still battling the urge to drop to all fours, which grew harder as the vegetation thinned out and I felt exposed and insecure. I was terribly thirsty, too. I hadn't seen anywhere to drink from in hours. The humans drank often, from metal flasks that hung from their necks. But they didn't offer me any, and I was too fearful to try to ask them. I simply scoured the bushes we passed for my usual drinking ports. But they didn't seem to exist in this part of the jungle, the conical leafy plants that I was used to seeing everywhere having been replaced by plants with much flatter leaves.

Everything was new and different. The trees had become shorter and much thinner in girth, their leaves just small shiny buds still awaiting their invitation to maturity. As a consequence, the canopy was sparser, and where shadows had been the norm, here the light reigned supreme, the forest floor becoming a feast of sun and space. The feeling of vulnerability was intense now. I had no roof above my head to shelter me, and I felt suddenly naked. It hurt my eyes to look up at the sky. It was very uncomfortable, all that space.

Eventually, the man had no further need of his machete and stowed it in a case he had strapped on his back. The landscape had changed radically and become hilly, even steep, and was no longer like anything I knew. The couple began slowing and eventually stopped, and as I waited in the sparse bushes, still bent in an unfamiliar, half-upright stance, I could see I was the object of some discussion. Once again, I had the strong sense of discord between them, such as I'd see if one of the young monkeys annoyed Grandpa in some way.

I stepped out from the bushes and drew a little closer. Why had they stopped anyway? It wasn't clear. But in moving only half a dozen paces I had my answer. They had no choice but to stop for we'd arrived at the end of the world.

The land – the very ground I was standing on – just ended. It stopped abruptly, a few feet ahead of the hunters, and dropped dizzyingly away to nothingness. I edged a little closer – the hunters, busy arguing, seemed to have lost interest in me – and my eyes could barely take in so much all at once. It was the biggest panorama I had ever seen, even from way up in the canopy. In the distance, there were mountains, undulating grey and purple monsters, and something seemed to tell me they were where I should be headed. But they were so far in the distance that they seemed more like a shimmering dreamscape, and between us and them was a vast and seemingly endless blanket of trees. We were at the top of the world, and I felt giddy just looking. I had to clutch a nearby tree trunk to keep myself steady.

The hunters had moved off now, disappearing to the side of me, and as I followed them I could see that the world hadn't ended. Instead, it dipped from the lip of the ridge and there was a steep path snaking down. I could also now see where the hunters were going: down the dirt track to something that initially confounded me – I had absolutely no idea what it was.

Again, I followed, my feet working hard to grip the steep incline, and as I drew nearer a new memory bubbled to the surface of my mind. This was a vehicle. A vehicle that wasn't dissimilar to the one that had originally brought me here.

The flash of recognition was accompanied by others. I took in wheels and windows, the bulk of an engine, an open back, pockmarked and dusty and weathered, that was covered by some sort of green and grey material, which was stretched over a series of metal hoops.

The couple were by now divesting themselves of the things they carried: their water flasks and machetes, their rifles and bags. They were then throwing them, one by one, into the back of the truck, along with various sacks and nets, which only now did I appreciate carried captured animals. Once they'd dealt with everything, the woman looked at me again. Her signal – to come to her – was unmistakeable. I duly left the sapling I was now clinging to and at her next gesture obediently clambered up into the back of the truck.

The air inside was so fetid that it almost made me recoil. It eddied in foul swirls, stirred up by my presence, and as I peered into the eerie greenish gloom of the interior it soon became easy to see why. The truck was almost full to bursting with cages. Some were made of mesh and contained a variety of unlucky animals, including lizards, giant butterflies and beautiful birds. There were birds that were familiar to me – parrots, parakeets and macaws – as well as some that were not, such as small, pretty blue ones. Not all the cages advertised their contents, however. Some were solid boxes with airholes I couldn't see into. They might, looking back, have contained tranquillised animals. Dead ones as well, perhaps, given the intense heat.

There was also a little monkey, next to whose cage was a space I could fit into, and I scrabbled up beside it to keep it company. It was not of the same species as my own monkey family and was speaking a language I didn't quite know. But the tone of his calls was very clear to me. He was making a sort of grunting noise that immediately seemed familiar as the sort of noise my own troop only made when sick or distressed. He was also hooting piteously, trying to project his feeble calls to the family he was so far from and would never see again.

What had I done? I couldn't stop thinking about these humans. I had entrusted myself to creatures who felt nothing for other creatures. No, worse than that – creatures who captured and caged other creatures, who routinely tortured them for their own ends.

I tried to comfort the monkey with my own voice, but it was pointless. I could see he was too deeply in distress. I pulled up my legs as the woman lifted the tailboard and locked it. Did he know something I didn't? Did he have a sense of despair? It was impossible to say, but as I felt the passenger door slam and the truck shudder into life, I wondered if, in my willingness to be led from the jungle, I had just made a very grave mistake.

15

We travelled all through the night. In the back, under the canvas cover, I could see very little, as the only view was from a plastic or glass panel in the back, much of which was out of sight behind the piles of boxes. But soon there was little to see anyway, as when the night deepened the darkness was absolute. The air was still thick and foul, choked with the smell of the captive animals' excrement, and bluebottles and other winged insects competed with the engine to provide a constant thrum of angry sound.

Up in the cab, I could hear the low voices of my captors, and from time to time one of my fellow animal prisoners would cry out in pain or distress. And I did feel like a prisoner. I had crossed the line and let these humans take me from the jungle, so I could no more think of leaving than if I'd been locked in a cage, too. I had loved my jungle life, and desperately wanted to belong to the monkeys, but the spell had been broken the day I'd seen the Indian woman. However many times I'd had it proven to me that humans were cruel, cold and murderous, I knew I would never rest until I'd been accepted by them. They were my own kind and that need to live among them had never left me. Whatever became of me now, I had to follow this through; it was a drive so strong inside me that it refused to be ignored.

I spent the night alternately wakeful and sleepy. The chugging of the engine would lull me into slumber only to wake me again moments later when we'd hit some small obstacle or pothole. I remember we stopped once, the slam of the cab door rousing me, and I saw the humans embracing each other up in the cab. I remember being fascinated but also a bit revolted to watch them touching mouths and stroking and playing with each other's hair.

I also recall the man disappearing for a while – presumably to relieve himself – and the woman doing the same a while later. Locked in the back of the truck, I had no choice but to urinate where I was, just like every other animal trapped there.

Every time I woke, I would feel immediately anxious about the monkey next to me. I would rattle the bars of his cage and coo to him, trying to get him to respond to me and only allowing myself to sink back into slumber once he had. At first, he would chirp at me, letting me know he was still hanging on, but as the night had worn on he'd grown increasingly feeble, and now, as I desperately shook the bars and tried to communicate with him, his stillness had taken on a different quality. I peered into the murk, trying to spot some reassuring sign of movement, but then the horrible truth hit me. He had gone.

I cried then. I let out a wail of such desolation that many of the other creatures stirred and began vocalising too. I think a part of me died as well in that moment, the loss of my little monkey companion summing up everything I had lost. Just as he'd been silenced, so I couldn't hear my family any more.

But if the hunters heard the commotion in the back, they took no notice. The truck still travelled on to wherever it was headed, stopping only once more, for the man to buy what must have been fuel from a man at the roadside. It filled the whole truck with acrid fumes as he poured it into the tank. And on we went. I could tell that the sun had travelled high in the sky before we stopped again.

Now it was fully light and I was wakeful, I pulled back a tiny corner of the truck's cover, as I was desperate to see out. My view was very limited, but what I could see was both tantalising and worrying. I could just make out a sliver of the road winding away behind us. It was partly blurred by the dust cloud the moving truck created, but to my astonishment it looked as if the jungle had disappeared. I tried to square this with the view I'd had of that enormous green plateau and found it incredible that there seemed to be no evidence of it here. Most amazing – and alarming – was that we seemed to be travelling along the side of a mountain. To one side, a great wall of rock seemed to loom upwards, while to the other, or so my severely restricted view seemed to suggest, the ground abruptly ended and the drop looked immense.

The journey in the intense heat was making me nauseous. By now, my mind had begun sifting through memories. I remembered this feeling. I remembered these sensations. The shaking and bouncing and being slung around. I well remembered the sensation of being lifted from the truck bed only to be slammed down again, hard, on my bottom.

As the sun moved lower and I drifted in and out of sleep, there seemed to be a new kind of light that seeped through the canvas cover. I could see very little, but such glimpses as I could get through the small plastic window opening made me gasp in wonder – it was so incredibly bright.

My first thought was fireflies. They were everywhere in the jungle, and their sudden streaks of yellow were tiny flames of night-time joy. But these lights were bigger and did not flash on and off. They seemed to be strung along the roadside, big and bold above me. A thought surfaced – these lights were not natural. Like the pots and the campfires and the huts I had seen, these lights had been fashioned by human hands, and they seemed to pierce my eyes and make them weep.

Other glimpses intrigued me too, making me momentarily forget my nausea. There were dwellings, but not dwellings made of woven grass and branches. These dwellings seemed to have solid, sandy-coloured walls. But these obvious signs of human habitation didn't reassure me. The more I saw, the more terrified I grew.

And the sights and the smells and the cacophony kept on growing as we travelled. Soon it seemed we'd entered an entirely new kind of territory. A human territory but one quite different from the Indians' jungle home. The dwellings grew denser, the lights brighter and more frequent, and the road teemed with trucks like the one I was being carried in. They swooshed past us so close and so fast that I would quake in terror as the eyes of fierce light they wore blinded me and fumes from their engines invaded my nose.

I was becoming increasingly agitated, my eyes darting around so I could see in all directions, trying to keep on top of all the possible threats to my life. But it was the noise that was the most terrifying. There just seemed no end to it. As well as the roar of traffic, the air was also full of new sounds. I could hear human sounds, noises that reminded me of the

Indians, but so many, and at such volume, that it began to hurt my ears. There were other sounds, too; sounds not so readily identifiable. Strange hoots and a loud and blaring background noise that seemed an assault on all my senses but which I'd soon learn was the sound of human music.

I had encountered music before, of course, even if I didn't know what to call it. I would make sounds of my own for no other reason but my own pleasure, and at the Indian camp they would sometimes make sounds by blowing into different lengths of sugar cane. But this was different. It had an unnatural, insistent beat, and to my highly attuned ears it was alarmingly loud.

By now I was petrified. For so long, I had tried to imagine what the land of the hunters might be like, and in my head it was like the Indian camp, just located somewhere else, not this vast teeming place, thronged with scary noises; this place full of strange smells and speeding machines.

Nothing reminded me of my human past at that point. Yes, those recollections would return over the coming days and weeks, but at that moment all I could think, as I clung to the handrail, was that I wished for all the world to be back in the jungle. Back with my real family. Home with those that loved me. Safe again. What had I done?

*

The journey ended in the same way it had begun. One minute we seemed to be travelling at great speed through the thundering traffic, and the next we lurched violently, the truck slowed beneath me and, with a shudder, it stopped and finally fell silent. I tensed my body and tried to get a glimpse of where they had taken me. All I could make out through the canvas flap was a fence made of woven canes. What would happen now? What would the hunters do with me? Had they brought me to their human camp?

I was soon to find out. I heard the doors to the cab slam and the sound of the bolts of the tailboard sliding back. All around me, a mass stirring of animals started up. Buzzings and flappings and hoots and high chirrups, though my poor monkey friend lay lifeless in his cage.

And then there was light, though I could see the day was

fast disappearing. I was being blinded instead by the lights on other vehicles that were still flashing past at terrifying speeds.

I hated speed. In my world, speed meant danger. It meant a predator, preying. The risk of sudden death. It meant a bullet, or an arrow, or the jaws of an aggressor. I shrank back into the truck and gripped the rail tighter, terrified at the prospect of getting out.

But it seemed the hunters had other things to do at that moment. Having opened the back of the truck and peered in at us, the man grunted then followed the woman towards the fence. I couldn't see what lay beyond it and had no idea what might be there. I was only glad they had gone and that I was still safe inside. I had no thought of running, though. I had no thought of anything. Everything outside that truck seemed too terrifying to contemplate, so I crouched in the darkness, squeezed my eyes tight shut and berated myself for the idiotic, reckless and dangerous folly that had taken me from everything I loved, knew and wanted, and brought me to a place I couldn't have conjured up in my worst-ever nightmare.

I didn't wait long. I could hear voices coming closer and opened my eyes enough to see that the hunters were back. Now the woman in whom I'd foolishly invested so much hope looked as scary to me as the man. I tried to make myself as small as possible and scuttled as far into the truck's interior as I could manage. They beckoned me out, but I simply bared my teeth and began making monkey distress calls, which seemed to quell their enthusiasm for touching me, at least. They beckoned again and then, saying something to the man, the woman climbed into the truck with me and reached for my arm. I quickly snatched it away and bared my teeth again.

I could see the man losing patience, and I felt even more fearful. I could also see that the man held some sort of filthy cloth in his hand. As he too climbed up to assist the woman in grabbing hold of me, I realised with sudden clarity what he was about to do. It wasn't a cloth but one of the bags that they would stuff the monkeys into. The monkeys they shot out of the trees!

This was enough to force me to fight. Speed of movement always meant attack in my world, and I felt impelled to defend myself from it. Making noises of aggression, I fought them with every shred of strength left in me. Shrieking in terror, I tried to slap them away and bite them, though they were always too quick for me – not once did I manage to connect with their flesh. So I was soon overcome and hauled roughly from the truck, where a group of people stood and watched us, presumably having come out to see what all the commotion was about. But these were not people like the Indians, with their solemn ways and blank faces. These humans seemed to find my distress funny.

The cloth turned out not to be a sack, after all. It was some sort of covering – looking back now, probably a towel – and, having yanked me out and hauled me up onto two feet once more, the woman draped it loosely round my naked body. Seemingly satisfied, she then gripped my wrist and, pulling on it roughly, led me up the stony path towards the fence and whatever destiny awaited me beyond it.

16

The ground beneath my feet felt cold, hard and painful, not at all like it was in the jungle. But within seconds we had reached the entrance to a building. It was a solid barrier and again not like anything I remembered. In the Indian village, the entrances to huts were just open apertures, hung with material at most, which could be simply pulled aside.

Both the hunters now had a firm grip on my wrists, despite my repeated attempts to bite them. Still holding me tightly, the woman pushed the door open, revealing a gloomy interior. She then yanked me inside, the man following behind us, and though I screwed my eyes shut in fear – as small children do – once again my feet found some welcome warmth. I was standing on some sort of strange, smooth red surface, and as I dared to look around, almost everything I could see was unrecognisable, with functions and forms I could only guess at. I recognised mats on the floor but almost nothing else. Things like beds, chairs and lamps had no meaning.

But it was warm and, compared to the nightmare of getting here, peaceful. Though I still felt scared, I could also begin to sense that this might be some sort of home. Perhaps it was just another version of the Indian camp I had so yearned to live in. A place where I might be welcomed and cared for.

But though my mind grabbed onto positives, a part of me knew better. If that were so, then why was the woman still gripping me so tightly? Why were the expressions on the hunters' faces so hard?

'Ana-Karmen!' The man's voice boomed in the small space. I didn't understand the words – it was just a harsh and sudden sound to me – but, as had been the case all along, the tone was clear. I followed his gaze and could soon hear the sound of someone coming. It was a fat woman who had shuffled in from another part of the dwelling and now approached us with an equally hard look on her face. Years of relying on my instincts for survival made me stiffen. She was old and tired-looking, with evil green eyes and a heavily lined face – no doubt the result of years of nurturing the sour, angry expression that occupied it now.

Nothing seemed good about this woman. Every fibre of my body seemed to want to shrink away from her. Happily, though, she seemed to want to keep me at a distance, too. The humans communicated in their weird, unintelligible language, the fat woman, whose many chins seemed to have lives of their own, repeatedly darting disgusted glances in my direction. I knew what her expression meant as she cast her gaze over me – I had seen the same look on the Indian chief's face.

This did not look as if it was going to turn out well, and I felt cold dread once again overtake me. The hunter woman still held on tightly to my hand, as if fearing that I'd choose to run away – which I might have done, had the idea of what was outside not felt every bit as terrifying a prospect.

I watched as the fat lady then waddled off and left us, aware that whatever trace of compassion had still existed in the hunters when we arrived here had now drained away as surely as the rains did.

The woman returned with something in her hands. Two things, in fact. On one hand perched a green parrot, its plumage bright and unusual. I wasn't even sure I'd seen one like it. And in the other hand she held several pieces of something – I didn't know what they were but they looked a little like a wad of dried-up leaves. They crackled slightly as she held them out and waved them towards the man and woman. More unintelligible babble was now exchanged, though not the wad of leaves, even though it was clear to me that the fat lady wanted the hunters to take them.

It was at this point that I felt a push in the small of my back. At the same time, my arms were released and the truth about what was happening became clear. I knew so little of this world, knew so little about so much, but some things, I think, are universally straightforward. This was one of them – I was being exchanged. I had seen it happen once at the Indian camp, when

I saw a man giving another his bananas. I had been surprised by it then: a monkey would never willingly give their food away. But in return, the other man had given him a pot of something. I didn't know what, but it seemed the same sort of thing was happening now. The fat woman had given the hunters the bird and dead leaves, and in exchange they had given her me.

As if to reinforce that I had just made the biggest mistake of my life by leaving my family in the jungle, the next few minutes and hours remain horribly sharp in my memory. I watched the man and woman leave, returning the way we had just come. I recall how they never so much as turned round. I remember the heat of my hand where the woman had held it, and how I flexed and released my fingers as I watched them go.

I felt as if I drowning, as if my heart were being submerged into a sea of regret. Why had I chosen this path? Why had I left my home for this? Why had I trusted that the hunter woman would save me and care for me? The devastation when the woman left was total. I would never trust a human being again.

In a state of shock but beginning to come to my senses, I started to take stock of my surroundings. I recall seeing food in a bowl, some pieces of fruit that looked familiar from the jungle, and something that looked similar to a kind of bread I'd watched the Indian women make. I remember my hunger. I was starving. I had barely eaten in two days, and to snatch some was almost an automatic action. I certainly didn't anticipate the wooden implement that slapped down on the back of my hand, however, nor the pain that went through me as it connected.

After a few days, I would come to anticipate that feeling all too well. I would also begin to learn the names of things. The vicious implement was called a 'wooden spoon'. Ana-Karmen kept it stowed in her belt at all times and would pull it out and use it at the slightest provocation. Right now, though, like Ana-Karmen, it was just an agent of pain. Just like the humans who had swapped me for a parrot and a pile of leaves I'd learn were called 'money'. I had a great deal to grasp and I would learn faster than seemed possible. But the first important lesson had already been absorbed. I would never trust a human again.

*

Ana-Karmen (whose name would so soon take shape for me) closed the door on the hunters and the night. I kept my head low as I studied this strange new creature. She had a big lump on her neck that wobbled when she spoke, and her eyelids were painted with smears of livid blue and green – like that of a beetle's wing case but not at all pretty.

I felt sure her intention was to harm me – kill me, even – though I perhaps had enough innate intelligence to realise that had she wanted to kill me she wouldn't have made an exchange for me. What would have been the point? Even so, I was riddled with nerves. What did she intend to do with me now I was trapped here? I felt so anxious that every part of me was taut and poised for action. If she attacked me, my body was already saying I would fight her in every way I knew.

That I could fight was something I didn't doubt. As well as fear, I felt anger. Anger at myself for having come here, anger on behalf of all the trapped animals, anger especially at the death of that poor monkey, though I consoled myself that he had at least been spared further torment.

Ana-Karmen spoke, opening her mouth and letting another stream of noise out, her chins wobbling threateningly as she did so. She reminded me of a bird I used to enjoy watching in the jungle. It was a nocturnal bird that had a big red-balloon chest and never failed to entertain me. He would stand up, pick up leaves, turn around, inflate his chest, then deflate it, turn around and sit down again. And then he would do it all again.

I had no idea why he did it, and it was the same with Ana-Karmen. I had no idea what she was trying to communicate, so I couldn't answer. Which seemed to infuriate her. She gabbled the sounds at me once again, this time pulling sharply on my ears for good measure. I shrieked in shock and pain, and perhaps it was at this point that she too learned a lesson: that however much she shouted, I couldn't understand her. And another lesson, too: that I couldn't talk.

'Sophia!' Once again the sound boomed around the tiny dwelling. It made me jump. And as I did so, another person arrived from somewhere. I didn't know where, quite; it would be a few days before I worked out the layout of my new home. But there were clearly other rooms here – who knew how many? And people, too. This new person was another woman, but younger. Though her face seemed slightly older and her eyes were dark and sunken, she reminded me of the mother I'd seen in the jungle having her baby. She was slender and more graceful, and the thing I remember most clearly was that she wore bright orange shoes. Like Ana-Karmen, she also had paint on her eyes: this time a bright blue with black lines. Like me, she seemed scared.

She was joined by another girl, who looked and spoke differently, and when I return to these memories now her difference still remains. I wonder if perhaps she was disabled in some way. They called her 'La Bobita', and she looked a little like the women from the Indian camp, with darkish skin and a long, shiny black fringe. She seemed to spend all her time stationed in the corner of the kitchen and apparently couldn't talk – she only made strange spastic utters. When she was beaten, though, she screamed. Just as I did.

After a burst of snapped orders – again, the tone was unmistakeable – Sophia duly led me to another room. I still had no idea what any of them planned to do with me, only that they seemed disgusted by my presence. They certainly looked at me as if they could hardly bear to touch me.

As soon as I entered this new, darker chamber and saw what was in the middle of it, I froze. In the centre of the space stood a big battered container that seemed to be made of the same shiny material as some of the Indian camp cooking pots and which Sophia began filling from huge containers of water. Was she filling this to cook with, as the Indians cooked the roots? And then another thought made me flatten myself hard against the wall. Were they filling it so they could cook me?

It's impossible to adequately describe the emotions that filled my head at that moment. I had survived in a wild place for a very long time. I had done so with nothing but my own wits to help me. I had made my own mistakes and I had made my own rules. And bar leaving the Indian camp all that time ago, I had never been made to do anything. Such memories that lingered of my time before the jungle were now so vague as to be nothing more than wisps of impressions: about the pea pods, the path to the allotment, my black dolly. I was as much a wild animal as I could be, and now I was a cornered wild animal. I tensed again, waiting for the woman to pounce, and made noises that I hoped would convey to her that I was not going in that water however hard she tried to make me, that I was an animal she would be unwise to take on.

Perhaps understandably, given the kind of animal Ana-Karmen seemed to be, Sophia decided to take me on anyway. Once she had poured enough water into the giant pot, she approached me without fear and grabbed my upper arms while once again babbling at me. Again, though I couldn't understand what she was saying, her intention was obvious: she was also pointing at the pot and trying to drag me over to it.

I hated being touched by her. It felt unnatural and violent. The touch of the monkeys had always been so gentle. A soft furry arm snaked around my shoulder in affection. The gentle probing of nimble fingers combing my hair for grubs. This was so different and also very rough.

Now she seemed to decide she needed help. 'Lolita!' her shout rang out. 'Imelda! Elise!'

Whatever the sounds meant, they got a swift reaction. Just as a warning cry made the monkeys react quickly, so this barked noise brought reinforcements. Now there were four women intent on subduing me, and even with my terror of the water making me stronger, I was no match for four fit, grown women. One I could have managed. I intuitively knew that. But together they were unassailable and seemed to know it. Within seconds they had lifted me, kicking and shrieking, and dumped me in the water.

The shock of it made my whole body tremble. Would I now dissolve? Would being immersed rip the skin from my limbs? I remembered how I would sit up in the canopy and listen to sounds far below me of jungle animals in the river in palpable distress. I could hear them splashing, bellowing and howling their terror, and often wondered what fate might have befallen them there. To my mind, no creature was ever safe in water. And similarly petrified, I began to shriek as well.

They took no notice. Instead, they went straight into action, one of them picking up an instrument of torture – a long stick with a rough-looking brush at one end. Another held a ball of something slimy on a string. I would come to understand that this was soap – a giant ball of soap made from leftover slivers of old soaps all stuck together. They attacked me with both, scrubbing my poor delicate skin and my matted hair. I had never felt so violated.

And I resisted – resisted with a strength I didn't even know I had – but it didn't seem to make a bit of difference. They continued to manhandle me, scrubbing my limbs with rough, fast-moving hands. This was nothing like the monkeys' grooming. They were scrubbing at my flesh viciously – invading me, it felt like – and taking no notice of my obvious shock and pain.

It's difficult to convey now how distressing all this was for me. I had no memory of my early years. I only knew the jungle. And once again, for all my nakedness and lack of self-consciousness, I had a powerful sense of being taken over, of being enslaved. For the first time in my life I felt my body was no longer mine and that I was just a powerless object for them to do with as they pleased. The loss of control was almost impossible to bear.

By now the water, which had started out clear, was a deep brown. I could no longer see the bits of myself that were under the surface, yet still the three women continued to manhandle me and scrub me, getting increasingly angry about my shrieking and splashing. And then, after some more gabbled speech, I was again lifted. They took me out of the filthy water and stood me on the floor, and while I stood and shivered, they dragged the pot of filthy water from the room.

So perhaps I wasn't to be cooked and eaten after all. But if I thought the worst of the ordeal was over, I was horribly mistaken. Within moments the pot was back and once again they began to fill it. They were going to plunge me into it all over again! This time my resolve was even stronger than before, and I made so much fuss – wriggling and shrieking and flinging my limbs in all directions – that they obviously decided they might as well abandon the second dunking and instead lifted me back onto a small, scratchy floor mat. Here they set about scrubbing me all over again, only this time using rough cloths that they moistened in the fresh water before setting about me as if trying to flay my skin off. Looking back, perhaps they had little choice in the matter. They needed to clean me and I was making it very difficult. It might have been as much about self-protection as anything.

By the time I was as clean as I was going to be, and dry, I had run out of both the energy and the will to fight back. Now, my shrieks of indignant protest reduced to desolate whimpers, I just let them get on with their next job, which seemed to be to encase me in clothing. But these were clothes unlike anything I'd seen in the Indian village. They were also unlike the teeny scraps of tops and skirts they wore themselves. They seemed to want to dress me up to look like the hunters.

First, an enormous, stained shirt that looked like it was big enough for three of me was hauled unceremoniously over my head. Then my feet and legs were channelled into some equally huge brown trousers, which were itchy and billowing and smelt horrible. They wouldn't stay up – that was obvious – so a belt was fetched. It was white and stretchy and, like the string that held the skirt of the young Indian mother, it was knotted to hold the trousers up around my tiny waist.

I felt wretched. I was too hot, and my body felt restricted and enclosed. But they weren't done with making me miserable. They also wanted to force me into a stiff pair of shoes: sandals with a top made from some kind of multicoloured stringy material. But again they drowned me. I couldn't walk in them, and they frightened me. They made such a loud slapping sound every time I moved one of my feet that I stayed rooted to the spot, afraid to move. My defiance flared again. I was not going to wear them, and this time, when I flipped them angrily from my feet, the women, thankfully, didn't argue.

The worst was still to come, though. My hair. Much as it had driven me mad on occasion – getting in my way and causing me to scratch in itchy hell – my hair was still a part of me: my protection, my coat, my shelter. So when one of them approached me holding a big metal implement, it was just as well I had no idea what she was about to do with it or I would have found the strength of twenty Indian chiefs. But before I could even begin to guess at the purpose of the caiman-jawed tool, there was a chopping sound and my hair – all my hair – was on the floor.

I now knew better than to fight. I reached behind my head to see if there was any left there, only to feel the cropped ends

The exterior of Ana-Karmen's brothel. (© Daniel James)

Park in Cúcuta – Marina's home as a street kid. (© Daniel James)

Marina's nickname on the streets, 'Pony Malta', was due to her resemblance to the short, dark drink bottle. (© Daniel James)

Viewing Cúcuta from Loma de Bolívar. (© Daniel James)

The Cúcuta bridge that exploded near the Santos family home, now rebuilt. (© Daniel James)

The exterior of La Casita convent. (© Daniel James)

Meeting the convent nuns during a research trip to Colombia in 2007. (© Daniel James)

Maruja (Marina's rescuer) as Marina remembers her.

Marina's earliest known photograph, aged
17. Now named Luz Marina.

Amadeo and Maria Nelly Forero.

Marina at home in a tree-trunk hole, like those in which she would find a bed during her jungle days. (© John Chapman)

The wild child in her natural habitat. (© John Chapman)

Marina aged 62. A day out in the countryside often involves some interaction with nature and wild animals. (© John Chapman)

Family portrait. (© Carl Bromwich)

of it bristle against my palm. My head also felt light – so incredibly light – and now sat so differently on my shoulders. Without my curtain of black hair, I felt exposed again. Vulnerable. I had nowhere to hide any more.

The skin on my body looked strange now I took time to inspect it. It was a revelation: so pale and smooth, it looked as vulnerable as I felt. It was as if I was a tree and my bark had been stripped back, exposing the pale, delicate wood underneath.

All trace of the jungle had been stripped from me. It was there, on the floor, in the form of my lost hair, and there, in the tub, in that cloudy brown water. All gone. I was beginning a new chapter.

17

I had still been given nothing to eat or drink. In fact, the only thing the women seemed to want to put into my mouth was a small bristly brush on a long stick. It was yet another physical assault, but by now I was exhausted and had no fight left in me to stop them. So they yanked my lips open and while two held me rigid, the third put some sort of white stuff on the brush and then applied it to my teeth with vigour. This too was a shock, for the taste was bizarre – like nothing I remembered having tasted in the jungle. And there was another surprise: it also seemed to fill my mouth with bubbles. But of all the indignities I'd suffered up till now, this was definitely the most pleasant. It tasted good.

Finally, the brushing done, they gestured that I should spit all the bubbles into the tub and allowed me a handful of water. And with that, it at last seemed they were done with me. My mouth was wiped, my hand taken by one of the three women, and I was marched back to be inspected by Ana-Karmen. Returning to the room reminded me of my stomach, and I glanced hopefully towards where the fruit and bread had been. But it hadn't been for me. It had gone and the surface stood empty. No one even seemed to care that I was starving.

Indeed, Ana-Karmen, having given me another sour-faced inspection, seemed to have other ideas. Huffing and puffing, she yanked my arm and pulled me into yet another room, this one being vaguely more recognisable to me as it contained things I had seen in the Indian camp that I remembered were used for cooking and eating.

But still there was no sign that I was about to be given food. Instead, Ana-Karmen pointed at a mat on the floor and gave me a short push towards it. I was to lie there, she seemed to indicate, and go to sleep for the night. The day was done. I duly did as I was told.

*

I thought of escape that night, but only very fleetingly. Traumatised as I was by being imprisoned in a confined space (I was used to confined spaces, but ones I could leave at will), I was much, much more frightened of what lay outside. I had already found myself frustrated by door handles – what were they? How did they work? My hands could make no sense of them – and my natural urge to climb had also proved fruitless, as the one small, high kitchen window was barred.

But it wasn't these obstructions so much as my own fear that ensured I stayed. I was an animal and I was in a place where there was food – why would I leave it? Outside, I felt sure I would be killed in an instant. The horrors of my arrival were still fresh in my mind, particularly the cars, which really scared me.

It was almost impossible to sleep that first night. Where once, so long ago, I had been confused and disorientated by the jungle, I was now deeply unsettled by everything that wasn't the jungle. For a start, unlike my cosy nest in the tree trunk, the floor I was trying to sleep on was hard and unyielding. How did these people sleep in such a fashion? How could they get comfortable without tree boughs to rest their heads on, or the soft warmth of a monkey nearby?

And where was the proper darkness? It never seemed to come. The moon was so bright without its gentle veil of canopy, and the bright lights the people seemed to want to fill their world with seemed to sneak under my eyelids even though they were tight shut. And the noise – there was so much disconcerting unfamiliar noise here. I was used to the jungle night brigade of darkness-loving animals, and though I'd sometimes be woken by the sound of a nearby predator, I felt safe in my cocoon and would soon return to sleep. Here, though, like the light, the noise was constant.

There also seemed to be some sort of machine in the room I lay in. I didn't know what it was, but it seemed to hum at me all night. There was also the sound of water dripping constantly from somewhere. But it wasn't like the gentle plip-plop of morning dew or raindrops. It was a tinny repeating sound that seemed to bore into my brain.

And when I did manage to sleep a while I was tormented by nightmares, something that would continue for many days and weeks. It was such a terrible thing to think that I had lost my beloved monkey family and even worse knowing I would probably never see them again. Through my determination to try to find a life with one of my own species, I had become an outcast: completely isolated, anxious and scared. And more lonely than I thought I could bear.

The morning brought no sign that any of that was about to change. It seemed hours after I'd woken that I was finally given food – a bread roll, which tasted strange, but, being ravenous, I soon devoured it. But that was all. What I mostly recall of that first morning was that I was left in the corner while everyone dashed to and fro, ignoring me, all speaking to each other in their unintelligible babble. I also remember needing to defecate and, unable to communicate my needs, going outside, unremarked, into the scrubby garden. It was such a sad place in comparison to the lush green of the jungle, with just a few sparse bushes and some sad rows of plants. I remember doing my business and thinking once again about escaping, but the fear of what might be beyond the fence quickly put all such thoughts out of my mind.

Ana-Karmen put me in the charge of one of the women and set me to work immediately. It was probably a steep learning curve for all concerned and not just because of our inability to communicate. I had very little idea what 'work' was, let alone the mechanics of how to do it.

I had, of course, spent many hours watching the Indians in the jungle. I had observed them going about many different aspects of their daily business, which included preparing food, washing clothes, looking after their children, and so on. But in this odd, enclosed environment, nothing seemed to make sense. I had no memory of 'houses' – not of this strange type, anyway. No memory of 'windows', much less that one would climb up and clean them. I had no sense of what dust was or why it was necessary to be rid of it. I certainly had no idea what a stain might be.

But Ana-Karmen was clearly determined that I would learn.

And quickly. So right away I was given instruction in how to clean things: how to wield a cloth and some spray and how the one worked with the other. I have a strong memory of one of the girls holding her own hand over mine and showing me how to make swirly movements with it. And I also began to understand the concept of 'names': Sophia, Lolita, Imelda.

It was the latter two that gave me my first-ever lesson in what would become my principal occupation: doing the chores no one else wanted to do. No more playing with pretty flowers or crushing leaves to make paint. All the colour was to disappear from my life and be replaced by the dull tones of servitude. And the most important lesson was how to mop floors.

A mop seemed to me to be a strange-looking thing. Reminiscent of a stringy upside-down flower on a thick stalk, it was first dunked in a large container containing foamy greenish water before being applied, for some unfathomable reason, to the floor. Why did they want the floor to be wet? It made no sense at all. When it rained in the jungle, for all the cooling relief of it, the wetness underfoot was mostly a hindrance. Yet, strangely, it seemed to be desired here. The mop was thrust towards me and the women gestured that I take it. So I did so and wet the floor some more.

'*Estúpido! Estúpido!!*' Imelda snapped, making me jump. She exhaled loudly, then wrapped both her hands around mine, pulling me this way and that as we weaved backwards across the floor. My feet were getting tangled in my flappy, too-long trousers, while the mop trailed glistening arcs of liquid in our wake.

She then let go of me and gabbled something else that meant nothing but which I took to mean that I should try doing it again. And I did – I tried so hard to do it just the way she'd shown me, but I just couldn't seem to make my arms work the way hers had, and both she and Lolita started shouting at me again.

And that was me all day – '*Estúpido! Estúpido!!*' I heard it millions of times – so often that I thought it was my name. I tried so hard – all I wanted was to please them so they wouldn't shout at me – but it was impossible, for I understood nothing.

I had spent long hard years amassing the skills of the jungle, but here I was useless. Worse than useless, in fact. I couldn't seem to coordinate my limbs the way they could. I couldn't even open a cupboard door, because I couldn't work out how to twist a handle. I could push and I could pull, but the action of twisting it eluded me. I couldn't scrub. I couldn't spray with their funny spray bottles. I couldn't wipe.

Ironically, once I got the hang of it, I really quite liked mopping. It was water, yes, but water that I could control. I liked seeing how the water in the bucket changed colour as the dirt from the floor was mopped up and swirled in. I liked splashing the mop-water on my bare feet, to cool them. I liked the gentle ploppy sound beneath my feet. I liked that the more water you put on the mop, the more came out. Such simple things, really, but a much-needed source of fun.

But my games irritated the girls. I irritated them daily because my domestic ineptitude knew no bounds. I had no memory of simple things like plates, for example – at least, not plates that went *smash*! if you dropped them. '*Esfragil*' was a word that had no meaning for me until the point when a wet plate, which Lolita had indicated I should dry, slid from my clumsy fingers and exploded into a million pieces across the floor. How had it done that? Why had it done that? I stared wide-eyed at the mess at my feet, fascinated.

I didn't associate the 'crash' sound with anything being wrong – why would I? I just looked at pieces on the floor, trying to understand it, because I'd not seen a texture like it before. Ana-Karmen came to hit me, so I naturally ran to hide, but for what misdemeanour, I didn't know. I was just curious. I didn't think, 'Oh, no, I broke a plate. Now I'm in trouble!' The whole concept was completely alien to me. Yes, I was shocked at the volume and intrigued by the discovery of a new noise. But again, I was in control of it. I knew where it had come from, so maybe that's why I didn't fear it so much. I was just desperate to understand.

The jungle now seemed so much more comprehensible to me. There were hard things and soft things, and each had its purpose. A rock was hard: good for lodging nuts in, to crack them. A flower was delicate, perfectly suited its purpose – to bloom. But what was this thing 'Esfragil'? Why did humans have so many things that weren't fit for purpose? Windows that got dirty, floors that got dusty and things to eat and drink from that broke if you dropped them? Perhaps these humans were the ones that were 'estúpido'!

They certainly seemed estúpido. Because the complexities of their world simply baffled me. Why exactly did they make everything so complicated? Clothes fastenings that confounded me, eating implements that irked me, rules and regulations that seemed designed to confuse me and which seemed to serve no other purpose but to do so. I was a picture of inadequacy with so much to figure out. And in the meantime, I got shouted at and beaten several times a day. I got beaten for doing wrong, and when I tried to escape the beatings, I got beaten again. Not a day went by when I didn't grieve for my lost monkey family and wonder why I had left them for this hell.

*

I didn't know it then, of course, but the hunters had delivered me to the village of Loma de Bolívar, a tiny place in northern Colombia about thirty minutes from the centre of a city called Cúcuta. It could have been a hundred metres or a hundred miles from the place where I'd been born. But it meant nothing, because the only home I knew now was the jungle: a home I had abandoned to be here.

The house I was now imprisoned in was owned by Ana-Karmen and seemed to be inhabited by a number of young women and several children of varying ages. It was single storey and very basic, with four or five rooms in total, in all of which there were beds – some covered by what I now recall as a hospital-style curtain rail. There was a patio to the side, with a big yard attached to it, and an ugly garden with few plants but several fruit trees. There were goats in the garden, and I loved them from the outset. There was also one dog – a scruffy animal, but a loving one – and sufficient bugs and creepy crawlies to give me at least a small sense of home. But, as with everything in this place, it was as if the sound and colour had been turned down. Compared to their jungle relatives, these creatures were dull and insubstantial.

I felt as dulled by my surroundings as they appeared dulled to me, my world now reduced to the dimensions of the tatty cane fence. I had been bought by Ana-Karmen to be her slave. I imagine the polite expression then might have been 'servant', but since I received nothing from her bar the rudiments necessary for survival, the word 'servant' would be wholly incorrect.

Naturally, as a child who was by now completely feral, such definitions were of no use or interest. All I knew or cared about were the things that mattered to me personally: how to understand what was required of me, how to make myself understood, and how to get through each day without being punished too much, all of which were very, very hard.

But since I had no thought of escaping to the even more terrifying outside world, all I wanted was to be able to fit in. I wanted to be pretty, like Ana-Karmen's girls. I wanted to play with the other children in the street. I wanted to be elegant and wear nice orange shoes and gold jewellery, bracelets and earrings that caught the sun and reflected it back again. I wanted to be decorated, garlanded, like I had been with my jungle flowers, only all shimmery and sparkly and golden. But none of this was for me – that was made very clear. I was tolerated only because I was potentially of use, and when I failed to be, naturally I was punished.

The wooden spoon in Ana-Karmen's belt – initially so terrifying – soon seemed the mildest of punishments. And I was punished constantly, because it seemed I could do nothing right: a situation that seemed to both enrage and delight Ana-Karmen since, though it angered her, it also gave her a reason to inflict pain.

She smoked cigars, so a cigar burn on my arm was a favourite. She liked to whip me, too, sometimes with a belt or a rope and at other times – the worst – with a length of braided electrical cord. Within days she had hit me more than once with a frying pan and more than once clenched my skinny neck between her sweaty, chubby hands. Within a fortnight, she had also learned about my profound fear of water and seemed to take particular delight in spraying me with the powerful hose out in the yard.

It seemed I could do absolutely nothing to escape her

cruelty. I was puny and terrified and had no idea what I could do. I had chosen this path – chosen to leave everything that mattered. So I put my head down and waited for the storm to pass.

18

Over the following weeks, I existed in a strange sort of purgatory, suspended in a place where I felt completely alone. I was no longer one of the monkey troop, and ached for them constantly, yet neither was I a part of this strange new world I lived in, where it seemed I could do nothing right. But at least I was making progress. Little by little I was beginning to grasp the odd word and phrase. It was by the tiniest of increments, and I had a long way to travel, but I was a child and trying to learn was instinctive.

Adapting physically to the sweeping change in my life was very hard. My spoken language was still made up of animal noises, and I didn't know how to smile or make facial expressions that corresponded to those I saw around me. I climbed constantly. It was an effort of will not to climb up things: in the house initially, where I would climb up onto worktops, and soon outside, up the trees in the garden.

I couldn't stand properly. It still felt unsettling and unnatural, and, left to my own devices, I would squat any time I was stationary. I especially liked to squat in corners. To be in a corner was to feel safe. My back and sides were covered. And though it wouldn't save me from a beating it still felt instinctive to do it, especially in those corners that held big plants in pots and where there was sufficient space to slide in behind them.

If I needed to move somewhere, I would still scuff along the ground on all fours. I knew humans walked on two legs and tried hard to copy them, but I was constantly hindered by my unconscious mind, which would have me back in my default position unless I made a huge effort of will. It was as hard for me as it would have been for a human in the jungle ordered to get around on four limbs instead of two. And every time I was caught doing any of these things that came so naturally, Ana-Karmen, equally naturally, would discipline me.

Perhaps the hardest discipline to learn, however, was how to behave at mealtimes. Simply learning to sit and eat at a table was so difficult. I had no idea about tables and cutlery and crockery (other than that the latter was so fragile), and would automatically take my food to the floor in the corner and set about quickly eating it with my fingers. That was the way things had worked in the jungle. You found something to eat and you took it to a quiet spot, wolfing it down quickly and guarding it as you did so. If you didn't, then it would obviously be stolen by another monkey. So to sit with others and eat together was unthinkable.

My table manners, consequently, were appalling. I would grab at food, stuffing it into my mouth in big handfuls, and with some kinds of food this inevitably meant chaos. I was given things I'd never seen before, such as meatballs in lumpy liquid sauces that would run down my forearms and drip from my elbows, as well as lodging on and in my face and hair. They would be served with another bewildering food called spaghetti – long strings, like vines, which seemed impossible to eat, especially with all that sauce dripping from them.

My fellow diners – the girls, Ana-Karmen, the other children – clearly found my manners repulsive. I could tell by the disgusted way they looked at me. But I knew no better and found it very hard to learn. Their lifestyle was just so incredibly complicated.

Most of the time I lived on bread rolls and a bitter drink called coffee, which would be given to me in something called a cup. It took me a while to understand the concept of drinking a hot drink in the first place, but served in a shallow bowl with a handle and a ring of gold round the top of it just seemed the strangest thing ever. So I would get my coffee by dipping my bread into the mug and 'drinking' my hot drink in that way.

If 'boiling hot' was a new thing for me, so was 'ice cold', and I remember my first experience of it clearly. I was given an ice lolly – actually frozen fruit juice set into an ice tray with a little piece of wood stuck into it – which was so cold against my lips it actually hurt me. I thought it was alive, too, because it stuck to my tongue when I licked it. Terrified, I threw it across the room.

Tastes, too, were as much of an adventure as temperature. As well as the bitterness of coffee, there was the lardiness of butter and the strange, rubbery texture and blandness of pasta, which was not like eating proper food at all. I mostly loved the fruit bowl and the reassuring familiarity of its contents, though being allowed anything from it was painfully rare. Mostly, in any case, I was permanently hungry, so these details were of only passing importance. If I was given food and drink, I gladly consumed it.

*

Eating and drinking were not the only things that involved an intense learning process at Ana-Karmen's. I was equally taxed by the way humans dealt with the other main bodily functions. After a few days of sleeping on the mat on the kitchen floor or in the garden, I was 'promoted' to being allowed to sleep in a bed. Once again, I didn't know what to do with it. I would sleep on the floor under it, believing the frame was a canopy, there to protect me.

Similarly I was flummoxed by the toilet. I had no inkling of what the toilet was for and had been making use of the bushes in the garden until one day I was caught in the act. A high-pitched scream was followed by a lot of babbling and the appearance of Ana-Karmen, who bellowed her disgust at me, gesticulating wildly. Sophia then thrust a pair of weird utensils in my direction, seeming to demand that I pick up my waste with them. I was appalled: not only frightened of Ana-Karmen's crimson-faced fury but also disgusted that she should want me to do such vile thing – pick up my own excrement? Why would I do that?

In the end, I kicked soil over it and fled into the house, closely followed by Ana-Karmen, Sophia and Lolita. I was then dragged by the latter two to a tiny outside lean-to. Suspended by my armpits over the thing they called the toilet, it was made clear that this was where my business should be done.

I was so frightened as they did this that I could hardly draw breath, for beneath me, buzzing with flies, was a deep and stinking hole, the stench from it so strong it made me gag.

But the old toilet was as nothing compared to the 'new' one they also had, for, though it didn't stink like the other, it was a hole filled with water, into which I was sure I could fall and die. I was even more terrified when they pulled a chain above my head and a sudden rush of new water gushed underneath me, accompanied by a loud roaring sound. Once again I bolted and, despite my fear of Ana-Karmen and her electrical cord, I continued to sneak out and secretly use the garden.

*

Within a few days, I was also given a new set of clothes. Whether they realised I would be less clumsy if I didn't have to wear the enormous trousers I don't know, but one day Elise came and measured my body. I struggled as she did it, as I had no idea what she was doing, but a couple of days later I was presented with the results of her efforts. I had been made another pair of itchy trousers, as thick and unappealing as the last pair, only this time they were the right size and stayed up on their own. I was also given a white short-sleeved blouse, which was decorated with bits of lace and within a day or two was spotted with bits of food, too.

I remained barefoot, but now my heels, already hardened by the forest floor, had begun to crack and were becoming very painful to walk on. It was in this that I saw my first glimmer of compassion. Sophia, on seeing them, found some sort of ointment and rubbed it into my feet, which helped a lot.

I liked Sophia. And I desperately wanted the girls to like me. I would listen to them chatting and try to understand what they were saying. Words began to stand out, and I unravelled their meaning. Then I started to pick up whole strings of words, making connections between them, and these glimpses into their world made me feel less alone. Eventually I noticed there was one word they used around me often and made the connection between the sound and them wanting my attention. They would say it, and then touch me, and then say it again, and it began to dawn on me that, just as with 'table' or 'blanket', this was the word they used for me. And so I learned the first name I ever remember having. The one they had given me. Gloria.

*

The weeks passed, and as I learned how to do things, my duties became more varied. I spent much of my day involved in food preparation. I couldn't cook – I had no idea how to do anything so complex – but it was my job to prepare the ingredients. I peeled potatoes and carrots, yucca and arracacha, corncobs and plantains, and many more. I cut my hands often, as I had yet to learn how to use a knife properly. It seemed so crazy to do all this cutting and use all these tools when you had the hands and mouth and teeth nature had given you. But I wanted to fit in, so I persisted and eventually managed to master it.

I was also, after a time, sent on errands in the village. This gave the local villagers something new and strange to look at, and me – too intrigued myself to be bothered by their scrutiny – my first proper glimpse of my new home. I would walk the dusty streets, weaving between the equally dusty cars, my ears picking up snippets of unintelligible conversation from behind intriguingly open doorways, the call of birds, the cries of babies, the blare of strange music. I was also more aware here of the feeling of constant heat: a heat that seared into my scalp and made my skin prickle with moisture, and which made the metal on the cars and trucks untouchable.

Initially I'd go out with one or two of Ana-Karmen's girls in attendance, to show me where to go and ask for what was needed, but as time went on and they trusted that I wouldn't run away, I was sent alone, with a basket and a shopping list. And they were right to trust me not to stray, for my main preoccupation was being fed. I lived to eat: it was the only enjoyable part of my day. And how would I manage if I left? I would surely starve. This was so different from the jungle, where there was food to be collected or picked from trees and bushes around every turn. In this grey world of concrete and fences and cars, there was no food to be found anywhere.

And no friends, either. Once I had been living there a few weeks or months – I'm not clear – I began sneaking out if Ana-Karmen was distracted. Not to run away but just to follow my normal childish instinct whenever I heard the sound of other children playing.

I had no relationship with the children of the house. In fact, I hated them. There were several, mostly babies and toddlers, who cried and fussed and annoyed me. They were the children of the girls who lived and worked there. My only contact with any of them was when I was told I had to feed them, which made me cross. I had to shovel food into their ungrateful mouths when I was given barely anything and was so hungry.

Outside the walls of the house, though, it seemed different. So beguiling. I would hear children that seemed so much more like me, playing and laughing. But nobody wanted to be friends with me. I was only just becoming aware of the concept of friendship, but the absence of warmth was something I felt keenly. The affectionate way the monkeys in the jungle had interacted with me was not something I had ever really thought about before. But it was as natural a thing to me as the squabbles and play-fights, and the isolation I now felt upset me.

But why would the other children in the street want to play with me? I had no human language, I made strange noises and looked different. I was only just learning to move around as they did and still had lots of monkey behaviours such as snatching at food, scratching myself constantly and pulling exaggerated faces to express my emotions.

I would watch them playing with their toys and, having none of my own, I would try to indicate my desire to join in. But if I was granted a few moments with a precious plaything of some sort, they would just snap at me or laugh at me for holding things strangely, stripping every ounce of pleasure I might have got from it.

The other children could do so many things that I still couldn't. They could run around on their confident legs, even kick balls while doing so, play games with counters and draw pretty pictures. I could do none of these things, so any time I had spare, I would increasingly retreat to my world of plants and animals, decorating the boughs of the trees in the garden with flowers and the skins of papaya and bananas, just as I'd done in my old home. My friends were the animals – they seemed to accept my presence unquestioningly, allowed me to get close to them and even entertained me, especially the goats, who made me laugh with all their antics such as nibbling at the clothes drying on the washing line.

I also found a new source of pleasure: making mischief. And in a village that had shunned me, there was great fun to be had in picking fruit and, having climbed the boughs of one of the trees in the garden, lobbing it into other gardens, aiming squarely at the villagers who were hanging out their washing.

Perhaps it was that, or perhaps just the odd way I went about things, but very soon I became an object not just of ridicule but of fear. Ana-Karmen clearly picked up on the sense of unease that the villagers were feeling about my presence – and perhaps she felt the same way herself – as another clear memory of that time was the appearance of two Catholic priests at the house. I was bewildered by their chanting and splashing of holy water, the waving of burning branches of incense, but I now realise they must have been performing some kind of exorcism. With most of the villagers being superstitious Catholics, it's not hard to imagine that they might have believed that this strange, animal-like girl who suddenly appeared in their presence was possessed by some kind of demon.

While this was clearly not the case, evil was a word that would come to have great meaning for me. And rather than a pair of chanting priests bearing incense, I only needed eyes and ears to see it all around me.

19

With little to compare it to, I didn't question the set-up at Ana-Karmen's. I just kept my head down and did my best not to displease her. But as the weeks turned into months and I adapted to my new environment, my expanding vocabulary meant I was better able to take in more of what was going on around me.

The house was always busy. There seemed to be girls who lived there all the time, such as Sophia, Imelda, Elise and Lolita, and other girls who would be around for a few nights in a row and then seemed to disappear for weeks. I struggled to understand why these girls lived in such a wicked, unfriendly home. Out of choice?

La Bobita, the cowering child I'd first met trembling in the corner of the kitchen, was more like me – she had no choice but to stay. But where I was beginning to master human language and could both understand and be understood, I had never once heard a proper word come out of her mouth. Something told me she was different in other ways too. She moved oddly and slowly, with a shambling gait, and cowered every time Ana-Karmen came near her. Which wasn't surprising, as Ana-Karmen hit her very hard and very often, and when not hitting her, shouted at her constantly.

Today, I look back and I wonder – was she Ana-Karmen's daughter? I can think of no other reason why Ana-Karmen would continue to take care of her – although 'take care of' is entirely the wrong expression.

There were also men. Men would visit the house every single day. A continual stream of them would come and go. And there was one who sometimes lived there, like some of the girls, for days at a time, though I never saw him very much. He was called Rufino, and when I did see him, it would be when he was sitting on the patio, drinking beer, peering over his giant belly and smoking cigarette after cigarette. When he was in the house at night, he would sometimes sleep in the same bed as Ana-Karmen but sometimes on the bed out on the patio – close to where I slept – and his snoring on these nights, presumably due to alcohol, was so loud and so constant it drove me crazy.

I was still, at this time, a little monkey. Having not yet had the cheekiness beaten out of me by Ana-Karmen, I would get up to mischief on many occasions, with a complete lack of thought for the consequences. And one night, having had enough of the man's terrible rumblings, I decided I would teach him a lesson by getting some ice cubes from the freezer and throwing them over him – anything to stop the noise.

It would prove to be a shock for both of us. For me, because when I crept out onto the patio it was to find him completely naked, and for him, because what other response could there be when you are fast asleep and someone chucks a cup of ice at you?

Rufino's roar was so loud it seemed to make the very walls shake, the freezing cold hitting him like a jolt of electricity. But I was quick and thought I had got away with it. It was dark and I was back in my bed in an instant, but he rightly worked out that no one else in the house would be as reckless and stupid as to do such a thing. I got a beating with his belt minutes later.

*

I was learning all the time, though. The months rolled by and I continued to absorb the ways of humans. Both by watching and copying, and also by making mistakes – for which I would get beaten but from which I would also learn. I still had no thought of trying to run away. The outside world, where, if possible, people seemed to hate me even more than Ana-Karmen did, held no kind of promise or appeal. One constant – which was sometimes a curse, sometimes a blessing – was that when I wasn't being set to work, or shouted at, or beaten for something, I was mostly left alone and ignored.

And then, at some indefinable point, the situation changed.

I don't remember when it first became evident what was happening, but I seemed to go from being treated like the goats in the yard to a creature in need of tuition. I was, in short, becoming an object that was starting to be of interest. Both Ana-Karmen and the girls started taking an interest in my manners, teaching me ways of doing things more 'nicely' and behaving more calmly at the table. They also seemed determined to get me cleaned up and groomed. And perhaps I should have liked that.

I had certainly missed the daily communal grooming of my former life. I so missed the monkeys: missed the physical closeness of being with them. I missed their silky fur, missed their gentle touch, missed their warmth and cuddles. But this new attention wasn't like that. The girls were always so rough with me, so irritable and unfriendly. Where the monkeys would gently tease bugs from my hair, Ana-Karmen's girls would yank and pull, dragging their vicious brushes through it and moaning about all the food I habitually got lodged in it from my repeated head scratching with sticky, dirty fingers. It was the same with my lice, which were just a fact of life in the jungle. Where else were lice to live? It was just normal. But here they were despised, and on seeing them the girls would always shout at me, calling me a filthy old rat, which I found incomprehensible.

I found it very difficult to adjust to being pulled and pushed around in this way. I had spent my formative years working out my own way to do things, so resisted all efforts to 'civilise' me. Naturally, this led to more beatings. But slowly I came to accept that if I could modify how I did things, my life would be more pleasant.

I was also opening up my eyes to the people around me. I had worked out that I lived in a house full of females who lived a life very different from that of the women in the Indian camp. Some of them had children – there always seemed to be babies and toddlers coming and going – but it was as if we inhabited different worlds. They certainly felt alien to me, especially the little ones, and what I mostly remember of them – the details are quite hazy – was that I envied them the love and care that I didn't have, not to mention all the toys they were given. There was no connection – I'm quite sure their mothers wanted it that way – so I saw them as just an irritating presence (especially when they cried) and continued to feel great anger when they refused to eat their food.

But this wasn't a house that nurtured little ones, not really. Regardless of whether they had children or not, Ana-Karmen's girls, it seemed to me, spent most of their time getting 'dolled up', as Elise called it, painting their eyes and lips and tirelessly styling their hair. There were lots of beds, and lots of men, who'd disappear into the girls' bedrooms, spend an hour or two there, then disappear again.

I had no idea what this meant back then. I was a child and still naive about the ways of the adult world. Perhaps even if I hadn't spent those years in the jungle it might still have passed way over my head. And as it did so, I was still very much Ana-Karmen's slave anyway. Though I was about to graduate – to be trained for a new purpose.

*

Increasingly, going out – getting a chance to escape the fetid, oppressive atmosphere of the house – would be the highlight of my day. Though the man at the local shop still didn't understand my garbled attempts at language, at least I wasn't being beaten or yelled at. And it also gave me an opportunity to steal food.

Stealing food was completely natural to me, and I still had no concept that doing so was a crime. I sometimes got caught stealing little things – a piece of fruit, a bread roll – but they never banned me because I was also a paying customer. Food was still the biggest treasure in my life.

These excursions gave me a window on the human world that I didn't get from being stuck inside Ana-Karmen's. I had no education, obviously – while the older children in the house went to school, I cleaned and prepared food – and though the girls would sometimes name things and try to make me copy them, formal learning, as in learning to read and write and count, was something to which I had no access. So what I knew I learned mostly from getting out and observing, taking in what I could of my surroundings.

Though a few were painted white, most of the houses in Loma de Bolívar were grey. They were crammed in together, in narrow concrete huddles, and the pavements outside them were dusty and dirty, the grey only broken up by the cars that were parked and the green shade of the Matarratones trees.

The village was a sociable place. At around six o'clock every day, most people would take chairs out onto the street to sit and chat, to swap the heat of the dark interior of their homes for the relative cool of the open evening air. Only Ana-Karmen, it seemed to me, was different in this respect, though I had yet to understand quite why she was shunned.

I would walk downhill, Ana-Karmen's house being up a slight incline, passing the tall scary building I'd been told was a hospital, and, if I was going down late with my basket and list, would pass the gaggles of seated people, most of whom completely ignored me.

The shop – *la tienda* – was the only one locally, the village, though packed with dwellings, being small. One afternoon, I had arrived at the shop with my basket and list when I spotted a woman I knew. She was a mother with three children, and I liked her. Of all the people I encountered whenever I left Ana-Karmen's, she was one of the few who treated me kindly, rather than as if I were some kind of filthy animal.

She was outside her house, just down from the store, and had been cleaning her windows, but when she saw me she stopped and beckoned to me. 'Gloria,' she called. 'Come over here a moment.'

There being no hurry to get back, I immediately did so. Where I baulked about being given orders at Ana-Karmen's, this was different. I knew she meant me no harm. I also trusted her. I don't know why – was it the fact that she had children? Probably, with my persistent sense of motherhood meaning 'goodness'.

I went across to her and set my empty basket down.

'That's right,' she said, speaking slowly, as she knew my language skills were poor. 'Stay there a minute. I have something I need to tell you.'

She disappeared into the house and returned with a small plate, on which was what looked like *longanizas*, a kind of sausage.

'You have probably noticed,' she said, gesturing that I should sit down with her on her doorstep, 'that lots of men come to your house, to see the women.'

I nodded. This was true. 'Yes, I have,' I answered.

'Well, let me tell you something,' she said. 'Before very long, you might find one of those men wanting to see you.'

This had never occurred to me. No one wanted to see me. I was invisible to the women, except for when work needed doing or when they wanted to scrub me clean. To the men, I was invisible always.

'Why would they do that?' I asked.

'Because they are checking,' she answered. 'They are checking to see if you're made of the right meat.'

I was confused. I had no idea what she meant. And she could obviously sense that, because now she looked down into her lap at the plate of sausage she'd brought out but hadn't as yet suggested I might eat. Besides, it was raw, which seemed odd. Humans didn't eat them raw, did they? And then she squeezed it. Now I was more confused than ever.

'Like you are a piece of raw meat,' she said again, saying the words slowly and squeezing the sausage again. 'Like this. And you don't want to be that. That's what the girls are up at Ana-Karmen's house. You understand? They are raw meat. For the men.'

It sounded horrible. 'To eat?' I asked, wide-eyed, imagining the sausage was made of human girls. It couldn't be, could it? I recoiled.

The lady thought again. 'Sort of,' she said. She put a hand on my arm. 'That's not important. All you need to know is that if they come in or try to take you from Ana-Karmen, that is what you will become. A piece of meat.'

I looked at the sausage on her plate, which looked like a chubby baby's arm. How would I become that? I didn't know. But I could see from her expression that it was probably something bad. 'Don't let her do that to you,' she warned. 'Don't let any of the men touch you. Ana-Karmen is training you to be the right sort of meat for these bad men. Don't trust her – don't trust them. You need to leave there. Run away. Do you understand what I'm saying?'

I nodded glumly. I didn't understand all the words, but I understood that this was a warning. The trouble was that I was still much too frightened of the city. If I ran away, where would I go, and how would I survive?

'You understand?' she said again.

'Yes,' I said. 'I understand', which seemed to satisfy her, because she told me I could get on my way.

I didn't sleep at all that night for trying to understand about becoming sausages. Or meat. The kind of meat that was liked by bad men. But one thing I did understand was a new feeling – fear. A fear different from that I'd experienced when I came here, and different from the simple fear of getting a beating for some silly thing or other I'd done wrong.

This was a different fear. A fear that went into the very core of me, and I couldn't sleep for days. I became fearful of all the men in the village – particularly one old man who'd always be dozing outside the shop, mumbling as he slept and making strange movements with his hands. Looking back I realise he was probably mentally ill or disabled, but all I could think at the time was that perhaps he was one of the men – the bad men who turned girls into sausages.

Though I struggled to understand the details, I believed what the lady told me, because, of all the people I'd met, she was the one I most trusted. Men, on the other hand, had now become like devils. I went into protection mode. I must really be on my guard now.

*

Up to now, I had no understanding of Christmas. No memories of it from before I was abandoned in the jungle and no idea what all the fuss was about now. Not that there was a great deal of fuss in Loma de Bolívar, as the people were so poor that extravagances were few, and the most Christmassy memory I have of that period was of seeing trees decorated with cotton-wool 'snow'. There were certainly no festivities in the house of Ana-Karmen – no special food, no sense of celebration, no singing. My strongest recollection is just one of seeing other children with new toys and feeling that same gnawing sense of abandonment.

But there was one event that happened two days after Christmas that will stay with me always. I remember it started with a commotion – a huge commotion outside the house. There was the sound of a blaring car horn, amid lots of shrieks and giggles. I rushed out into the street to see what all the noise was about, and what I saw almost took my breath away. I had seen lots of cars and trucks by now – they were just another part of the landscape. But parked outside Ana-Karmen's was the most beautiful machine ever. A convertible motor car the colour of creamy milk. I had never seen anything so pretty, or that looked so expensive. I had developed an idea of what money was for now, and what it could and couldn't buy, and I knew this was something way outside my experience.

The car dazzled me as I approached it, the light dancing off it and making diamonds in the air. The sun caressed it, too, bouncing joyfully off the car's dazzling chrome curves and making its creamy panels glisten as if liquid. It was finished with a paint trim of olive-green detailing and was the most beautiful thing I had ever seen.

It belonged to a man from Venezuela, who had come with two friends to see some of our girls for the day. I could see it was his from the confident way he 'owned' it. The way he twirled the keys around, demonstrated how the fabric cover was raised and lowered, and the way he stroked it – as if it were one of Ana-Karmen's women. The men were from something which I think might have been called 'the mafia'. It had nothing to do with Italy, I've found out since, but I'm fairly sure that was how they were referred to locally. In any event, they were potentially dangerous, powerful, criminal 'guerrilla' men.

They were probably bad men. I knew nothing about their activities, obviously, but my instincts were strong, and they just had the aura that if you crossed them you would put yourself in danger. But whatever they did or didn't do, it was clear that they were wealthy. Be it good or bad, what they did bought them beautiful things. There was so much about the world still to understand.

That the girls approved of the young men was not in any doubt, though. By the time I had come outside, there were several clustered around the car, all laughing, tossing their hair back and jutting out their bosoms, all trying to win the attention of the young Venezuelan man. And he was lapping it up.

For the first time in my life I felt a stab of jealousy. I wanted nothing more than to be one of those girls now, just so I could go for a ride in the man's car. And luckily for me, it seemed I might get a chance.

Soon the gaggle of adoring females followed the men into Ana-Karmen's to conduct the business necessary to free up the girls for the ride. For me, this provided an irresistible opportunity. I was tiny – I still am – and was used to squeezing into small spaces. It was the work of moments to clamber into the car over the hot, slippery boot and quickly wedge myself into the rear footwell, covering myself with the blanket that had been tossed over the back seat.

I felt sure I would be discovered very quickly, but I didn't care. There was always a chance I wouldn't, and that was enough for me. As it was, I heard the crowd returning, and within moments two of the girls had swung their legs over the back, their sandalled feet planted on the rear bench seat, inches above me. I risked a peek and could just see enough to work out that they were going to ride sitting with their bottoms on the boot, so they could parade down the street for all to see. The engine roared then, startlingly loud from my position under the blanket, and with a judder we roared away.

Not being able to see anything that was happening was frustrating, but I was so energised and excited by what I'd done that I didn't care and was happy enough with the senses that I could use. I could smell alcohol – an odour I knew well from living at Ana-Karmen's – and I also knew enough to realise that at least one of the men was drunk. Probably all of them, I reasoned, listening to their loud voices, though one in particular was slurring his words a lot.The girls, too, were very noisy, even more excited than I was. And as the car thundered up and down roads I couldn't see, I felt the heat of the sun on the blanket, the whistle of the air rushing past us, and experienced a surge of pure joy at this sudden freedom. If this was the life these girls lived, would it be so bad a thing? They seemed almost delirious with joy to me.

After a time, I decided I could risk another peek. What were the chances, after all, that the girls would be looking downwards? Their eyes, surely, would be on the road and the view. I slid the blanket from my eyes and looked straight up to the sky. It was a deep blue, completely cloudless, dazzling. More dazzling still to my eyes, though, was what was rushing past beside us. It was a rock face so tall that it exceeded my sight line – so we must be travelling upwards, along a high mountain pass, perhaps along the very one that had first brought me to Cúcuta. I instinctively craned my neck to try to see more.

'Aeey!!' I heard Elise shout. 'Look, Lolita! It's Gloria! Aeey, Gloria,' she commanded drunkenly. 'What are you doing here?'

Unmasked now, I pulled the blanket off my whole face and grinned up at her. 'Elise,' I asked her nicely, 'can I sit up there with you?'

'No, you idiot!' she snapped at me. 'Get down or they'll see you!'

But I kept popping up again – I was too excited to stay down now. And Elise flipped. 'Right, that's it! You will have to get out! Marco, stop the car, please!'

I pulled myself up to sit on the seat itself, next to Lolita's coppery shins. 'Please,' I said. 'Let me stay. I want to come with you!'

Marco turned, which alarmed me, since he was doing the driving. 'Oh, ho!' he laughed. 'Boys, it seems we got ourselves a special offer! Three for the price of two!' They all burst out laughing.

Elise's face, however, showed that she didn't share their happiness. 'Gloria, you idiot!' she hissed at me. 'Get back down in that footwell. You shouldn't have come, you idiot! You stupid girl!'

I slunk back down to the footwell, though this time I stayed sitting rather than lying. Her tone had been harsh, and I huffed, feeling very told off, but I could see she was concerned as much for me as for having their fun spoiled. Was she thinking about how much Ana-Karmen would beat me? And what did they mean when they said three for the price of two?

We travelled on for some minutes, the atmosphere now subdued by my presence, though I felt not the slightest pang of regret that I might have spoilt Elise's day. I was just so thrilled to be out with them. It was such an adventure! I'd never done anything like this in my life before.

The landscape had changed. We were now travelling on a much wider mountain road. We were high up still, but the road followed the route of a plateau and after another few moments, the car came to a stop. But this was not a stop for a picnic or to pick mountain flowers. Straight away the car leapt back into tyre-skidding life as the men began to play with their very expensive toy, driving as fast as they could and then slamming the brakes on, and sometimes yanking up the handbrake so the car slewed round wildly. I had no idea why they'd want to do that, and I was petrified.

But it seemed I was the only one, because the girls seemed to love it, whooping and cheering and commanding that Marco drive faster, even as they had to shimmy down onto the back seat. If they didn't, it was clear that they'd both be thrown off. I shut my eyes and curled into a tight ball again in the footwell. The air was now full of dust and it caught in my throat. This was madness, and I wanted it to stop.

And stop it soon would. I began to hear a noise in the distance. A noise that grew and became identifiable as the wail of a police siren. I risked a look and saw flashing lights heading straight towards us. I felt relieved. The police obviously wanted Marco to stop his crazy games as well. But knowing this seemed to send his drunken mind into madness. Far from stopping, he actually stood up as he spun the car around again, waving his arm even, as if mocking a rival team.

But the car now had its own idea of where it wanted to go. Gouts of dry dust engulfed us, so it was difficult to see, but, craning upwards, I could just about make out where we were headed. I froze in fear. We were skidding straight to the edge of the plateau, which was now mere yards away and getting closer by the second.

Marco, at least, seemed to sober up slightly and jumped back down into his seat to try to control the spinning car. I heard the girls scream and felt the ground disappear from beneath us. Could this really have happened? Was the car really in space now? Were we really going to plummet to our deaths?

I heard the sound of the siren fading, heard the girls' screams snatched from their lips, heard the rush of air moving as the car knifed silently down through the air, to ground that was who knew how many miles beneath. I had no idea how far we would fall – from where I was I couldn't see well enough. But in that instant I remember my mind being quite calm. It was going to happen: my life was going to end. All our lives, probably. This was back at a time before seatbelts and safety – what were the chances of any of us surviving this?

But my half-second's worth of philosophising was brought

to an abrupt halt as we suddenly smashed into something unseen and I hit my head so hard I thought it would explode. And now I saw a sight that would stay with me for ever: four of the other passengers, two of the men and both the women, being launched from their seats as if flung from an unseen giant hand – flying as far and fast as the pods would from the towering Brazil trees and just as surely destined to crack when they hit the ground.

I clung desperately to the seat mechanism, wedged in my footwell, listening to the screams of Elise and Lolita, which travelled with them. And then, finally, finally, the screaming faded. Silence. I strained my ears, but I didn't hear them land.

All I could hear now was the creaking and squeaking of the car. I didn't know what had stopped us or whether the car would fall now, too, but I was also aware of rustling and could see a mesh of branches. I tried to move to see better but without moving too much. We were wedged in the boughs of a sturdy-looking tree that had grown huge despite its crazily steep and inhospitable home.

I didn't move far. Trapped in the car, the tree's swaying was a terrifying feeling, but to climb out and trust my body to lead me to safety was impossible. I was clearly hurt – the smallest movement caused excruciating pain in my neck. But I could see enough anyway. I could see Marco, the driver. He was smashed against the windscreen, the car's bonnet hanging vertically beneath him. I stared at him, appalled and yet fascinated by what had happened. He was completely broken and very obviously dead.

But I wasn't. I remember making a mental inventory before passing out. I was trapped. I was in agony. My body hurt all over. I was still alive, I remember marvelling. But for how long?

20

It might have been hours or it might have been days. All I knew was that at some point I must have lost and then recovered consciousness, because one minute I was trapped in the car, staring at the body of a dead man, trying to clear my clouding vision, and the next there was the sense of pain crackling and sparking through my body, and a voice in my ear saying, 'Hello?'

I tried to move, but the pain was like electricity inside me. Some deep instinctive sense told me to stop trying to do that. And where was I? In the car still? I tried to gather my thoughts and make sense of what had happened. Make sense of what was happening right now. But I couldn't. I opened my eyes, but the vista was white and blurry. I blinked away a bright light and it began to clear a little. But the light was still above me. Was that the sun? And who was that speaking to me? A ghost?

'Hello,' the voice said again. It sounded high-pitched. A female. 'Hello, young lady. Are you awake now? You know, you're very lucky. Very lucky to be alive.'

I tried to focus. It was a female. Dressed in white. Wearing something on her head. Was she an angel? I'd heard about angels. They lived in heaven and they were good. Was I in heaven now? I was confused. She was saying I was alive, wasn't she? Which meant I hadn't gone to heaven. So where was I?

She seemed to know the answer even though I hadn't yet asked the question. She moved closer. 'You're in hospital,' she told me. 'How are you feeling?'

'I hurt,' I said. 'Everything hurts. Where are the others? Did they die?'

Her expression changed. 'I'm afraid so,' she said. 'You're

159

the sole survivor. Like I said, you really are very lucky to be alive. Lucky to be awake, too. You hurt your head quite badly.'

I looked at her. Was I in hospital? If I was in a hospital then she must be a doctor. I had heard that doctors worked in hospitals and they made people better. I knew nothing of nurses. All I knew was that she had a kind voice. Perhaps she was an angel on the earth.

I tried to move again and found it hurt just as much as last time. 'Will I die as well?' I asked. Judging by the pain I felt, it definitely seemed as if I might.

She shook her head immediately. 'No,' she said. 'You're not going to die.' Her tone was clear. 'You are going to be OK. You have lots of cuts and bruises, but they have done something called an X-ray and nothing's broken. You just need time for your body to heal.'

She pulled a board from the end of my bed and then came around to the side of it. My face was close to a cabinet made of shiny metal. I could see my face in it. It didn't look like mine any more. It was too big. Like a balloon. And all red and blotchy, with bandages wrapped around it. There were also bandages, I realised, on my arms and bottom.

The lady smiled. 'You were lucky,' she said again, 'that there were police already there.'

I remembered the police suddenly, but I didn't answer. It hurt to talk.

'And when they saw the driver,' she continued, 'they called for help. And they got the car up from the ravine using a helicopter. And there you were!' She grinned again, and I immediately decided that I liked her. 'Tucked in the back, you were, wedged under the seat, which was what saved you. A complete surprise to everyone is what you were, young lady!' She looked pleased. 'And you've been sleeping since you got here, and no one knows where you came from. But now you're awake. So we can find out who you are. We need to contact your parents, of course. Where can we find them?'

It was then that I realised the lady wasn't alone. I turned my head and saw that there were two men in smart green uniforms standing at the end of my bed. They both had guns on their hips and one held a pen and a pad and was writing. I had no idea who they were or why they were there. The only thing that was clear was that, unlike the lady, they weren't smiling. In fact, they looked cross. I didn't like them.

'Young lady?' the woman said again. 'Who can we contact? Who should we get in touch with to let them know you're safe?'

My head filled with thoughts of the poor dead girls who'd been with me. I couldn't quite take it in. I was the only one left alive. I then thought of Ana-Karmen. Her girls. Her girls were dead. Did she know yet? Had anybody told her what had happened? I thought what she might do to me. I shouldn't have even been there. I would be in trouble. BIG trouble. I shook my head as much as I could bear to. Which wasn't much. 'No,' I mumbled through cracked lips. 'No. No one to contact.'

One of the men spoke then. The one holding the pad. He still looked angry. 'How did it happen?' he wanted to know. 'And who were the others?'

'Where do you live?' said the other. 'Are you local?'

They weren't even giving me time to think how to answer. 'Loma de Bolívar,' I managed to get out. Then immediately regretted it. Would they now take me back to Ana-Karmen?

The nice lady leaned over me. 'Don't be upset,' she said gently. 'These two men are here to help you. Once you're a bit better – in a couple of days or so – they're going to take you home, OK?'

'Loma de Bolívar,' one of the men said, scribbling on his pad.

*

Of those couple of days, I recall almost nothing, bar the white walls of the hospital. The nurse (for it was a nurse, I later realised) tended to me. Other nurses came and went as well. I think I ate a little, drank a little, and my aches and pains subsided. What I mostly recall is a feeling of dull acceptance. I didn't want to go back to Ana-Karmen's, but what else could I do? I had nowhere and no one else to go to.

And so one day, perhaps a week or two later, the men in uniforms came to get me and took me away again in a jeep. I'd obviously been in a hospital in the city, because I remember them announcing when we arrived back in the village. And then, by a process of many questions – plus my finally getting out the word 'Karmen' – the men delivered me back to the hellhole I'd come from.

Seeing the house again filled me with dread. I stared morosely out, seeing the tatty cane fence, the tumbledown house, the wealth of weeds that sprouted defiantly from every crack in the broken pathway. Reluctantly, I pointed.

'This is it?' asked one of the men, half turning around.

'Yes,' I whispered. 'This is it.'

I was escorted up the path, my arrival heralded by the bleating of the goats. The door had already opened before we reached it.

I watched Ana-Karmen's face as we approached. Her expression was one of first surprise and then anger.

'Hello, madam,' said the taller and more talkative of the two men. 'We believe this young lady belongs to you.'

Ana-Karmen seemed momentarily at a loss for words. All she could splutter was, 'I thought that dog was dead!'

The men looked shocked, which was understandable, because she lunged for me and grabbed me. 'Get inside!' she hissed, clapping me painfully around the back.

'Isn't she your daughter?' the other man said. 'We thought she was your daughter.'

'My daughter?' Ana-Karmen spat. 'How could this animal be my daughter? Not in a million years would I have a daughter like that thing!'

She yanked me inside even so, which must have confused them. But not so much that they seemed worried about leaving me with her, because such rough treatment was quite common in Colombia. They talked for a while, but most of it passed over my head. I remember, though, that Ana-Karmen seemed upset. She clearly already knew about Elise and Lolita, and the men told her they were sorry for her loss. I also recall them saying I'd not quite recovered from my injuries. But I'm quite sure she couldn't have cared less.

As the door shut behind the men and took the sunshine along with it, I cowered in the gloom, already anticipating the next storm. 'What have you said to those men?' Ana-Karmen railed at me. 'Have you told them my business?'

I shook my head and assured her I had not.

'Don't you dare open your mouth about what goes on here!'

she shouted anyway. 'You hear me? This business is a secret!'

I continued to reassure her that I had said nothing to anyone. How could I have done? I had no idea what Ana-Karmen's business even was. Looking back, it seems so obvious. They must have pieced things together, must have already worked out that the girls who had died were not Ana-Karmen's daughters. And neither, it was now clear, was I. I didn't understand why she was so anxious that I might have said anything to the men. It wasn't as if they had come to charge her with any crime, just to return me to my 'home'. That was the extent of it, and now they'd left. But it didn't make any difference. Ana-Karmen wanted to punish me in any case. She grabbed a frying pan and whacked me with it, hard, on my back, just, I think, for still being alive.

I remember that strike so well. It was the hardest I'd ever received from her. I remember my vision going cloudy and the feeling I might be sick. But most of all I recall feeling this great sense of despair. I had gone back to her. What had I been thinking?

*

Returning to the house after the crash seemed to awaken something in me. I don't know what, but I know that I began to see things with new eyes. Bit by bit, I began to build a clearer image of humans – how they did things, how they acted, how they liked to live their lives. It wasn't the prettiest of pictures.

I began to make sense of what I'd been warned about by the mother I'd met – the one who'd told me that I was going to be turned into 'the right meat'. I began to understand what that 'meat' was required to do, to understand that what Ana-Karmen was running was indeed a brothel. I didn't know the term, of course – it was not a word I'd encountered – but the meaning was becoming clearer by the day. I lived in a house of women whose job it was to 'entertain' visiting men. Old men and young men, anonymous men and well-known men. I found out that among the 'clients' were even a couple of famous footballers – or so the girls said – men who played for Colombia's finest teams.

I learned that the girls were only allowed to work at certain times of the month. At other times they needed to rub their stomachs a lot and drink herby water. I also realised that sometimes the girls would grow big and disappear. And I found out the reason, too – that they would go off to have babies. Like the woman in the jungle, they would have their babies in secret, but, unlike her, they would then give the babies away. There was a sign in the local shop that I saw more than once. 'We sell babies,' it said. I will never forget that. They would sell their own babies and people would buy them. It's no wonder, perhaps, that I was developing the idea that humans were an unusual species.

Ana-Karmen, for all that, was very simple to understand. After the car accident, she seemed to hate me even more than before, and I began to harbour a dread that her whole purpose in life was to think up a way to be rid of me. I had thought it wasn't possible for her to treat me more cruelly, but I was soon to be disabused of that notion. She mostly ignored me – a state of affairs that suited both of us fine – but if I did the slightest thing wrong, she would fly into a fury. Where she'd always been vicious and free with her punishments, now it seemed that when I angered her she lost all control, and I really began to fear for my life.

Yet on the day she nearly took my life, I had not seen it coming, which is perhaps why the incident is still etched so clearly in my mind.

It was a few weeks after I had been returned to the brothel, and the atmosphere following the loss of both the girls and a big client remained dismal, unsettled and very low. I remember I was scrubbing, removing some stain from the patio floor. Perhaps tree-sap, perhaps beer but definitely the remnants of something sticky, because, still weak from my bruising, I was struggling to get it off.

We were alone in the house for once, and I felt Ana-Karmen's eyes on me. This in itself was unusual because she barely acknowledged me, and when she spoke my name and I looked up at her, it was to see a rare smile on her face. She also had one hand behind her back – concealing what? I wondered. Used to her cruelty as I was, I still had a child's hopeful mind. Could it be that she had some treat to give me?

She beckoned me with a finger and motioned that I sit down

THE GIRL WITH NO NAME

on the floor. And then, before I could begin to comprehend what was happening, she produced a length of rope from behind her and swiftly tied my ankles together.

She was a big, strong woman and was now suddenly furious, and, despite my wriggling, it was impossible to escape her. By some clever manoeuvre she soon had my wrists tied as well and had dragged me a couple of feet to where a drainpipe climbed the house and managed to tether me to it. She then pulled a piece of old leather from her pocket and stuffed it firmly in my mouth, making my stomach heave. I wasn't getting a treat from Ana-Karmen; I was going to die. I felt as sure of that as anything I'd ever felt.

Ana-Karmen turned around then and opened one of the kitchen drawers, pulling out what looked like a long fabric pouch. It was tied with string and it was only when I watched her untie and unravel it that I could see what was in it. It was a collection of knives and what looked like other weapons. I felt myself choking. Suddenly I couldn't breathe. So I was going to die. And I was soon to know why.

Ana-Karmen chose a knife – not the biggest but not the smallest – and began to wave it in my face while she barked out my list of crimes. 'No one wants you!' she spat at me. 'None of my clients want you, and you're no use to me. Because of you, two of my best girls have DIED! All you do is cause trouble – trouble in the house, trouble in the village. And everyone wants rid of you – do you hear me? So now you GO!'

I watched horrified as the flailing knife reflected the sun at me. Ana-Karmen, always aggressive, seemed almost to have lost her mind.

'I'll go!' I tried to entreat. But the leather in my mouth wouldn't let me get the words out.

She looked at me with eyes that seemed unfocused and unseeing anyway, gabbling on as if deranged. 'Ayee!' she said, almost to herself rather than me. 'You've no parents. You have no one. No one will even know you've gone. No one will ask, either. You will be such an easy kill.'

My body, steeped in terror now, took matters into its own hands. As I sat and trembled beneath her, I felt a heat spread around me and realised I'd urinated on the floor. But Ana-Karmen didn't notice. Her eyes were still unfocused. They had an odd look about them, a greedy look almost. As if she was locked in the moment, losing all sanity and control. All her attention seemed to be on the knife in her hand and where best to place it so she could finish me.

I braced my body for the impending stab, swinging my head frantically from side to side, trying to plead with her not to kill me. But with the gag in my mouth, all that came out were strangled grunts. She was still shrieking at me, waving the knife around, but I had no idea what she was saying. What had I done? Why did I deserve this fate? I didn't know but I kept trying to say sorry for it anyway, sobbing the words out as best I could through the gag, while my heels scrabbled on the urine-soaked floor beneath me.

Ana-Karmen seemed oblivious. I could see she was preparing herself to stab me. She raised her arm, all her attention now focused on my face. But then there was a creak – the door opening – closely followed by a loud masculine roar. It was Rufino – her man. The same man I'd tortured with the ice cubes and who hated me almost as much as she did. Yet it seemed he was now my saviour. He roared again at Ana-Karmen, who, clearly incensed at his intrusion, flung the knife across the floor.

So it seemed it wasn't my day to die, after all. Soon the pair of them were locked in a furious screaming argument, while Rufino leaned down, roughly unbound me and ordered me to my feet. I needed little persuasion to do as he ordered. I scrambled up, slipping on the puddle of urine beneath me, and scuttled out to seek refuge in the garden with the goats.

But he wasn't done with me. 'Get back here right now!' he ordered. 'Get back here and clear up your filthy stinking mess!'

Quivering all over but terrified that he'd change his mind and let Ana-Karmen kill me after all, I ran back in to grab the mop and start doing as he said, but I was shaking so uncontrollably that it kept slipping from my hands.

'Can't you even do that?!' he roared, the vibrations from his shouting reverberating in my bones. 'You idiot! Pick it up and finish it! Do not even think of stopping till every trace is gone!'

And with that, he took a still gabbling Ana-Karmen by the arm and shoved her roughly through the door, while I continued to move the mop around, my throat burning and choking with sobs that wouldn't fall. It took hours for my shakes to subside.

I am still not quite sure what happened that day. I wonder now if Ana-Karmen might have had some sort of mental illness and on that day had a breakdown. That she meant to kill me – and cold-bloodedly, not in a moment of passion – I remain sure. But perhaps I am being kind. Perhaps she'd always intended to kill me, but as the house was never empty she had just never had a chance. And perhaps the man's wish wasn't to rescue me in order to spare me; rather it was to spare them both from committing a crime that could so easily be found out – at least till they'd worked out what to do with my body.

That was what I thought then, though it really never occurred to me to analyse. It's only now I question my own sanity that night. Why didn't I run? Whatever might be out there, why didn't I run? Yet I didn't. I was terrified but at the same time mentally paralysed. I was in danger, I knew. I was living on borrowed time. Yet I left things to fate. I don't know why.

Ana-Karmen, after that day, at least kept her distance. And I was aware of how the man had begun hanging around more, watching for that mad glint in her eyes. It was reassuring to have him there, but I still lived in terror. I kept out of her way as much as I could, and, once my panic subsided, I tried desperately to figure out what to do. I wanted so much to run away, but my fear was still too great. A greater fear, clearly, than I had of Ana-Karmen's murderous intentions, despite my years in the jungle. Fear of where to go and how to survive.

But it seemed events were about to outrun me anyway. It was nearing the end of a hot day. It was still sticky and humid but with the sun low in the sky when I heard a sharp knock from outside. The front door was often open in this sort of weather, but now the doorway was darkened by the bulk of a big man who had just rapped his knuckles on the wood.

I heard Ana-Karmen's voice. 'Come, Sergio,' she greeted him. 'Come in. Welcome.'

'Thank you, Ana-Karmen,' he said politely. 'How are you?'

I glanced up from where I was cleaning a door in the kitchen. I could see the man himself, who was wearing a suit and a tie, and beyond him, parked outside, was what looked like a taxi.

I kept quiet as I polished and listened in to their conversation. 'So who's your youngest?' I heard him asking her. 'Do you have any in today?'

I glanced across again and saw him pull out first a large pocketknife, which he transferred to his other hand, and, following that, a fat wad of notes. By now I knew exactly what he meant by her 'youngest'. Ana-Karmen's youngest girls were around fourteen years old. It was a fact that consoled me. I was only around eleven – surely too small and too young to be the right meat for her clients. And she'd already told me, hadn't she? None of them wanted me in any case.

There was a silence, and then Ana-Karmen mumbled something I didn't catch and raised an arm to point in my direction. Horrified, I saw the man then start to turn towards me. I bobbed back behind the door, mortified, but too late. He'd seen me, and his mouth had formed a smile.

I then heard Ana-Karmen's voice again. 'Don't worry,' she said to some query of his that I hadn't managed to hear. 'She'll follow you to the car if you give her a handful of *patatas fritas*.'

I froze, my hand gripping the doorknob I was supposed to be polishing. It was me. It was my turn. I had finally become the right meat. I had spent so long putting the whole terror of it out of my mind that I couldn't quite believe what I was hearing. But the man's smile had told me anyway. I was going to be his meat and he would turn me into sausages.

I pulled the door open, crossed the hallway and scampered into one of the other rooms – the one with three beds in a row. Here I scrambled, terrified, under the first and then the second one. Under the third – which would have been best – there were too many boxes. I could still hear Ana-Karmen muttering at him about how much I liked crisps – had she gone into the kitchen to fetch some? I presumed so. She'd give the man the crisps and the man would offer them to me. And then, in Ana-Karmen's mind, clearly, I would meekly follow him to his car.

I watched the two pairs of legs disappear into the kitchen and gave thanks for the encounter I'd had with the woman who had warned me that this dreadful day would come. 'Run, Gloria,' she had told me. 'Run as fast as you can.'

This, I now realised, might be my only chance to run. Where I'd run to, I had no idea, but that didn't seem to matter. Just 'away'. That was all I could think. Run away.

I wriggled my body from the cobwebby space beneath the bed. Then, barefoot, I bolted for the open doorway.

21

I ran as I had never run before, with fear snapping at my naked heels. Was I being followed? I had no idea, but I didn't dare turn to look. I was too frightened I'd stumble and be caught. So I pushed on with no thought but to keep my legs moving.

I ran for what seemed like hours. The sky grew dark and my legs began to quiver with tiredness. I had come such a long way and had no idea where I was going. I'd passed the silent houses of Loma de Bolívar, where the slumbering residents were indoors having their siestas, past rows of shops, playing children, animals. And as I'd run, the sound of the traffic had grown louder, the cars denser, the street corners more populated, and the lights of shops had grown correspondingly brighter, shining their synthetic glow up into the night sky. Though I had never been there, I realised I must be heading into the centre of Cúcuta.

Eventually, I slowed and risked a glance back. Had I seen a raging Ana-Karmen lumbering along in my wake, I would probably have been paralysed by shock. But there was no one there, and as I looked around my eyes latched onto a patch of trees and bushes. I would later learn that this was San Antonio Park, the violent heart of the city, but at this point, as far as I was concerned, it was just a big open space with a fountain that I ran to and drank from gratefully, splashing water over my head as well, to cool me down.

The sight of such a welcome patch of greenness sent a wave of relief flowing through me. I jogged across to the bushes that surrounded the park and, seeing there would be no place in the low canopy that I could sleep in and remain hidden, I curled up under an old mango tree.

For some minutes, I lay curled there, focused wholly inwards.

As well as my tired feet, my leg muscles were burning, and for a time I could concentrate on nothing else. But soon the noise of the city began to infiltrate my thinking, and then I noticed different, closer sounds. I looked up and around, my eyes now adjusted to the relative darkness, and what I saw made me catch my breath. I was not alone. Far from it. I was surrounded! Under almost every other tree and bush lay the curled-up, whispering forms of other children just like me.

My brain whirred with questions about who they were and how they had come to be here, seemingly homeless. I wondered if they had been through a similar experience to mine at Ana-Karmen's. I didn't know, but I had the immediate sense that we were all in the same boat. My eyes met other eyes – wide eyes that were full of sad stories. Nothing was said, but there seemed to be an immediate understanding, a sympathetic welcome to their world.

For all my terror of leaving and my fear of the future, seeing those children made me feel so much better. I had felt alone at Ana-Karmen's. I had felt alone running away from her. Now I wasn't so alone. This was the start of a new life for me. I didn't know it yet, but I was to become a street child of Colombia, just like the children all around me. I fell asleep in seconds, and I slept very well.

*

When the sun rose the next morning and I gazed on my new 'home', I realised I was back in the jungle, though it was a very different kind of jungle and perhaps even deadlier than the one I'd known before. I would soon learn that the streets of the city were riddled with violent criminal gangs, and where before I had learned to flee from predators, how to find food and how to prosper, I would now have to acquire a new set of skills to avoid being gang-raped or beaten, and to avoid being shot or getting caught by the police.

Cúcuta was a typical Colombian city. The houses had tiled roofs and were usually one-storey affairs – in a land of earthquakes, you don't build very high. The buses were yellow and old-looking, and most other types of transport also looked ancient and as if bought from a scrap yard. There were few visible signs of wealth in the city.

The markets sold all kinds of fruit, vegetables and meat. And much of the meat was still alive. I remember seeing rows of chickens hanging upside down with their legs tied, and goats, pigs and other animals tied to stakes in the ground. Customers would take them home and kill them to feed their families. There was food for free, too – mangoes grew on the trees in the parks – which was just as well, as many people lived in great poverty.

The very poorest didn't live in the city itself. Unable to pay rent or buy food, they lived high in the surrounding mountains where they could at least eke out some sort of existence growing vegetables, keeping animals and building their own shelters. One of my clearest memories was of these mountain people toiling up and down to Cúcuta, travelling many miles to collect water from the city's river. I found this odd – did they not have any water in the mountains? Clearly not, because they would also linger in the city river, washing both their bodies and their pitiful rags. I would then see them trudging back with huge metal water tins hanging from their shoulders, suspended from yokes by fat lengths of string.

The equatorial climate was unchanging. With no seasons, Colombia was always hot and stuffy, and in the warm, humid atmosphere, diseases spread easily. There was also little hygiene or clean water, and sickness was rampant. The infant mortality rate was very high.

For those who did survive, life was often very difficult. With work the overriding priority of every man and woman, there was little time to nurture infants. Mothers of the tiniest newborns had to get straight back to work and would either leave their babies at home alone – and the working day often began before dawn – or take them with them and work with them slung across their backs or placed in a cardboard box beside them. There was no child benefit or state-organised childcare. Only on the Sabbath – for Colombia was a devoutly Catholic country – would children get time with their parents during the day.

Older children went to school, but there was no real policing of attendance, so while parents toiled, their children would often play truant, learning street skills in place of letters and numbers. Their education – how to steal food, clothes and handbags – was very different from the one their parents probably wanted. As they stole, so their futures were being stolen too.

There were many homeless children. With no contraception in this devout Catholic country, families grew large and expensive, and with accommodation and food in short supply, older children were often kicked out of their homes. Girls, in particular, were very vulnerable. Many were raped or got into prostitution to earn money, and as a result the city was filled with babies born into unimaginable poverty, sometimes living on the streets from birth.

I felt such powerful anger for these children. I was so young, and I knew little of the circumstances of these mothers, but my rage for their infants was intense. I would rail at the broken world these feckless young mothers had brought their babies into and feel furious at their selfishness in doing so.

I might have been wrong, of course – and who was I to stand in judgement over these girls anyway? What did I know of the circumstances in which their children were conceived? But my adolescent mind, with its black and white view of the world, perhaps did me a very great favour in that respect. My experience at Ana-Karmen's had taught me a valuable lesson – that sex, for many men, at least, was a different thing from love. In the world of the brothel, the prostitute was seen as a commodity – something to be bought and sold for cash. And the consequences were there for all to see. The man promising everything, the girl believing all of it, and then, nine months later, another unwanted street baby being born with the father nowhere to be seen.

I didn't want that. I wanted a home, I wanted a husband and I wanted children. So, hard though it would be later, when a boy would try to woo me, or someone would try to entice me with a plan involving drugs, drink or crime, I would listen to the voice in my head that said, 'Hold on – one day you're going to be someone.'

I look back now in some awe at my young teenage self and how strong and self-possessed I seem to have been. And, if it's not too immodest a thing to reflect, how far-sighted. I have no idea where it came from, but it was definitely in me: this sense of the future, and any children and grandchildren I might have.

I wanted to 'be someone' as much as for their sakes as my own, because I didn't want them to have to suffer as I had. Mostly, though, I think I had learned to understand choices and how the making of them could so drastically alter your life.

My years in the jungle had taught me so many useful things. How to defend myself, how to feed myself, how to escape danger – how to survive all the things that should have killed me. And my time at Ana-Karmen's had taught me more. I now knew about sex, about how men could be – that women could even sell their own babies. I knew enough to know that sex could be the road to a girl's ruin.

*

But back on that first morning in the city, all I was thinking about was getting something to eat. I roused myself fully and began to take stock of my surroundings. As I had found a spot in a mango tree, this meant free food in abundance. The air was full of the scent of it, the ground littered with fallen fruits. That felt so good to me: the knowledge that I could simply help myself again. And I wasn't being shouted at. I was in control. That felt good as well.

As I ate, the city provided a feast for all my senses. The many smells – of car exhausts, food frying, hot tarmac – the noise of the other children all around me, with their sassy ways and their ragged clothes; the sounds of car horns and shouting, bottles breaking, music playing – the very abundance of things to see, smell and hear made it feel as if the world was once again in colour.

But I couldn't sit in a tree eating mangoes for ever. I needed to get out and about and explore my new environment. Everything happened fast in this new, high-octane life, it seemed. Though everyone was a stranger to me, I soon felt a sense of solidarity. Where the children I'd encountered in Loma de Bolívar seemed to want to avoid me, the children I saw now didn't seem repulsed by me or want to shun me. Though we were all wary of one another, I had this sense that we had a greater enemy – the adults, like Ana-Karmen, from whom I had only just escaped. And though the feeling was based on nothing more solid than instinct, it felt like I'd become part of a new troop, part of a team.

I made a name for myself very quickly. My time with the monkeys had taught me the art of blending into the background. I was tiny and skinny anyway, but I had an extra talent – stealth. So, although I spent as much time scavenging in bins for food as everyone else did, I also soon became skilled in the delicate art of theft. At first I would steal food in order to survive, but after a while the bug got to me and I would steal just for pleasure. I took some pride in it, and where some kids dined on leftovers out of bins, I would find ways to steal food from posh restaurants.

Again, my diminutive stature served me well. I could tuck myself behind some outside chairs and keep an eye on the chef. Then, as soon as he'd put a plate of food on the pass, I'd dash in and steal it. Sometimes they'd bother to chase me for a bit, sometimes they wouldn't. On a good day, they wouldn't even notice.

If I went into a shop, sometimes I would keep close to an adult customer so the shopkeeper couldn't see me, and this allowed me to grab sausages, buns and pieces of fruit. Not that I didn't get spotted sometimes – I did, often. But I could run fast, which was a big asset when being chased by angry shopkeepers, and was also nimble enough to shimmy up fences and trees.

I learned fast and thoroughly, with one of the most important lessons being that I was just as vulnerable as any other street child when I was asleep. Not long after I'd arrived in the city, I was awoken from an early evening doze. I was on a bench in the park, worn out after a busy day's scavenging, and was startled into wakefulness by a bright light and a firm hand on my shoulder. I opened my eyes to see two policemen staring down at me.

I immediately panicked, fearing the influence of Ana-Karmen. Had she sent them to find me? 'Let me go!' I cried. 'Get off me! Let me go!'

I wriggled and wrestled with them, my monkey aggression automatic. 'Keep still, *gamina*!' one barked at me. *Gamina* was slang for street kid. 'Stop struggling! You're not going anywhere!'

I was still sleepy and it felt like I was punching under water, but I kept at it anyway. I had too much to lose to stop. I knew the best defence was to attack your attacker's weak spot, so I tried to jab the closest policeman's eyes with my fingers.

He was too quick for me, however. 'Nice try, gamina,' he said sarcastically. 'Give it up, OK? You're coming with us.'

I was duly marched to a car that had lights flashing on its roof and bundled roughly into the back by one of the policemen. Then I was driven to what was obviously a police station. Men in uniform thronged inside, and there was a very high desk, behind which sat a well-fed and stern-looking man. He had a pen in his hand that he used to point at me. 'What's your name, kid?' he asked me. I didn't know how to answer. I didn't want to say Gloria, because it was the name Ana-Karmen had given me. I didn't want to be saddled with that connection, and I definitely didn't want her to find me.

'Erm . . .' I said, in my broken Spanish, 'I don't really have one.'

'Of course you do,' the man snapped. 'Everybody has one. Like Ricardo here, or Manuel. What do your little friends on the street call you?'

I paused again. The other kids did have a name for me by now. But I didn't want to tell the policemen that either.

'You understand what I'm saying to you?' he said. 'What do all the other gaminas shout at you when they want to get your attention?'

I considered. I would be safe. It would mean nothing to Ana-Karmen. 'Pony Malta,' I told him.

'What? You want a drink? Is that it?'

I shook my head. 'No. That's what they call me. Pony Malta. Really.'

'What? Like the drink?' The man rolled his eyes but wrote it down anyway. 'Well,' he grumbled. 'I have to put something down, I suppose.'

Pony Malta is a sweet malt drink that comes in a small, dark, thin bottle. A bottle that reminded some street kid of how I looked. Skinny, small and dark. Just like the Pony Malta bottle. It stuck right away. It was another name that I hadn't chosen, but it was something to tell the fat man behind the desk, at least.

My name taken, the two policemen then escorted me to a room. It was square, without windows and had a table in the middle. One of the officers sat down at the table and beckoned for me to take the seat at the other end. The other policeman sat down in the corner.

'Who are your parents?' the man opposite me wanted to know.

I wondered if they could tell that I had only just arrived there. And I feared, once again, for what Ana-Karmen might have done. I kept silent.

'Look, your surname, your family name,' he persisted. 'What is it?'

I remained silent. The man opposite glanced at the other one and rolled his eyes again. 'We've got a slow one here, Ricardo. OK,' he went on to me, 'so where are you from, anyway? Where were you born?'

Still I had no answer – I really didn't this time.

'Can't you speak, girl?' the officer snapped, now looking angry. 'What's your problem? Can't you answer a simple question? Are you hiding something we ought to know? You're making us very suspicious here, you know that? And if you don't cooperate, trust me, you're in big trouble!'

Where did I start? I still had only a patchy grasp of language. But I was frightened now. I had to tell them something.

'One last chance,' he said, his face red and beaded with sweat. It was hot in the room, and I was making them both cross now. I had seen the same thing at Ana-Karmen's, and I knew I had to say something. Still I faltered.

'Who are your parents?' he shouted, clearly fed up with waiting.

'M . . . m . . . monk . . .' I began. I had started to shake now. 'M . . . m . . . monkeys are my parents. I have no home here. Come from monkeys,' I tried to explain. 'Trees are my home . . .'

'What?' the man snapped. There was silence before he let out a sigh. And then, to my surprise, it turned into a laugh. The other policeman joined in. How could they suddenly find me funny? I no longer felt so scared now. Just ridiculed and humiliated. I had told no one about my family in the jungle before this, and now I finally had, I wished I hadn't.

The man opposite me finally stopped laughing. 'You stupid child,' he told me, his tone less aggressive now. 'You think you're from monkeys? You're just a little bit crazy, aren't you?' He glanced at the other man. 'Got ourselves a bit of a retard.'

It was then that I vowed I would never speak of the monkeys again. In fact, I said nothing, so some paper was produced. Their attitude different now, both officers tried to explain things to me differently, even drawing a picture of a house and some stick people. Another policeman also came in and tried to explain what they wanted to hear from me, but I kept silent. I had already told them the truth, hadn't I? So, for all their drawings, there was no house they could deliver me back to. In the end, they gave up. 'Lock her up,' the new policemen said. 'She's just a lunatic, filthy gamina, that's all. Lock her up for the night.'

So they did.

*

Even though I had been locked in a tiny room and felt so small and ridiculed, I actually slept well that night. I slept better, even, than I had the first night in the park. And as the sun came up and I waited to see what the new day would bring, it occurred to me that if they kept me here, it wouldn't be so bad. I had heard rumours of bad things happening to children in Colombia's prisons, but it didn't seem so bad here. I wouldn't go hungry, I'd be safe, and I'd have a roof over my head.

But they didn't seem to want to keep me, because a little while later two different policemen came and marched me out of the police station and round the corner. They didn't say a word to me while they did this, and I couldn't imagine what might happen next.

I was soon to find out, though. We arrived at the entrance to a small restaurant, where they ordered me a meal. Of course, I had no idea that I might have looked malnourished. I felt strong. But to the policemen I clearly didn't look well-fed, because the plate of food that the waitress brought for me looked fit for one of Ana-Karmen's wealthy clients. It was some kind of chowder, made with milk and spring onions, plus a poached egg and a pile of melba toast.

She smiled and told me to try it, and I didn't need telling twice. I shovelled it in, using my hands – I hadn't realised I was so hungry – which seemed to amuse the policemen greatly.

'Holy carajo!' one said to the other, laughing. 'She must be part animal!'

More food came out – fried eggs now and *arepas*. These were delicious fried corn patties: the bread of Colombia. It was a feast – a meal I knew I'd remember my whole life. And I ate till I could eat no more. I even finished the food they had ordered for themselves, and once I'd done so I looked quizzically at them, wondering what was to happen next. Were they going to take me back? Apparently not. They both smiled at me.

'Off you go, then, gamina,' one said to me kindly. 'Off you go, and keep out of trouble!'

I ran off, the food jiggling in my huge grateful belly, and after I'd travelled a while – the park wasn't too far from where I'd eaten – I saw them a bit behind me. I realised they'd followed me to see where I'd gone. Perhaps they'd hoped I might lead them to the home they were so sure I'd come from. Perhaps they were just curious. Perhaps just happy to see me safe.

I look back now and I still wonder. And I wish I could thank them. Street children are criminals and treated like vermin in Colombia. Most policemen, I would learn, did (and still do) treat them like dirt – arresting them and throwing them back to where they'd come from, unfed. I have no idea why these two acted as they did. No clue why they were so kind to me. But I'm glad they did, because they showed me that not all humans were cruel.

Even more than that. That maybe angels did exist.

22

Those policemen did me another important favour. They introduced me to the restaurant and the lovely smiling waitress. I went back there pretty much every day after that. I would go round the back and wait by the dustbins, hoping to see her because I liked her and wanted her to be my friend.

It was a posh restaurant. That I knew. It sold something called lobster, which was delicious. I'd never seen it before, never tasted anything like it. It was one of the boys who worked there who pointed it out to me and told me to try it. It was another moment in my life that has stayed with me always – the taste of the lobster, with its delectable pink sauce, and the boy's grinning face as he watched me.

I would wait very patiently when I visited the restaurant. I knew I could easily slip inside and steal something from the kitchen, but I wanted to be given food, just as I had the day the policemen took me there. And because I was small and would always ask nicely, they never minded giving me their leftovers. It was at this point I learned another lesson – food that is given to you tastes better than food you have to steal.

The first day I went back there, the waitress recognised me immediately. 'Hey,' she said. 'How are you today?', giving me a friendly smile. I don't know what she thought of me turning up barefoot, in my dirty brown rag of a dress, but she was kind and let me have some food she was going to throw away.

She also asked me what my name was, and I told her it was Pony Malta. She laughed, just like the policemen had, but not in a mean way. She said it suited me. And she told me that her name was Ria.

Now I had a source of food that I didn't have to steal, my

days got better. I would still steal, of course – I couldn't rely on Ria for everything – but having somewhere to go each day where I could be sure of a welcome was worth as much to me, almost, as having at least one guaranteed meal.

But it wasn't to last.

'Hey, Pony Malta,' she said to me one day. 'You know, I can't do this every day. I will get into trouble. You can't keep on coming here all the time. I'm sorry.'

It was a bitter blow, but I had an idea. 'Please,' I said, 'let me work for it. I clean for you, I wash up for leftovers. Anything.'

Ria shook her head. Then looked at me and back to the restaurant. 'How can I,' she wanted to know, 'when you're so dirty? You have no shoes, and you're not clean enough to be around a kitchen. It would be disgusting. You could end up making us have to close down.'

I took this in. I hadn't even thought of something like that. 'But, Ria, you help me. Please? You help me be clean. I don't know how to. There is nowhere for me to get clean on the streets.'

Ria looked doubtful, but at the same time I could see she was thinking about helping me. It felt good to have someone looking at me like that. It had been such a long time. Not since the jungle had I felt that.

'Well, we'll see,' she said. 'I will have to ask my manager. Go on, now. Go. And come back tomorrow.'

'Oh, thank you, thank you!' I said to her.

I went then, but just as I turned the corner she called to me.

'Hey, Pony Malta!' she called. 'Just don't get your hopes up, OK?'

I tried hard not to get my hopes up, because another lesson I'd learned during my time at Ana-Karmen's was that hope was a pointless emotion. But when I returned the next day, it seemed that maybe I should have got my hopes up, because Ria brought out a lady whom I recognised. She was the restaurant manager, and she, too, remembered me from that first visit.

'You were the little girl eating with those nice policemen, weren't you?'

'Yes, *señora*,' I said politely. 'And I could help you in your restaurant. I don't ask for any money. Only food.'

She looked at me carefully, the way Ria had, as if inspecting me very thoroughly. 'Well,' she said finally. 'I don't know what you did to get involved with the police, but they said you were a nice little girl, and by the looks of it you are . . .' She paused to think for a moment, rubbing her chin as she did so. 'Hmm,' she said finally. 'You look about the same size as my Belinda – very skinny, very short, doesn't get her looks from her mother, as you can see!'

Her laugh was good to hear. She laughed like she meant it. No one had laughed much at Ana-Karmen's. Only the drunken men. 'I have some old clothes you could borrow. Only for the restaurant, though – not to be worn on the streets, OK?'

I nodded vigorously. I couldn't believe it. She was actually going to hire me! Useless Gloria, who always did everything wrong. But I wasn't Gloria any more, I was Pony Malta, and I was clever. 'Thank you, señora,' I said. 'I will be a good, good worker.'

'So,' the jolly woman said. 'Ria, show her where the hose is and help her get cleaned up. And go and find Belinda and tell her to look out some old clothes.'

She waddled back into the restaurant and Ria winked at me. 'Hey, Pony,' she said, grinning. 'You got in!'

I have no idea how old I was. My hair was growing longer again, that I did know. And I liked it. But I never seemed to get any taller. I am still tiny today – no more than four foot nine – so I must have been a pretty tiny, skinny, puny twelve year old. But, for all that, I was still turning into a teenager.

I had had the best possible luck. Someone – several people – had taken a shine to me. They had treated me so well – the best since I'd left my precious monkey family. They had trusted me and been kind to me and given me an opportunity. I was a filthy street kid – one of thousands – yet Ria had been kind to me. It was a miracle. But I soon tired of this new, more honest lifestyle even so.

At first, I was so excited. I remember going with Ria to the shower and getting myself clean. I was still so scared of water, but I didn't let fear get the better of me. I stood under the shower and scrubbed myself till the water ran black down the drain. Then I donned Belinda's soft, clean clothes. They didn't quite fit; the knickers were much too big, so I pulled them together with the rubber band Ria gave me. But they were better than anything I had, and I was grateful.

Now respectable, I set to work as a washer-up in the restaurant kitchen. The rules were clear. I was not to be seen by the restaurant's owners or the wealthy customers. I was to do the washing up and clean the floor and whatever else they needed doing. In return, I would be fed daily and once a week I would be treated – I could have a dish of my choice from the restaurant menu.

Almost immediately, I began to fill out and feel better. I was full of energy and worked as hard as I could every day. I would work for six or seven hours straight and go back to San Antonio Park each afternoon with a full tummy. I also had a full feeling – a feeling of delicious tiredness, which meant I slept all the better and woke up raring to go.

But as the days passed, the novelty of my new job began to wear off. Though it was not like being at Ana-Karmen's – where I'd been a slave and a virtual prisoner – I began to wish I didn't have to trudge off to work every day. After all, some scheming part of my brain kept reminding me, I was good at stealing. I was an expert – I'd been taught by the monkeys. So why should I work all day – which did feel like being at Ana-Karmen's – when I could get what I needed for free?

And so my resentment about not being like the other street kids began building and was made all the stronger by the fact that by the time I returned from my shift, all the best sleeping spots in the park had usually gone. I also felt different from my compatriots – separate from them, isolated. I had been one of them but now I wasn't. Which felt all wrong.

And so, a mere few weeks after being given the chance to find a future, I turned my back on it. I finished my shift one day and quit. I felt grateful for the chance, grateful for the trust that had been placed in me, but I simply didn't want to work there any more. I left my little uniform and Belinda's shoes in a neat pile on the doorstep and walked away. I wanted to become a professional street kid again.

23

My day would start early. The smell of the local bakeries would wake every sleeping gamina, and the noise from mechanics and builders, which seemed constant in the city, would always keep us from falling back to sleep.

The first thing I did was carefully check my shoes. They were favoured by scorpions and snakes. And, being city-dwelling reptiles, if you disturbed them, they would retaliate. They were far less shy and timid than their jungle counterparts.

My shoes safe to slip my feet into, I would head off to find breakfast. Early mornings also saw the setting up of street stalls, which sold all sorts of things from toys and gadgets to household goods and hot and cold food. Breakfast would often be something stolen from a street stall: sometimes bread, sometimes a delicious string of barbecued sausages, though with the latter it was always a case of getting your fingers burned – I would have to bounce them in my hands to cool them while I ran away.

Being a street kid meant you were essentially running your own business. Exploiting ways to make money to survive. By far the most common way of doing that was to sell drugs, but for me that was never an option. It made no sense: the kids who sold drugs were all addicts. How stupid would it be to take something that made you worse off than you already were? It was hard enough to feed yourself and survive, without having to feed an addiction as well.

Everywhere I looked I saw the effects of drug-taking anyway: the orphans who'd deteriorate right before my eyes – from nice kids into ugly people, pathetic characters obsessed only with getting their next high.

With time on my hands now I had given up my job in the

restaurant, I would spend chunks of the day just watching the world go by. I loved sitting on the benches and kerbs just observing people going about their lives. I got to know some of them, too. There was Guillermo, who ran the bicycle shop opposite the park. He was in his forties and always smiling. He would wave to me. Consuela, who worked at the dressmakers close by, was apparently his much younger girlfriend. Consuela entranced me; she seemed to be so clever. She could take what looked like a rag and, sitting on a bench herself, she would stitch it into something useful, like a pretty blouse. I always felt like I was watching a magic show when she did this. I couldn't imagine ever being so dextrous.

Consuela was always friendly – one of the very few who were. And sometimes she'd pat the bench and tell me to come across and chat to her. I loved our chats. When I was with her I forgot I was a street kid.

But never for long. The park also held the promise of rich pickings. Businessmen, too, sat on the park benches at lunchtime with their jackets off, and I could always be tempted from my silent reverie or bouts of chatting by the irresistible lure of an unattended wallet.

I was unscrupulous. I loved sweet things, always had done, and so the food children ate particularly appealed to me. Snatching an ice cream from a child in the park was, literally, child's play. It was as easy as plucking fruit from a tree. I was breathtakingly confident – far more than my fellow street kids – because the monkeys had raised me to be so. Where other kids would mostly get by on begging and rummaging in dustbins, I never thought twice about breezing up to anyone dining at an outdoor table and stealing the food straight off their plates. No matter how violent the city and how numerous us street kids, they simply never expected it to happen. My unorthodox upbringing had trained my imagination and my wild ways gave me an edge.

I would range around the San Antonio Park area, getting rides on the backs of buses. On occasion I'd also cling on to the back of a truck. We gaminas often did this – it was the mark of being a street kid. But ranging far and wide was a sensible tactic, too. It lessened the risk of getting caught.

A busy shop was always a good source of income, and as I

grew more confident I began perfecting my art, following my own street-kid rules for success. You must not rush; you must on no account appear to panic, and you must first wash your face, comb your hair, clean your teeth and look smart. Also speak slowly and properly, and make sure you've already stolen some good clothes.

That done, the execution was easy. I would saunter into a shop and greet the owner politely. 'Some bread, a jar of jam and a brush, please.'

The shopkeeper would get the items and place them on the counter. It was at that point that I would send him to fetch something else. 'Oh,' I'd say, my eyes wide and innocent. 'And a can of cola.'

The minute he turned his back, I'd scoop up the other items and, before he could stop me, be out the door and have melted back into the crowd.

If I got a buzz from stealing, I got an even bigger one when I joined a street gang. Within a few months, I'd got to know lots of other street kids, and when I was asked to join their gang, it felt like I'd passed some sort of test. Me included, there were six of us – three boys and three girls – and we were quite a mix, not least in our odd assortment of names.

There was Sincabow, the black boy, then Daggo. Daggo was probably the oldest – he behaved that way anyway – and also the angriest. He'd run away from a vicious and violent father who would beat him and his siblings daily, while his mother just looked on and did nothing. Then there was Hugo – the one who wanted to be a bank robber. The girls were me – Pony Malta – then Mimi, probably the youngest (she was even tinier than I was), and finally Bayena, which means 'whale'. Poor Bayena. She got her name for pretty obvious reasons – she was the biggest-bellied girl on the streets.

Bayena was very weak, and she didn't like stealing. She was one of those new ones who'd not long been kicked out of home – too many mouths to feed – and knew nothing whatsoever about surviving. Hardened myself now, I sometimes got annoyed about how fussy and wimpy she was, but despite our differences we were a good team.

The clever thing about our gang was that we each had our strengths – our own trademark talents for stealing. But I could teach them all things, I realised, because I'd been learning my craft thoroughly. I had all the tricks of the trade up my sleeves. I knew, for instance, who the best targets were on the streets, and one of my favourites was to target women who wore skirts and carried brown paper bags.

A woman in a miniskirt was the best sight to see, ever. As long as they were also clutching a pair of brown paper bags, it meant the chance of some easy pickings. I'd stalk my target for a while, just to be sure of a decent exit, and then creep ever closer, till I was in range. I'd keep low, which wasn't difficult, and also silent, and then I'd pounce, yanking their pants down to expose their bare bottoms, enjoying the sound of their mortified shrieks as they dropped the bags and struggled to pull their knickers up again.

I was always amused to see how hard they seemed to find this simple task, which taught me another lesson: embarrassment makes you all fingers and thumbs! It worked every time. There'd be ample opportunity to gather up everything I could fit in two hands before I scooted off to enjoy my spoils. In fact, one of my best memories of being a street kid was my very first Christmas. Ladies in skirts, carrying paper bags containing their Christmas shopping, were, for me, almost like Father Christmas.

I was constantly adding to our repertoire of schemes. During the football season, I always did particularly well. I would steal people's tickets while they queued to get in and then sell them on for double the price at the gate. I would also steal road cones and make my own impromptu car park – always on someone else's land, obviously. Sometimes I'd even charge for a single free parking space, and people – particularly if they were late and just desperate to get a parking space before the game started – would cough up without even protesting. Over time I built up my own stash of cones that I hid away in a secret place so I could maximise my profits.

I also made money, for a time, as a shoe polisher. That didn't last long, however, as a couple of months after I'd stolen my shoe-polishing box, someone else stole it. How rude.

Despite the odd setback, I grew more and more successful, and I became one of the best burglars and money-makers on the streets of Cúcuta. Eventually, my success – and my bravery

– meant I was widely respected, and I was asked by the others to become leader of our gang. Even now, I remember how proud I felt to be admired by my peers.

And also how much fun we had. I remember that, too. We were still children, after all, and when we weren't busy scavenging or stealing we'd play hide-and-seek, chase, sometimes ball games (if we'd found one) and 'chicken', a game children from all parts of the world know. In our case, it involved running in front of cars on the teeming city streets. It's amazing I never saw anyone get hit.

*

I lived on the streets of Cúcuta for around two or three years. I struggle to remember the time in terms of years, first because I didn't really know my age to start with and second because when you lived in the way we did, the concept of time – work days and rest days, term times and holidays – had no meaning at all for me. It never had done, as there were no 'weeks' or 'months' in the jungle.

It's only now, having watched my own daughters growing up, that I can recognise, through noticing their stages of development, how old I might have been at each stage in my own life. I now believe I must have been around twelve or thirteen when something happened to me that would make me want to turn my back on the life I was living.

As lives went, looking back on it, it was really pretty bleak. Almost every night, our sleep would be interrupted. People would urinate on us, throw rocks at us and kick us for no reason. Drunken men would stroke the girls' legs, while laughing dirtily. The only safe places to sleep would naturally also be the filthiest places, where the air smelt of sewage. We couldn't ask for a glass of water if we were thirsty, because everyone despised us – and no wonder, for we stole from them daily, to survive. Passers-by would taunt us by holding out a hand to us, a hand that might hold a burger, and then, when we tentatively reached out to take it, they'd snatch it away again, laughing. People looked at us in disgust, because to them we were disgusting.

Although there were highlights to my day – like my meals from posh restaurants – life on the streets, despite the odd thrill and success, was difficult, scary and uncomfortable. We never really knew where our next meal was coming from, or if today would be the day when we would get caught by the law. Our gang grew, but it also, from time to time, shrank again, as children would get arrested, never to return to us. Daggo, in particular, I remember disappearing one day. He used to attack drunk men and steal their wallets – that was his speciality. He was my friend, but he had a dark, violent edge. I wonder where he is now. I wonder if he's still alive. I wonder where they all are, what became of them.

We were always on our toes, keeping alert at all times in case we fell victim to a mugging, a rape or an arrest. And although we were all in the same boat and had an intense, loyal friendship, none of us could care for one another in the way that a parent could. Inside I was still searching for a mother's love. It was what I thought about often as I tried to go to sleep.

At night, it was hard to find a safe and comfortable place to sleep. Older and wiser, I didn't risk the trees in the park any more. The best place I knew was the secret children's place. If you ever visit Cúcuta, or maybe other similar cities of the world, you will see secret places under bridges that kids can wriggle into. I don't know what they're called, but they hang beneath the main structure. Perhaps they are some integral part of the engineering, to support the metalwork and roadway above them. In any event, they felt hard to reach and so secure. So that's where the street kids like to sleep.

Back then they were the safest place, because the police didn't really know of them, and even if they did – and I'm sure this is true the world over – the gaps were child-sized, and no policeman could fit through. It was, however, horribly smelly. Inside would be a small contained area, with no through draught, and the kids would urinate, drink alcohol, eat and take drugs there. The odour of unwashed bodies – mine included – seemed to permeate everything. It was an acrid stench that seemed to singe your nostrils; it was a stench you could never get used to.

Yet you adapted to being filthy and living in gutters. On some nights when I was too tired to get to a bridge support, I'd simply curl up in whatever smelly drain I could find.

Unsanitary living was my norm. I would rummage around in dustbins, drink water from drain pipes, and washing myself didn't even cross my mind any more. I would only do the minimum required to carry out my little scams, and my minimum standards were dropping by the day.

And there was another dark side: what street life did to your psyche. There were so many damaged, abandoned children. So much pain and so much anger. When people don't respect you, it makes you want to lash out, and bit by bit you then lose all respect for yourself as well. Eventually, you start to wonder why you were ever born. Gradually, I was turning into a different sort of person, my mind focused more and more on my criminal plots and schemes, and the bad part of me, the part that exists in every human being, was taking over from the good.

The reason for this was probably anger. Of all the emotions I have described during my time on the streets, anger was by far the strongest one. And it wasn't just me – it was felt by every child in that situation. Of course it was – we had so much to be angry about. No child asks to be born to a life of such hardship. No child deserves to be treated as scum by complete strangers – strangers who probably had the luxury of being brought up by people who loved and cared for them. We could turn to no one. Of course we were angry.

But then one day I bumped into a street kid I knew. Except she wasn't a street kid any more. She wore nice clothes and looked clean, and she'd lost that hunted, tense look. So much so that it was she who recognised me. I wouldn't have even known it was the same girl.

'Pony Malta!' she called to me. It was towards the middle of the day. The sun was high and I was sweating and on my way to a restaurant, hoping to steal something filling for lunch. She was out on an errand, shopping. She carried a bag, though not a paper one. She must have been fourteen or so, not much older than I was. But in every other sense, light years away.

'Millie?' I said, shocked. 'Where have you been? Where have you gone?'

'I have a job,' she said, smiling. 'And a home. And I get fed.' She explained that, fed up, she had just gone knocking on doors one day, asking if she could work for food and shelter.

'And they let you?' I was shocked. People had actually accepted her? I was such a long way from those early days when I had been treated similarly by a lovely waitress that the idea now seemed unthinkable.

She nodded happily. 'Yes! Oh and, Pony Malta, you should see it. Their home is so lovely, and I have a lovely comfy bed. And it's not just me. Several kids like us have done it.'

This was news to me, but then perhaps I'd been so blinded I couldn't see it. I lived and breathed my gang to the exclusion of everything. There were people out there who would give work to hardened street kids?

'It's not permanent,' Millie said. 'They just use you and then you have to move on. Before this family I would work and get fed and maybe have one night or two. And you have to be prepared to do whatever they ask you. But it's so much better. You should try it.'

My mind was whirring now. Could I do as she had? And have a bed and be given food again? But I was a different person now. A criminal. Who would trust me? 'Wouldn't they just slam their doors in my face?' I asked her.

'Some will,' she said. 'But if you're lucky, some won't. But, Pony Malta, you have to go alone. No one will even speak to you if you knock on doors with your gang. It has to be just you, or they'll just be scared you'll rob them.'

I felt a wave of disloyalty as I pondered what she'd said to me, especially towards weak Bayena and little Mimi, who'd have to fend for themselves. But not so much that it stopped me from wanting to try it. I had nothing to lose, after all.

24

It took a while for what at first seemed like a workable idea to transform into an actual plan of action. For all my bravado on the streets and my courage as a burglar, I was actually nervous about knocking on doors to ask for work. And perhaps I was right to be. After all, stealing is a private act, really. You do it alone, you do it for you, you seek no one's approval. Speaking to strangers when you wanted something legitimate from them was asking them to judge you, and perhaps I wasn't ready to make myself vulnerable like that.

But eventually my desire to find a better life wrestled my fear into submission, and once I was as clean and presentable as I could make myself, I set out on my mission.

I chose the El Callejón district of the city, as, from what Millie had said, it seemed the most likely option. It was the place where the people with money lived. I suggested to my gang that they might want to come with me, and at first we went together and tried lots of likely-looking houses. But, as Millie had warned me, it soon became obvious that, as a gang, we looked intimidating. People naturally distrusted groups of scraggy street kids, and we decided we might do better knocking separately. So that's what we did – just saying a quick farewell in the street. No big deal. I didn't know I'd never see any of them again.

It was a soul-destroying, miserable, thankless, lonely mission. I walked up and down street after street, footsore and thirsty from trudging in the heat. And everyone, without exception, still told me to go away. Disheartened, I decided I would simply give up – it seemed so pointless – but then a memory surfaced that took me by surprise. I remembered the first time I'd watched a monkey get a nut from its casing – how long it had taken and how hard he had worked. How he'd searched for the right rock, with a hollow to place the nut in – a job that in itself took a long time – and how he'd then found another rock and toiled away for so long, repeatedly hitting it till he was rewarded with that first small encouraging crack. Even then it took a lot more effort to break it open. The tastiest nuts didn't give up their treasures lightly. You had to earn them. Just as I would have to earn this.

So I continued. I stuck at it day after day. There were many streets and many houses, and often no one was home anyway. It would be a good while before I exhausted the possibilities, and I vowed I wouldn't abandon my mission till then.

And just as the monkey who makes the effort is rewarded with a richer diet, so my persistence, it seemed, was about to reward me. I was at the end of a street I had tried several times now, knocking on a door I had tried at least once already. And this time, when it did open, it revealed a kindly face.

In front of me stood Consuela, the girl I used to see in San Antonio Park. One of the few ordinary people who ever smiled and said hello to me. She said hello now.

'Well, I never. Pony Malta!'

I said a prayer of thanks that I had never thought to steal from her as she sat on the park bench, sewing clothes.

I smiled my best smile, which wasn't difficult because I was so happy it was her. 'Consuela,' I said. 'Hi!'

'What are you doing round these parts?' Consuela wanted to know. 'What are you up to?'

'Well, I was hoping that maybe you could help me.'

She looked a little less pleased to see me than a second earlier. 'OK . . .' she said slowly. 'As long as you're not here to ask for money.'

'Oh, no, Consuela. I'm here because I want to help you. As a servant. As a housemaid. But for free.'

She looked surprised. 'Why would you want to do that? You must surely want something . . .'

'All I want,' I said, 'is not to be a street kid any more. Not to live on the streets any more. If you let me work for you and live in your house, that's all I want.'

I didn't know what else to say. But she could see I was

sincere. 'I promise I won't get in the way,' I added. 'And I am a very hard worker.'

Consuela smiled. 'I'm sure you are,' she said, 'but this is my parents' house, Pony. I would have to ask them . . .' She hovered for a moment, as if thinking about whether she ought to, and for a minute I thought she would send me away. Perhaps I would have to come back tomorrow. But then she seemed to decide. 'Wait there,' she said firmly, then shut the door.

I stood on the front step for a few minutes. It was a very grand house with a heavy, old-fashioned-looking door. It looked big, solid and substantial – not at all like Ana-Karmen's shabby brothel. These people were clearly very respectable.

The door opened again, and a middle-aged man and woman were standing in the entrance. The man looked very grand – tall and elegant, like his house. He was well-groomed, with neat black-grey hair and a moustache, and a face that would have once been very handsome. The woman was less daunting, being short and a little plump. She had a face that reminded me of a hamster more than anything, and a plum dress. She wore lots and lots of jewellery.

'These are my parents,' Consuela explained.

'Euwww, she looks dirty,' the older woman said. They both looked me over, inspecting me as if I were a piece of fruit or a new car.

'I could make her a dress,' Consuela suggested. 'And I have known her for a long time. She is called Pony Malta. She's very nimble, and I know she'd work hard. And she's not really that dirty. Not when you consider how she is forced to live.'

I could have hugged Consuela that day. She made such a strong case for me. She continued to have answers for all their objections, convincing them that I would be the perfect cleaner for their family and, best of all, they wouldn't even have to pay me.

'All right,' the man said, in the end. 'But only for a trial.' He fixed his dark eyes on me, and the eyebrows above them gathered themselves together. 'Just don't steal anything. Promise?'

'I promise,' I said happily. 'I promise not to steal. Oh, thank you, thank you.'

So, I thought, as Consuela led me inside, there are some

good people in this city after all. And now I had a job and a home. I couldn't have been happier.

'What's your name again?' said the woman.

'Pony Malta,' I answered.

'I told you,' said Consuela. 'Because she's so small!' She proudly placed her hand on my head, as if I were her new pet, to indicate just how small I was.

'That's not a name,' the man said. He looked me over once again. 'Hmm. I think we'll call you Rosalba. Consuela, take Rosalba to the bathroom to get washed.' His nose wrinkled. 'I could smell her from the other room!'

*

Another name, another life change. By the end of that day, I had a freshly cleaned body and had settled into what I thought of as a higher way of living. Which it was, for at last I had clean clothes and a bed, and no longer had to steal in order to eat. I was also the new cleaner for a family called Santos, who had done me a great service by allowing me a place in their grand home.

It was a big home, housing a big family. As well as Mr and Mrs Santos, there were their five children: Juan, the oldest, who was around forty-five and very frightening; Alfonso, who was in his thirties, and Pedro, a little younger than the two girls; Estella, just a little older than Pedro, and finally, my saviour, Consuela, who I think must have been around thirty to thirty-two.

I was set to work straight away, and my first job was dusting. I was told to brush the steps and dust the big square brick patio out the back. It was a pretty place, full of potted plants and home to a couple of tame birds, but, open to the elements, it got very dusty. Cúcuta is a very dusty city, so it was a constant problem for those who lived there, but Consuela gave me tips for how to deal with the surplus. Before sweeping the floor I had to splash it with a little water, to prevent the dust escaping up into the air. It was such a good idea that I adopted it from that day on and still do it now in my own home.

For a shovel, she showed me how to use a newspaper, again wetting the edge so that it stuck to the floor, making it easier to collect every single particle.

My other duties were exactly the ones you'd imagine. I

washed up, I cooked for them, and I cleaned and collected rubbish, just as had been agreed at the outset. In return, I had a bed – well, a mat under the porch table by the back entrance where the dogs slept. I had no pillow, bar the pile of newspapers I would collect, but I did have the company of the dogs, which was good, and I was fed as well as they were.

Yet, once again, within weeks, I was miserable. For all the advantages I had gained, I had lost something so important: the friendship and company of my street gang. I had become a ghost again – no one spoke to me, no one acknowledged me, no one seemed to want to have anything to do with me. They fed me and housed me, but I was every bit as invisible as I'd been when I was living at Ana-Karmen's.

I was also, once again, a virtual prisoner. The door to the street was always locked and also barred. There was a heavy pole, set on two hooks, that rested horizontally against it, which, small as I was, I couldn't have moved in a million years. So there was no way of getting out, except via one little glassless window up a short flight of stairs that led out, if you were small and sure-footed like I was, onto a branch of a large Mamoncillo tree.

The Mamoncillo tree produces fruit that look like limes on the outside and lychees on the inside, and has a sturdy spreading habit and glossy spear-shaped leaves. The one in the Santos garden was huge, and it soon became my favourite place of refuge. I would climb out there whenever I could and sit hidden in the boughs, enjoying the company of the many birds and insects. Being with nature was still the only place I felt I belonged and would always turn my thoughts back to my lovely monkey family: how they would sit and groom me and tease me – sometimes to distraction, so much so that I'd get cross with them and chase them away. How I longed for them now that my life was the very opposite and I lived among humans who didn't even want to know me.

But, for all that, my resolve was still strong. I was grateful to them for giving me a chance to start again, and perhaps when they saw my dedication to being a good servant, maybe, bit by bit, things would change. Maybe one day soon they would ask me to come and sit with them at mealtimes, or greet me in the mornings.

Or maybe not. Maybe I would regret the day I ever came knocking, much less moving in with the Santoses. There are plenty of good people living in Colombia, so it was unlucky that I knocked on the door that I did. For the Santoses were one of the most notorious criminal families in the city.

As such, they were understandably secretive. What I learned, I learned slowly, by observation and by chance. I regularly saw expensively dressed businessmen coming and going, though I had no idea what kind of business they were involved in. They would carry expensive-looking briefcases and smoke fat cigars as they trooped back and forth from the office, part of the house that was strictly out of bounds.

Whatever the Santoses did to earn money, it was obviously successful. Evidence of their wealth seemed to be everywhere – their home dripped with it – and sometimes, if I was quietly cleaning in the hallway, I could pick up snatches of their conversations. The family thought I had less understanding of language than I did, because I hardly ever spoke. And when I did, I still had something of an imperfect way of speaking, having picked up my human language so late. But they underestimated me. I could understand so much more than they realised, and what I picked up, when eavesdropping on the men's conversations, was often about money – great quantities of money – and what sounded like elaborate plots to get it from other people, including framing innocent bystanders. I even heard them mention the word 'kill'.

I was not shocked by any of this. I'd been a street kid for long enough to know that lots of businesses in Colombia did bad things to make money – this was normal for Colombia at that time. But I was scared of their oldest son Juan, as I learned that he was involved with a powerful Colombian 'mafia' group. He therefore seemed the most powerful member of the family, his mafia associates being so dangerous that his parents would assist him in his crimes – they had no choice.

The whole family, it seemed, made their living through crime. Alfonso was a professional burglar and Pedro always seemed to come home with lots of jewellery. Even the women were involved, helping in any way they could with the spoils of their criminal activities. The Santos men would often come home at three in the morning and unload things they'd stolen

– precious stones, long rifles, ammunition and watches. And one of my jobs, when they arrived, would be to quickly hide the guns, which would be stashed under the bins out on the patio.

Even compared to life as a street kid, this was frightening stuff. The more I learned about how they ran their business, the more scared I was for my own safety. They would burn down the homes of rivals and kill without a second thought, always planning everything carefully to ensure they'd get away with it – they were masters of making everything look like 'an accident'.

So it was probably naive of me not to consider the fact that bad men did bad things in lots of areas of their lives. And that, just as had been the case at Ana-Karmen's brothel, I was an adolescent girl with no home and no family, so when and if I was noticed by any of these men, it would be for entirely the wrong reasons.

25

It soon became obvious to me that life at the Santos house was no different from life at Ana-Karmen's. What had I been thinking? I was treated like one of the family's dogs, tied to a tree or to the washing pole on a regular basis, never really sure what I'd done. My meals consisted of the family's leftovers: chewed bones, scraps of bread and vegetable skins. I'd fight over these with the dogs, too, and they were stronger than I was.

But in one respect I was different from the family pets. Within a couple of weeks of my being there, I saw a look in Mr Santos' eye that chilled me to the bone. His gaze seemed to be on me all the time now, as if assessing me, which made me feel uncomfortable and defensive. It was a look I'd seen many times before.

Mr Santos mostly worked at night and slept during the day, so, as Mrs Santos and her children were usually out working – or doing whatever it was they did – the house was empty, bar the two of us, most days. On this day, it was late in the afternoon and I was in the kitchen preparing dinner when I became aware that he had come in and joined me.

I was by the stove, making arepas, and I could see his reflection in the shiny black tiles behind the hob. He was standing in the doorway, and I noticed he was wearing only underwear. I felt a shiver run up my spine, but I pretended I hadn't seen him, only stiffening as he approached and crouched down slightly behind me. The next thing I felt was the rough and clammy touch of his hands sliding up and down my bare legs.

All too soon, the movement changed and I could hear his breathing quicken. His hands had started sliding even further up my thighs. Was this what was required of me now? That I must do every single thing the family wanted, including allowing Mr Santos to grope me – or worse? My street-kid anger was never buried deep and now it surfaced, my mind racing to consider if and where there might be an escape route. He was a big man, and strong, but I had the advantage of surprise. He didn't know me, and of course he would expect me to acquiesce. But no one – not even powerful Mr Santos – was going to rape me. Not when I still had air in my lungs.

I looked down at the metal rack of cooling arepas, forcing myself not to flinch under his touch. As soon as I did, he might realise I planned to escape. I needed him to think I would let him have his way.

I slowly curled my fingers round the blackened metal cooling grid. It wasn't the best weapon, but it was heavy, and if I hit him with sufficient force . . .

I whirled around and slammed it down on him. He was kneeling behind me, so it hit him square across the head and shoulders, while the warm arepas flew everywhere, rolling across the stone floor. He let out a roar of shock and, unbalanced on his knees, toppled over sideways to the floor. I hit him again, then, and a third time, just for good measure. It wasn't the heaviest of weapons but I made up for it in fury. Then I ran.

There was no real escape for me, of course. The doors were locked, the windows barred, the high wall topped with barbed wire and shards of glass. I could only run up the steps to the little glassless window and then climb out to bury myself in the boughs of the Mamoncillo. I wriggled out and launched myself into the tree boughs, hearing his voice bellowing behind me, 'I'll kill you, you bastard!'

I knew he'd come after me now, wielding his fat leather belt. So what to do next? I sat, panting heavily, in the fragrant green shade, nausea rippling through me as my pulse started to slow. What should I do? How could I deal with this situation? Should I try to escape? Try to lift the huge pole behind the door? But I knew I couldn't. I could barely reach it, not without climbing on something. By which time Mr Santos would be there to stop me anyway.

The thought made me want to weep with frustration. But

then I thought some more. What would be out there for me anyway? I'd just be a street kid again. And was that going to be a better life than this? I had so little now, but at least more than I'd had as a street kid. How could I go back to that? That dead end of a future. At least I had hope now. If I could work, I had a chance of a future. And the thought of losing that made me even angrier. How dare he, with his filthy lust, try to take that away! If I tried to escape, what would happen to me? Would the Santoses come after me? Would they worry that I knew too much about their business to let me live? It seemed terrifyingly simple to answer that – of course they would.

And then I hit upon an answer: Mrs Santos. I would simply stay in my tree till I saw her come home. Only then would I show myself, and I would tell her the truth about what had happened. Mr Santos would lie to her – I knew that for certain. But something told me she would believe me when I told her the truth. My hunch was that she knew her husband and the sort of thing he got up to. And perhaps she would put a stop to it and I'd have my chance back.

When she arrived home, Mr Santos got to speak to her before me, and I could tell by her expression that he had already told her tales. I hadn't heard what they said, but I didn't need to. I could tell by the sour expression on her face, and my hopes that she'd back me were immediately dashed. 'Where have you been?' she snapped as she entered the kitchen. 'Mr Santos tells me you've been hiding and that you've not done your work!'

She threw a slipper at me then, which I didn't try to dodge. 'Mrs Santos,' I said. 'Please . . . I need to speak to you.'

'Then speak, Rosalba! Speak!' She stood and glared at me, hands on hips.

'Mr Santos,' I whispered, flinching as the words left my mouth. 'He tried to have sex with me. He had his hands up my legs –' I stopped and mimed it. 'Like this. But I hit him with the grid and I ran away.'

Mrs Santos fixed a look of dismissal on her face. 'What?' she said. 'You think he would want to have sex with a little rat like you? I don't think so! Stop trying to get attention and just do your job!' She stabbed a finger in my direction. 'You'd better be careful, Rosalba. Do not get in our way. Do not make him angry, or you will pay for it, you hear me?'

She turned her back on me then, but before she stomped off she turned again. 'And do not tell a soul about any of this, you hear me? Or I shall drown you.'

I stood for several seconds, trying to take her words in. I had misjudged her. She knew. I was so sure she knew. But she obviously didn't want to know. Not about her husband. I thought back to what I'd been told and why I'd left Ana-Karmen's. Now I was going to be meat after all.

*

The cruelty from Mrs Santos now escalated. And with no fear of his wife's wrath, Mr Santos held the power. He never raped me, but I knew his intentions were sexual. Every time Mrs Santos went to work or even just nipped out to the shops, I would feel traumatised knowing we were alone in the house together. He even offered me money, which I refused, but he only tried to force himself on me once more. That time I went for his eyes with such ferocity that he never tried to put his hands on me again. Sometimes I think it was to my advantage that people still thought I was a wild animal.

Both husband and wife, however, had no compunction about regularly beating me. Mr Santos, I think, because he was a sadist, a monster, and Mrs Santos perhaps because she knew he had his eye on me and hated me for that, on top of despising me in general. Whatever the reason, I was beaten all the time.

Looking back, I wonder if I was in the middle of a big marital breakdown. Or perhaps it was just because I was such a poor, inefficient slave. I still did most things wrong, was clumsy and cack-handed. I did the washing wrong – forever leaving soap on the clothing – and my washing-up was hopeless: nothing was ever properly clean. When I ironed shirts, I was always putting the lines in the wrong places. I'd sweep rubbish under cupboards instead of picking it up. Oh, I was a pretty poor slave. I know I was.

Compared to Ana-Karmen, the Santoses were more sophisticated. Being part of a criminal fraternity, they were experienced in violence. They understood how much electrical cable hurt. They also knew that with a plug attached, it could unleash even more pain, so that was their preferred tool to use on me. Sometimes the pain would make me pass out completely, and I would wake to find myself in a puddle of blood and urine. And, like Ana-Karmen, they would beat me for creating that, too. My only place of safety was my branch in the Mamoncillo tree, where I would crawl once my body had been discarded for the day, and I would be forgotten till the next day's chores began.

I would sit out there and often wonder about Consuela. She had been so kind to me, befriended me, and where was she now? I hardly saw her, and when I did, it seemed as though she could hardly meet my eye. If she had, then perhaps she'd take more notice of all my bruises, but it was as if she no longer wanted to know me. Did she even really know what they did to me? Perhaps not. I also felt sure Mrs Santos had poisoned her against me with tales of goodness knows what transgressions just when I so badly needed a friend.

I would think of the monkeys – of Grandpa, bold Rudy, little Mia – and of my street gang. How was Bayena doing now? Was she safe? I missed them all. I missed them so much that it was like a physical ache in me. Right then, I felt as alone as it was possible to feel.

But the Mamoncillo tree didn't just bear clusters of glossy green fruit. It brought me a friend.

*

The Santos house was situated on a fairly wide street. The fences were high, but from my branch in the Mamoncillo I could easily see into the next garden. The neighbour from that house was middle-aged, a little younger than Mrs Santos, and there was something about her face and manner that made me like her. It was like the day when I'd watched the Indian lady looking for a place to have her baby. There was just something that drew me to her – a gut instinct that I'd learned to trust. I didn't show myself, however; life in Cúcuta had beaten that out of me. But I would watch her often from my eyrie in the tree.

She had several children: older ones, who helped with washing dishes, and younger ones – a little younger, I judged, than I was – who would play and laugh together in a way that reminded me of my monkey family. This was a family, too. This was where I wanted to be. I would watch her endlessly, noting all the time how loving she was towards her children. How she'd smile at them, even when they weren't looking in her direction, and how she'd instinctively stroke their hair whenever they streaked past her in play. The children looked so happy, so content, that I couldn't help but wonder. Did children in the city often live like this? Happily, free of fear? Was I the one who was odd?

Eventually, my need for her acknowledgement grew too strong to resist, and one day I changed position. I moved slightly lower in the tree and slightly closer to her garden, and the rustling this created made her look up. Our eyes met, and once again I could see compassion and sympathy. I felt safe, so I risked showing myself a little more.

She smiled at me then, and it was a smile of warmth and understanding. But she must have known the Santoses, I imagine, and known the kind of people they were, because her silence, together with the way she glanced around nervously, made it clear that she knew I might be in danger. She then lifted a finger and pointed towards their house, shaking her head to indicate that she was aware of my situation.

Then she pointed to me and put her other hand over her ear. I mustn't speak. I mustn't be heard, or we could both get into trouble. Which made me sure that she had heard – heard my cries, heard the beatings, heard my sadness.

She put her hand on her chest next and whispered her name: 'Maruja'. I did the same, for at last I knew I might have found a friend.

'Rosalba,' I excitedly whispered back to her.

Knowing Maruja was there gave me hope and courage. I had become truly isolated, no longer allowed out of the house in case I talked about the family's business. So the only company I had was of the animal kind. And why wouldn't it be? To them I was an animal. And a badly bruised one, which might make people talk.

But every day now I had the solace of my lair up in the tree and my new friend Maruja to soothe my hurt away. We would meet regularly, and if I couldn't see her once I'd climbed the Mamoncillo tree, I would shake the branches a little to attract her attention. She would always come, and then we'd chat – her down on the ground, me up in my branches, developing a way of communicating that didn't require either of us to speak.

It was a whole new language, in fact – a mix of sign language and miming – a language all of our own that would one day be my saviour. I loved Maruja from the day I met her. I still love her today. Finding Maruja was like stumbling upon precious treasure. It was almost as if there were another angel walking the earth now and I'd been the one lucky enough to find her. I wanted to shout it from the rooftops, but, of course, I could not. I knew if the Santos family found out that Maruja had befriended me, her whole family could be in danger.

*

I was very soon to be in danger myself. I had been with the Santoses for around a year or so when one day two men visited the house to have a meeting with Juan. I no longer had any desire to listen in to the family's business affairs, but on that afternoon I was working in the downstairs rooms, cleaning, when I couldn't help but overhear what sounded like a row.

The men were in the living room – not the office, for whatever reason – and they were all shouting loudly. And, despite not wanting to know – what I didn't know couldn't hurt me – it was impossible not to catch words that made me go cold. Unable to resist, I stopped my polishing and approached the living room, which had double doors. There was a sliver of a crack down the middle, through which I could see a chink of light and movement.

Juan's voice was the loudest, and they were talking about some plan. A plan, it seemed, to kill a wealthy couple. I knew they must be wealthy because of the words they were using – stealing their possessions was apparently going to make the firm rich.

'It's too dangerous, Rico,' I heard Juan say. 'I don't want to get involved with this. We just don't know. It might be them trying to frame us for murdering those people. They might be the police, and then we'll never see the money.'

I tried to make sense of this – so other people were going to pay them for committing murder? I listened on, clutching my rag and bottle of cleaning fluid to my chest.

'Maybe you're right, Juan,' another man said, presumably the one called Rico. 'But just think about it – it's such a lot of money!'

'I know,' said Juan. 'And I'm very, very tempted. But something just doesn't feel right. And I always trust my instincts. Besides, there's something else we should be concentrating on right now, don't you think?'

There was a short silence and then a sigh. 'Fabio? Yes, you're right. He is a problem.'

The third man spoke. 'He's getting to be big trouble. He's just not moving with the group's rules any more. Betraying his family.' Someone let out a sound of great disgust at this idea. 'He could be a danger, too.' Another silence. 'We can't let this get any worse.'

'And he refused to do his last job.' Juan sighed again. 'Yes, I think it's time now.'

I held my breath. Time for what? Were they going to kill him as well?

'So,' I heard the first man say. 'How best to eliminate him?'

'My mother Maria,' I heard Juan tell the others. 'She's our best bet.'

Mrs Santos? She was a murderer as well? This really shocked me, and in my surprise I dropped the bottle of cleaning fluid from my sweaty hand. Crash! It went clattering to the floor, though thankfully it didn't break. I snatched it up with shaking fingers and fled to the kitchen.

Juan, who must have heard it, followed me in there moments later. And when he saw it was me, I saw something like relief flood his face. 'Was that you?' he said. 'Making that noise out there?'

I nodded hurriedly.

'Stupid animal,' he barked. 'Just be more careful!' He then turned to go back to his friends, but before he did, he had one more comment to make. 'You,' he said, not even bothering to turn around, 'you, little orphan, will be dealt with.'

26

It was the summer and perhaps a public holiday in Cúcuta. I'm still not sure which, but perhaps it was a saint's day of some sort. All I know is that it was definitely a time for family. There seemed more people on the streets than usual, and no one appeared to be working. There were children about, I remember, and family members visiting. I recall it being lunchtime, and because of the heat – given that there was a houseful of people – someone had left the front door open. For them it was a chance to allow a welcome breeze in. But for me it represented a very different opportunity.

It was a chance to get out.

The Santoses were very careful about keeping me a virtual prisoner. Which was hardly necessary, because by now it was clearer to me than it had ever been that to try to run away would not be the answer to my misery. I think I had become so used to being beaten, to being thought worthless and useless, to being ignored, that a part of me believed I must deserve it. I had been treated so badly and for so long by so many people that why wouldn't I believe I deserved it? If I did choose to run, I was sure they would track me down. And even if they failed to, running away would just return me to the equal or worse misery of living life again on the city's streets.

And by now there was another reason to stay put: Maruja. For the first time in my life that I could remember I had been shown love and care, and our fledgling relationship was very precious to me. Maruja was like a diamond – the only shining light in a world of darkness – and there was no way I was going to give her up.

And it wasn't just that I didn't want to lose her companionship; I genuinely hoped that at some point she might take me in. I had no idea when this might happen, but I believed that it was possible, so I was prepared to wait for as long as that took.

But to get out for just a little while was a beguiling idea. I was a caged bird and I wanted to fly just a little. Not far or for too long – just for a little while. I wanted to see other children, perhaps play. I had no fixed intentions. Though if I got the chance to scavenge while I was out, then I would. I had so little of my own, and there were things out there somewhere that I wanted and that I knew I could get for myself. A comb and a toothbrush. Perhaps some soap, even. So, with the family all so preoccupied by lunch and conversation and siestas, I sneaked out of the front door and melted away into the heat.

The road the Santoses lived on ran down to the river, and there was a bridge about twenty-five feet from the house. I was soon there, my direction governed by the sound of nearby children who were buzzing around the large bins nearby. I liked bins – I well remembered the sorts of treasures you could find in them. So, seeing the children pulling various items out, I decided I would go down and join them.

The bins in Cúcuta, which were like small rusted skips, had always been a draw for me. You could find every kind of thing inside them. As well as food, you could get your hands on parts from rifles, old tools and all types of clothing, as well as broken toys, pots and pans, and thrown-away gifts. Today, though, I was to find something the like of which I had never seen before or would wish to again.

Once at the bin area, and being too small just to reach in, I quickly clambered up into one and began my inspection. I knew I shouldn't be out too long or someone would notice my absence, so I rifled through the contents of the first bin at speed. Finding it lacking in anything that was of immediate use to me, I climbed nimbly down and moved on to the next.

It was here that I found something more intriguing. It was a rectangular metal box that looked a little like a moneybox. It put me in mind of the cashbox I'd seen in the Santoses' office, though a little longer and deeper. It had the same slot in the lid for coins. Excited now, I held it up to my ear and shook it, imagining the great wealth that might be stashed within. To have money could change everything. It might even bring me freedom. Money could buy things that I could only dream of having, but, more importantly, it could buy me a way out of my miserable existence. I had no idea quite how, I just instinctively knew it could.

Whatever was in the box made a sharp metallic sound. Coins, at the very least, I thought excitedly, inspecting it more carefully. All I had to do now was find a way to get into it. I scrabbled further in the rubbish, looking for something that might help me. The box was heavy in my hands, clearly made of thick metal, and looked very secure, just as I'd have expected it to be. There was no way I would get inside it using my fingers.

Clutching the box under my arm, I scrabbled down from the bin, with the intention of finding a rock, or perhaps even a discarded hammer, with which I could force the lid open. Once out, I became aware of two boys, both around my age, who had the unmistakeable look of young drug dealers. I knew they were focusing on me and my new treasure.

I had good reason to be nervous of their attention. There was no honour among street children beyond their individual gangs, and stealing from other kids who'd found useful stuff in rubbish was obviously less effort than having to find it yourself. I knew this because on lazy days I'd done it myself.

By now I'd left the bin area and was up on the bridge itself. Across the river and across the city, the air was full of the sights and smells of a lazy summer afternoon. The scent coming from the barrows that sold lemonade and *empanadas* would normally have made my stomach rumble and commanded my attention, but I was too preoccupied. I had only one thing on my mind now: how to get inside my box. And, as yet, I had found nothing I could use.

'Hey, gamina!' I heard a voice and turned around to see the two scruffy street kids. They'd followed me up onto the bridge and now stood before me. Close up, I could see that they were a little younger than I was. One pushed me. 'Hey, gamina!' he said again.

'What?' I answered, pulling myself up to my full height and scowling. I wasn't big, but I could still carry myself like the leader of a street gang, even if by now I wore a maid's simple dress. I was just thinking things through – should I just save myself the trouble, let them steal the box, open it and then steal back the contents? – when the decision was taken away from me. The bigger of the two boys just yanked the thing from me, and the two of them sped away, laughing.

'Say goodbye to it, gamina!' they hooted.

Naturally, I followed. Cross at being so easily stripped of my treasure, I forgot about the fact that I needed to return to the house. All that concerned me was keeping up with them and finding out what was in the box. If it turned out to be worthless, then I could leave them to it, obviously, but if it did contain something of value, then I wanted it. There was no way I was going to give it up – no way. I was the expert and somehow I would take back what was mine – probably by scurrying down and taking it back while they were rejoicing.

I followed them downriver, intending to stay close till they stopped and opened it, but was dismayed to watch them scale the high fence on the bank and disappear far below me to the dry riverbed. They were taller than me, plus one had been able to give the other a leg up, and alone I had no chance of following. I knew where they were headed: to the underside of the bridge's arches. It would be a good place to get the box open out of sight of prying eyes. One of them had something to use to do it, too. They were too far away to see exactly, but it looked like a large nail, and from my vantage point it looked like they were having some success. And that was the moment when the world exploded.

Inside the box had been a bomb. The whole bridge went up, right before my eyes. And in the middle of it all I could see both their bodies. They were lifted high into the sky and returned to the ground in separate parts. I watched their limbs fly through the air and their stomachs being torn open, the insides spilling out as they landed. I couldn't believe what I was witnessing, couldn't speak, couldn't hear. I was trapped inside my head, silently screaming. They shouldn't have died, my mind kept telling me, they shouldn't have died. It could have been me lying dead now. It should have been.

Sound returned slowly, then it gathered pace and clarity. 'Are you all right?' someone was asking me. 'Are you hurt? Are you OK?'

'What happened?' someone else was saying. 'Did you see what happened?'

I couldn't answer them. I was numb with shock. All I could do was cry.

It seemed the whole street, the whole area, the whole city was on the scene now, and in the middle of the smoke and the clamour and the screams of frightened children, I picked out Estella, who was gesticulating. 'Get back in the house!' she snapped. 'Quickly! You shouldn't be out here!' She obviously assumed I'd just arrived at the bridge, as she had, having heard the explosion.

Then, presumably seeing my lack of reaction, she beckoned Consuela over and inspected me more closely. 'Consuela,' she wanted to know, 'what's up with Rosalba?'

'She seems sleepy,' Consuela suggested. 'Maybe she only just woke up.'

Estelle slapped my face to try to get me to focus. 'Ayee!' she shrieked. 'Look – she's wet herself!'

I then felt myself being half-lifted, half-dragged, as they both manhandled me back to the house.

Inside, they made me soup to try to revive me, but I couldn't eat it. There was meat floating in it, and it was meat on the bone, which filled my head with the horrible images I'd just witnessed. My stomach heaved violently just seeing it. But if I expected sympathy, very little was forthcoming. Instead, the Santos men, who seemed increasingly sure I must know something about what had happened, spent the rest of the day interrogating me.

'Stop it!' Consuela kept crying, as Juan repeatedly shook me to try to get some sense out of me. 'Can't you see she's traumatised by something?'

He ignored her. 'What d'you know?' he kept shouting at me. 'What happened? Was it a bomb? Did you see anyone?' On and on and on it went, well into the evening, and I realised that with the bomb being so close to where we lived, the Santoses had decided it must have been intended for them.

*

I was in a haze for days and have only the vaguest memories of what happened in the immediate aftermath. I'm sure the police must have been involved and there would have been some kind of investigation. It would also have been reported in the local newspaper, *El Diario*. But as the boys appeared to have been street kids, with no family to mourn them, interest would probably have soon died down.

Their deaths haunted me, however, day and night. I couldn't get the image of them out of my mind and was plagued by the thought that it should have been me who died instead of them. Why had fate arranged it for those boys to snatch the box from me? Why had I been unable to scale that high fence? Why had I been spared and their lives taken so violently? I had no idea, but I was alive. It appeared that I had cheated what fate had planned for me and I figured that there must be a reason. That thought made me determined to find myself a better life.

And my dear and only friend Maruja seemed to feel the same way. Living so close by, she would hear me crying, hear my screams as I was beaten with the electrical flex, and hear my whimpers as I tried and failed to sleep. Some mornings, anxious to see her, I would climb the boughs of my special tree, and it would hurt so much to do so that she'd hear those cries too. But, strange though it might seem, the anger and upset in her eyes would immediately make me feel a little better, for it meant she cared about me. I'd never felt sympathy from someone before, and it was a wonderful thing to feel. It meant everything.

But there was another emotion growing in Maruja: fear. By now our private language had become more sophisticated, and we could communicate easily, albeit silently, when we met. And increasingly Maruja spoke about the danger I was in. Since the explosion at the bridge, there seemed to be a new tension in the area, and one day, a few weeks later, Maruja told me she felt certain the Santoses had become paranoid about me, fearing I knew things about their business that could harm them badly. And so they wished to get rid of me as a matter of urgency.

I was already aware of this feeling myself, particularly since I'd been caught overhearing Juan's heated conversation about getting rid of one of the members of his group. I could tell something was going on, as the Santos sons had begun acting strangely around me. I was sure they were just waiting for the right opportunity to arise to dispose of me, and I was as scared as I'd ever been. Yet I knew that to run away would be to just prolong the agony. With all their criminal connections in Cúcuta, they would soon track me down and, alone and penniless, where else could I go?

It seemed I was about to get my answer. While I would have given anything to go to Maruja's, it was not an option for her to take me in. I wished for nothing more than to be cared for by her, as she cared for her own children, but I knew it was something I could never ask of her. She would then be in danger herself.

But one day when I expressed my despair at my situation, she told me she might be able to help. She had been thinking about what she could do for some time now and had come up with a safe place where the Santoses wouldn't find me. All I had to do, she explained, was get out of the house somehow and meet her at San Antonio Park at noon the next day.

'Could you do that, do you think?' she mimed at me.

I nodded. It would be difficult to escape the house again. It might even prove impossible, but I didn't want to think about that. I would find a way to do it. I would have to find a way. I would rather die, I decided, than not do so.

As I lay on my mat on the back patio that night, I tried for hours to come up with a decent plan. The best-case scenario would be for most of the family to be out, but since that was unlikely, I had to think of something that could conceivably work even if they were in.

By eleven the following morning, things weren't going my way. Mr Santos and Juan had been in the office since breakfast and were showing no signs of going anywhere. As the minutes ticked by, I kept imagining Maruja waiting and waiting in San Antonio Park and the chance of my escape slowly dissolving. Now Maruja was helping me, everything suddenly seemed so urgent. If she was as frightened for my life as I was, then how long did I have? I could be murdered the very next day.

I was interrupted in my gloomy reverie by the phone ringing. I could hear Mr Santos barking gruffly into the receiver, followed by the sound of chairs being scraped back and keys being grabbed. Yes! I thought, feeling relieved as the office door flew open and both Mr Santos and Juan emerged.

Consuela, who was sitting at her sewing machine and listening to the radio, barely looked up as they passed.

'Consuela,' said Mr Santos, 'Juan and I have to go out on business. Tell your mother we don't know when we'll be back.'

Consuela, who wasn't interested in their various comings and goings, muttered, 'Yeah, OK.' And of me, standing in the kitchen doorway, they took not the slightest bit of notice, which was probably a good thing, as they might have seen the relief flooding through me reflected in the grin on my face. Finally. My chance. Now it could happen.

I carefully closed the kitchen door on Consuela, who was once again engrossed in her sewing. Now I could put my plan into action, which first involved a liberal spraying of cleaning fluid around the kitchen, to disguise the smell of what was to come.

My plan involved a request to go to the shop to get kerosene, and with only Consuela to contend with I thought I had more chance of being allowed to go. But first I needed to create a need for kerosene, which, with a half-full bottle, we currently didn't have.

I didn't have long, so I wasted no time in pulling apart the cooker on which I had just begun cooking lunch. The fuel was dispensed from an assemblage of pipes at the back, consisting of an inner bottle that hung upside down within another larger fuel bottle, the kerosene being dispensed via a wick. As the level of fuel in the outer bottle dropped, so air could enter the smaller bottle and allow more kerosene to be dispensed. The fuel would then travel along a pipe to perforated rings on the hob itself and so provide a flame on which to cook.

All I had to do was disconnect the kerosene supply bottle and carefully tip the contents down the sink. And since I'd disconnected and refilled the bottle scores of times before, it was a job – were my fingers not shaking quite so badly – that I could almost do with my eyes closed. It was soon done, shakes or otherwise, and once the now empty bottle was re-attached, all I had to do was to relight the stove and wait for the flame to peter out.

'Consuela!' I called, as I watched it slowly splutter into nothingness. 'There's no flame. I think we must be out of kerosene!'

I pulled the kitchen door open slightly and made a big show of cursing and moaning about the time and wondering how on earth I'd cook everyone's lunch. But Consuela was clearly more engrossed in whatever she was listening to than I thought, as she took no notice of me whatsoever.

I went into the living room. 'Consuela,' I whined again. 'No fuel! There's no fuel. I need to go get some so I can cook the lunch.'

This finally produced a response. And it was even better than I could have hoped for. With an irritable sigh, she pulled her bag onto her lap and began rummaging for her keys.

'Right,' she said, thrusting a note into my hand as she got up. 'Come on, then. I'll open up the door.'

I needed no further invitation. Time was short. Perhaps too short. Consuela unlocked the door – the heavy bar was currently propped at the side of it – and I was out of it, clutching the gallon drum, in seconds.

It was as if I had wings. Dumping the drum, I sprinted barefoot all the way to the park. My feet could have been torn to ribbons on the way – I didn't care. I was running for the biggest chance of my life, and I was terrified I'd miss Maruja. Nothing would have stopped me that day.

I entered the park minutes later, my lungs almost bursting from the effort of getting there and also from elation. I had done it! I had escaped the Santoses! I was free! There was just one problem. I couldn't see Maruja.

I glanced left and right, anxiously scanning the people all around me. Where was she? Why wasn't she here? She had promised, and I'd trusted her. I still completely trusted her. Which made a horrible thought surface. Had Mr Santos got to her? Was that why he and Juan had gone out earlier on? I sat down on the kerb side, dejected and now frightened. Had I got here too late after all?

Moments later, a taxi rolled to a stop beside me and I tensed for the door to open, expecting the worst. But it wasn't Juan or Mr Santos. It was Maruja! And she was beckoning me to hurry and climb in.

Once again, I needed no further invitation. I got to my feet, opened the door and slid onto the seat beside her. And met her properly for the very first time.

'Well done,' she said quietly, indicating that I should put my head down so no one could see me. 'Well done for getting out.'

'Hello,' I said, wriggling down, my heart leaping with happiness. This was it, I thought. I was at last going to have a better life. This, in fact, was the very best day of my life.

Maruja smiled. 'Hello, Rosalba,' she said more formally, smiling down at me. 'I'm Maruja. You're safe now.'

27

Although my prayers were answered that day, I never felt drawn to God. Yes, I had the same sense of wonder as any child would; I wondered as much as anyone where I had come from and what had made me, and how the beauty of nature had come about. But even if such an all-powerful creator did exist, I would be angry with him. What sort of God gave little children lives such as the one he'd given me?

In Colombia, a Catholic country, almost everyone is a Catholic – it's just not normal to turn away from religion as I did at that time. It's as much a tradition as it is a faith – if not more so. But, for all that, I could never have imagined where Maruja was taking me. I certainly never expected the next stage of my life to be located among people for whom a creature such as me would be as far from their ideals as it was possible to be. Yet it soon became clear that this was going to be the case. Maruja was delivering me to a convent.

We travelled in the taxi for around twenty minutes, to a part of the city I was unfamiliar with, Barrio Blanco. It looked different from the parts of the city that I did know: cleaner, less scruffy, perhaps a place for high-class people. Finally, we pulled up outside a large, clean white building – perhaps indicative of the good souls inside.

The metal entry gates, too, were clean of rust and painted white, though as we walked up to the entrance it was on cracked burgundy tiles. Maruja, perhaps sensing my innate distrust of this fine place, held on to my hand as we approached the oak door.

She clasped the knocker – a heavy-looking cast-iron ring – and banged it down twice on its plate. She also read the sign for me. '"Barrio Blanca,"' she read. '"La Casita", which means "the white district, little house" in Spanish. This is a safe place,' she explained to me. 'Do you understand, Rosalba? Nothing can harm you here. You are safe.'

I thanked her shyly but also sadly. I didn't want her to leave me. But it seemed she was going to, even so. I had tears in my eyes as the huge door swung open to reveal a lady with greying hair, wearing a baggy black dress and a headscarf, who introduced herself as Sister Elvira.

Maruja explained who I was and how she'd come to bring me here. 'Her life is in danger,' she added, when she'd finished telling the nun about the Santoses. 'So will you please take her in and keep her safe?'

Sister Elvira reassured Maruja that she could definitely do that. 'No one can enter here to harm her,' she reassured her. 'And no one,' she added, looking at me, 'can escape from here either. Don't worry. We will educate her and feed her.'

I couldn't help but screw my face up at Sister Elvira's words. They made the convent sound more like a prison. A friendly prison, but a prison even so.

'Come, child,' the nun said, as Maruja was obviously anxious to leave. 'Let me show you where you will be sleeping.'

Sister Elvira beckoned me to step into the building. So this was it. I'd met Maruja, and she was already leaving me. She'd been my salvation, and the price I had to pay was our parting. I had no idea if I'd ever see her again. Fresh tears began to flow down my cheeks.

'Don't worry, Rosalba,' Maruja whispered as we parted at the convent gate. 'I will come back every Saturday to see how you are doing, I promise.' She paused. 'Please be good. Please behave. This is your chance now, OK? I know you won't be used to this, but try. Please do try for me, won't you?'

I told her I would. I promised. And it was a promise I aimed to keep. I would do it for Maruja.

*

I had never set foot in a convent before and it felt unlike anywhere I had ever been. I knew nothing about convents or churches or nuns. I'd seen nuns in the street, but I didn't know what they were, only that their white habits and metal crosses were a kind of uniform. Arriving at the convent was confusing and also frightening, albeit briefly, as the only connection I could make was with the priests at Ana-Karmen's who'd attempted the exorcism. I had this sudden idea that nuns might be a kind of witch.

The convent itself was a big, echoing place. It was very spacious, with tiled floors laid in an intricate pattern. The words *La Casita* were painted in big letters on an arch above our heads, though, as I couldn't read, this obviously meant nothing. A flight of stone stairs ran up one wall to a big galleried landing, which led, Sister Elvira told me, to the dormitories above, from where I could hear the sounds of children laughing. I felt better.

The convent was apparently home to many orphans, street kids and abandoned little ones – anyone who needed a home, the Sister told me. We walked up the staircase and along the balcony corridor to the dormitory that housed the girls.

'Good afternoon,' she said once we'd entered the huge room. 'Attention, please!'

'Good afternoon, Sister Elvira,' they chorused back, in unison.

'This is Rosalba,' she continued, 'who has just joined us today. She'll be staying with us now, so please make her feel part of our family and help her wherever you can. Now,' she said, clapping her bony hands together, 'let's all welcome her in, shall we?'

And with that, every girl in the room started clapping, which made me feel odd, exposed and slightly anxious. I had never been welcomed anywhere, much less been clapped at and stared at, and I was relieved when the noise finally died down.

'There,' said Sister Elvira, beaming and placing a hand around my shoulder. 'Welcome. Now, then, let's get you some clothes.'

*

We were sent to bed at nine o'clock that night and every night from then on. To bed. It felt strange. I had never had a proper bed before. As beds went, it was probably a pretty poor specimen. It had a stained mattress and was covered in a pair of thin grey sheets, which matched the pale grey of the dormitory walls. But it was still a bed, which made it better than the tatty mat I was used to, and far, far better than sleeping in drains on the streets.

No one really spoke to me that night, but I was happy to be left alone. From my bed I could see the tiny square window at the end of the dormitory. It was too little for all but the smallest child to squeeze through but had iron bars across it even so. I thought about the Santoses and the beating that I wouldn't get tonight, and wondered if they were out there somewhere, looking for me. I feared for Maruja and what might happen to her if they found out she'd helped me escape. I worried terribly about her family as well. Saturday couldn't come too soon.

It took me a long time to fall asleep, because I was frightened of having nightmares, but once I did, I slept soundly and deeply. So deeply that when the sound of a whistle woke me in the blackness, it took some moments to figure out where I was. And what time it was as well, which was four in the morning – time to get up as far as La Casita was concerned.

'Time to pray,' the nun bearing the whistle commanded. 'Half an hour,' she explained to me, as the new girl. 'You have half an hour. Prepare yourself, wash and dress, and then make your way down to church.'

Still confused and bleary-eyed, I did as I was told and followed the rest of the girls. The church was on the second floor and was entered via double wooden doors. It was full of bibles and rosary beads, big statues and fancy crosses – to someone like me, a big assault on the senses. We sat in things called pews, which were high-backed wooden benches set out in rows facing the front, and sometimes, instead of sitting, we knelt in front of them to pray. It was all terribly confusing and a bit scary.

Unlike the dormitory, the windows in the church were tall and massive, and made of pieces of coloured glass that, come the daylight, would create pretty patterns on the stone floor. The church also housed a big machine that made music and which one of the girls told me was called an organ. Soon I would hear it and be amazed at the sound all around me, so powerful it would seem to make the air and floor vibrate. But for now all was silent and still dark, apart from the ranks of candles that flickered in tall holders and a giant centre light that seemed to drip crystal droplets.

I had no idea how to pray, what to say or how to act, so that morning I just watched what the other children did and tried to copy them as best I could. After we prayed, a priest in robes came and spoke to us. I didn't understand what he said, and as his voice was so monotonous, I didn't really care what it was anyway.

The service went on for what seemed like several hours, though in reality perhaps only an hour and a half. There was more praying, more talking, some chanting of strange words and something else called Holy Communion.

'Say you've taken it,' the girls around me all urged once it started. 'They'll ask you, so just say you've taken it, and they'll feed you.' I didn't understand what 'it' was, but when we were all told to line up, I could see a little better what was happening. The priest was leaning down and giving each child something to eat and drink, and I definitely wanted some of that.

Then it was my turn. 'Have you worn a white dress and taken your first Holy Communion?' he asked me.

I eyed the bread and wine that he and the nun by him were holding. 'Yes,' I said. 'Yes, I've done that.'

Church, I soon realised, was about following the crowd. As was almost every aspect of living at the convent. Within a matter of days, I realised that, though I wasn't being beaten, much of life would simply continue as before. After church there came breakfast – a dry roll and a glass of water – and after breakfast came the inevitable work. I was first assigned to clean the toilets, which felt a particularly bad start. In time I'd do every cleaning job that needed to be done there. But for now I was on toilets, which I scrubbed until lunchtime, when the whistle blew to call us for our next meal of the day: a watery soup with something green floating in it.

I saw the nuns tucking into meals of roast meat, and it occurred to me that my first impression had been an accurate one. I had definitely ended up in yet another kind of prison. We were being punished – that's what it felt like – with meagre meals and endless drudgery, and, most importantly, none of us could escape. But we could steal, and, being hungry, that's what many of the kids did. Most were street children anyway, so it was already in their nature, and soon, when I was ravenous, I would steal too.

It was easy. I would scuttle into the kitchen and dive under the table, where I was hidden from view by the tablecloth. Then, when the staff in there weren't looking, I would snatch a few bread rolls from near the window and stuff them into my pockets before sprinting back out of the door.

Only on one occasion did I steal something more precious: a banana. It sat in the middle of a glass bowl of fruit, almost like a decoration, and it seemed to be calling to me. I couldn't resist it.

I was almost certainly one of the oldest children in the convent, the majority eventually being reclaimed or adopted into a life that no longer required iron bars. But I wasn't quite the oldest. That title went to a lady called Francisca, who was around sixty and would sit in the corner of the convent and gossip with anyone who passed by. She told me she had been at La Casita for over half a century now, having never been claimed or adopted. Had it not been for Maruja, I could have been the next to take her title, because no one else knew I existed. I would think of Francisca often as I worked at my chores. She was my reason to keep doing them, in the hope I would be thought of as a good girl and somehow get out.

I saw every day of that first week at La Casita convent as just time to be ticked off until Maruja came to visit and I could show her what a good girl I'd been. But it was hard. For all the beatings and drudgery of life with the Santos family, this felt little better. The life I'd dreamed of wasn't supposed to be like this: being made to get up at four in the morning to pray to a God who I still felt had abandoned me.

Where was this bountiful God everyone else seemed to worship, anyway? For if I had come to understand anything since leaving the jungle, it was that every human I encountered seemed to worship him. And seemed to want me to do so, too. As street kids, we'd sometimes be offered cheese and lemonade as a bribe to visit the city's churches and sit through a short service inside. I always liked the cheese, but I hated the droning sermons, so when the bits of cheese got smaller and the lemonade changed to water, I stopped bothering – you could get better on the streets.

I didn't like God. I'd watch the endless Catholic street processions, but I couldn't reconcile this with what I knew of him. To me he was a punishing God – he'd even let his own son be crucified! – and if he was so good, then why hadn't he found me my mama or given me a better life? The one he'd chosen for me so far seemed so unfair. To be starving all the time, to have every minute filled with work, to be told what to do, when to do it, how to do it, to be expected to see 'obedience' as the most important thing of all.

I should have been grateful. I was safe from harm, I was being cared for, I was with other children, but my principal memory of that time is of stultifying boredom, coupled with what was probably, looking back, a typical adolescent mindset. I railed against everything, almost as if by instinct.

There was one shining light and that was having Maruja in my life, and the knowledge that, unlike many of the children around me, I at least had someone, someone who cared enough to visit me. I had someone I belonged to. I wasn't alone. And when Maruja came that first Saturday, I was almost beside myself with happiness. I was able to give a good account of myself as well, to let her know I had done as she asked and tried my best, and that my best, in the main, had been good enough.

And it was enough for me to see her – to know she was safe and well and that the Santoses hadn't tracked her down and killed her for rescuing me. However grim my 'better' life was, that knowledge – and the belief that I would one day grow up and be able to leave the convent – kept me going.

But then the next Saturday, Maruja didn't come.

28

Like children do everywhere, I tried to adapt. As Saturday followed Saturday and still no Maruja came, I tried to rationalise why that might be. At first I was terrified. Had the Santos family found out what she'd done? And if so, what had they done to punish her? Or perhaps she was in hiding, or maybe had had to leave the city altogether? Round and round my thoughts kept going. Why had she abandoned me?

I kept telling myself that she was safe and well, and there must be a good reason for her to stay away. I couldn't quite believe the Santoses would hurt her – not really. She was the mother of several children and would be known to lots of people. So whereas they could kill me and no one would know or care, they surely couldn't do that to Maruja.

But thinking that – believing that – was actually even worse, because that meant she had simply given up on me. Perhaps I'd displeased the nuns and they had let Maruja know, and not coming to visit was her way of punishing me. So I became bitter. It had always been too good to be true. I knew how humans worked, didn't I? How badly they treated one another. After so many years now of unkindness and abuse, surely I should have learned my lesson.

But still I yearned for her and refused to give up hope. Still I believed I would one day find that fantasy figure who would love me and care for me and nurture me. And in the meantime, I would just have to get on with it.

And I did adapt to life in the convent, in that I found ways to make the time pass a little quicker. It might be difficult to imagine, if you've never been a prisoner yourself, just how mind-crushingly boring it is to be locked up all day. Yes, I was fed and cared for, and nobody beat me, and I was grateful for that, really grateful. But I still had no freedom. I saw the same view each day, ate the same food, saw the same faces . . . It was a predictable routine with no end in sight, and I was beginning to find it unbearable.

I was still trying to make the most of it in the early weeks of hope, because that's what Maruja had asked me to do, but as the time passed I felt my will shrink within me. What was the point of living if this was to be my existence: one of a huge number of invisible kids – no more than numbers – who were so unwanted and unloved that they had been locked away?

I'd seen more life in a day on the streets, I recall thinking. I'd eaten lobster and steak, seen more sights, smelled more smells, lived more life. I'd been raised in the jungle, lived each day with the thrill of the unknown, seen animals and plants I might never see again and survived. Here, I felt I was dying.

Perhaps predictably, I found refuge in being naughty. At first cheeky – it felt so good to make people laugh, for them to notice me – and gradually just downright bad. With the life I'd led so far, I had no tolerance for rules and regulations, and couldn't understand why such strictures were even necessary. But breaking rules – which I did for the sake of my sanity – had consequences. I didn't mind being caught and told off by the nuns, though. To me, this meant attention. It meant I existed. Which, in a perverse kind of way, meant I mattered.

And I definitely became something of a comedian, very quickly adopting the role of ringleader and class clown, which gave me a degree of notoriety. I was also an endless source of ideas of mischief. We girls would often lie in bed late, whispering to one another. We had always been curious about the fusty old nuns and one of the perennial topics of our night-time conversations was what they might wear under their clothes. One night, I decided we should find out.

Only the bravest of the girls were up for 'operation underwear', the aim of which was to discover what went on behind closed doors – to find out where the nuns bathed and washed their clothes. This was one of the great mysteries that needed solving at La Casita, and we were determined to be the ones to do it.

So we made a plan. We stuffed our beds carefully with our pillows, to stump any night patrols, and set off in a flurry of suppressed giggles. I was partly responsible. As we left the dorm, I announced that 'Sister Ramona must have the biggest, ugliest knickers ever! And let's not even go there with Sister Dolores – woof!'

We searched the convent, high and low, over a period of an hour, climbing up to see in windows and peering through cracks beneath doors. It was fun, but it wasn't exactly fruitful. But then I spotted a high window that appeared to be out of reach – a narrow pane of glass above a tall wooden door. It stood to reason – this was their living quarters, so this must surely be the place, and at this time they'd all be busy praying.

My monkey skills now came into their own. No other girl could shimmy up things the way I could, and with a leg-up, and to the amazement of all the girls below me, I hit the jackpot. This was indeed the place. Beyond the window was a sitting room, and in the middle of the sitting room was a row of identical, not to mention enormous, beige knickers, all hanging drying on an airing stand. But they weren't all identical; some sported frills, a most un-nun-like thing, to my mind.

'Whooaa!' I said. 'Whooaa! You should see this!' I whooped.

'Rosalba!' hissed Janette. 'We can't!'

So, one by one, I helped each girl climb up and peer into the room, and finally our curiosity was satisfied.

But as there were many girls who'd still not witnessed the giant knickers for themselves, we planned another raid, which was even more audacious. There were a few times each day when the coast would be clear and, crucially, the door would be unlocked. Armed with this information, Janette and I set off a couple of days later and this time managed to pinch several pairs of the enormous pants off the airing stand.

It was perhaps an indicator of how dull and uneventful our lives were that prancing around with Sister Ramona's enormous frilly knickers over my clothes was the best fun I'd had for a long time. And it was true for all of us: we laughed till we had no breath left for laughing, and our sides ached so much we were in real pain.

But it was nothing to the pain I had coming. Naturally, Sister Ramona reported her missing knickers to Sister Elvira, and Sister Elvira, quite sure who the ringleader must be, accused me of the crime. Which, of course, my teenage mind found extremely galling. She had no evidence it was me. She just made the assumption and acted accordingly.

'Rosalba!' she barked at me, her eyes ablaze with suppressed fury. 'I know it is only you who could be so un-holy that you'd steal a sister's private undergarments!'

She was right on this occasion, but I wasn't about to own up to it, especially when I heard the other girls trying to suppress their chuckles.

'You can't prove it,' I argued. 'And I've been here all along!'

My defiance sent Sister Elvira's anger into overdrive. She actually gasped. 'In the presence of God, you lie!' she cried dramatically. 'Child, you have much coming to you!' She glowered at me. 'When will you learn? Now stand over there, by that wall, and turn to face it. And wipe that stupid smile right off your face!'

She then swept from the dormitory only to return moments later with a pair of building bricks, one in each hand. She transferred them to my hands after barking her instructions. I was to stand with my arms held above my head – I was on no account to bend them – and I was to stay like that, as punishment, for thirty minutes. 'If the bricks drop, they hit your head,' she explained, her tone waspish. 'And that, Rosalba, will teach you a lesson!'

Easy, I thought defiantly. I can do this. It will be easy. But it wasn't. After five minutes, all the blood had drained from my arms, and after ten both my elbows began quivering. But I did it. I held out. I would not drop those bricks. Which made it a victory. But, of course, it really wasn't that at all. It was just evidence that I was turning into someone I didn't want to be. A bad girl. A rude girl. A girl who didn't care. I was slipping back into the mindset of a cynical, bitter street kid. The only solution? To get out of there, and fast.

*

The weeks in the convent soon rolled into months, and, as a prisoner, each day felt like something I needed to tick off. It was either that or become like poor Francisca. I was desperate to see Maruja and find out what had happened. I thought of her all the time and couldn't allow myself to believe that she'd abandoned me of her own free will. She just couldn't have.

But, once again, I would need to think carefully. The convent worked on a simple principle: it was locked at all times. (Locked to keep the nuns secure in their chosen vocation, and locked to keep the outside world away.) In the middle of all this, there were all of us – the orphans – responsibility for whom the nuns took very seriously. Charged with our care – which was actually a part of their vocation – they could not let us wander, or we might run away, and then their work to keep us safe would have been pointless.

It would first be necessary, therefore, to make a thorough inspection of the place, to see where there might be a chink in the convent's armour – some security failing that I could exploit. It was on one such inspection of the inner walls, having snuck out of the refectory, that I came upon Imelda, washing up. She was an old fat woman who lived at the convent, not a nun herself but just someone who had found refuge among them. She was disabled, with two walking sticks, and had to sit down a lot.

'You want to escape, don't you?' she asked me, eyeing the dry roll I was holding and had been nibbling from.

I blinked at her, shocked. 'How do you know?'

'San Antonio told me,' she explained, as if the saints regularly engaged her in idle gossip. 'I can pray to him, if you want,' she added. 'And the Virgin Mary, too. If I ask them, they'll set you free. It will happen.' She screwed her eyes up a little against the glare of the sun. 'But there's a condition. You must give me all your breakfasts for a week.'

I was worried now. Imelda might tell the nuns what I was planning, and then they'd keep an even closer eye on me than they were doing already. I couldn't have that. I screwed my own eyes up a little, to match hers, and, since she was sitting and I was standing, tried to look menacing.

'I don't need you,' I told her. 'I can do it on my own. And if you say one word to the nuns, I'll cut your tongue out.' I thrust the roll towards her. 'Here,' I said, 'take this and pray for my escape. And if nothing happens, I will kill you in the morning.'

It was never my intention to harm a hair on Imelda's head, but it might at least stop the fat lady from singing.

When I returned to the refectory, Sister Elvira pounced on

me. 'Rosalba!' she hissed. 'Where have you been? What are you doing walking away from breakfast?'

'Please, Sister Elvira,' I said, 'I just felt so ashamed of all the bad things I've been doing that I decided not to eat breakfast and instead to fast, pray to the Virgin Mary and ask for forgiveness from God.'

Sister Elvira glared at me, not buying my story for an instant. 'Open your mouth!' she commanded, then inspected it carefully, to see if there was any trace of bread in there.

'Hmm,' she said, finally. 'Well, I suppose this is good. All right. I will allow you to continue, child.'

'Thank you, Sister,' I said politely, and continued on my way, silently thanking the Virgin Mary as I went.

And perhaps Imelda's prayers, in the end, did bear fruit. Because it was only the next day that I found exactly the thing I'd been looking for: a means to scale the high convent walls.

It was another tree that was to be my salvation. Looking back, trees have played such an important role in my life. There was my special tree in the jungle, the tree in the garden of the brothel, the trees in San Antonio Park, the Santoses' Mamoncillo and this time the tree was another mango. It was a big, spreading one that grew just outside the convent wall, and some of its boughs leaned over it, above the *lavaderos*. These deep concrete sinks had been built against the wall, and the branches of the mango tree provided shade above them, a boon for anyone out there washing clothes.

And also a boon for me. If I could just climb high enough to reach the branches, I could then crawl across them, above the wall, and climb back down on the other side. At which point, I realised with mounting excitement, I would be free.

I made a closer inspection around the lavaderos, albeit a sneaky one. There was hardly any time of day when the sinks weren't in use, and this morning was no exception.

But I didn't need to look for long to see that there were some potential hand- and footholds available as well. There were a number of metal protrusions above a couple of the sinks, which had perhaps been put there in order to hang a washing line up. This would be it, I decided happily. This would be my escape route. All I had to do now was think of a way that I could arrange to have the area to myself.

Once again I thought hard, and over a period of days a plan began to form in my mind. My first idea was to start a small fire in another part of the convent – perhaps the church, because I hated it so much. But I soon dismissed the idea. How would I feel if it got out of control and in my haste to escape I caused harm to my friends, maybe even somebody's death? No, I decided, I would have to think of something safer. But before long I returned to my original idea. Why not just pretend there was a fire in the church? If I made enough fuss, then surely everyone would run there to see what was going on? Shouting fire alone would create enough panic, surely? And I was nimble and fast. I was confident that I could be up the tree and over the wall in seconds.

I would do it, I decided, in the middle of the morning, while everyone was busy and preoccupied with work. It would be the last thing they expected. They would have to stop what they were doing, and, with luck, the whole place would be full of squawking headless chickens. Except me. I would be on my way to freedom.

*

'FIRE!!!' Even to me, my voice sounded strange and desperate. 'Fire!' I bellowed. 'Help! There's a fire!!!!'

It was around eleven-thirty in the morning, and I had made sure to look the part. I had upset my hair – which took little doing, for it was a mass of wild curls anyway – and adopted the expression I had been practising for days now – wide eyes, unfocused and terrified. I had also left nothing to chance. There was a girl in the convent who was something of an artist and would do face painting on the children for fun. She was very talented, and her speciality was to paint on realistic cuts and bruises. I had asked her to paint some bruises on my neck and shoulders so I could tell Maruja, when I found her, that the nuns beat me. It was a wicked lie, but I was just so terrified she'd send me straight back that I needed a convincing reason why she shouldn't.

My plan was at long last in action. I had bellowed my warning from the steps of the church and now ran, arms flailing, to the lavaderos. Shocked faces greeted me. 'Fire!' I screamed again. 'The church is on fire! Oh, please come!!'

231

Sopping clothes were thrown down, hands wiped hastily on aprons, and nuns and orphans alike began running towards the church. Watching them go – and still yelling, just to keep up the momentum – I was shocked at just how simple it had been.

I hadn't just chosen the church in a fit of pique, either. It was the place furthest away from where I now stood and was also out of sight of the branches of the mango.

But I had no time to waste. I hauled myself up onto the lavaderos, then up the wall and, by stretching as far as I could, got my hand around a sturdy mango branch.

Now I was in my natural territory it was only a matter of a few more seconds before I was high up in the tree, on top of the wall and on my way to liberation just below me.

I allowed myself to breathe out. I could hear confused voices by the church, as, one by one, everyone wondered quite where the fire was. But I was safe. The dense foliage shielded me from view, and, besides, who'd even think to look up?

I looked down, then, to see the best place to climb over, and realised it might be slightly trickier than I had thought. The top of the wall was studded aggressively with little shards of broken glass. Very God-like, I thought. I had purposely left my *alpargatas* (the thin sandals we were made to wear) in the dormitory, as I'd known they'd hinder my climbing, but how would my bare feet cope with such mean and treacherous terrain?

I didn't have very long to ponder. I had perhaps been optimistic about how long everyone would be duped before realising it was me who had raised the alarm and coming to find me and discipline me. And I had perhaps been naive about how likely the nuns would be to work out the reason why I'd done it. Had Imelda shopped me? I didn't know. But I did know one thing. The nuns were running back and, yes, they were looking up. I had to get on the other side of this wall, fast.

There was no time to edge along and down to other lower branches, no time to consider and plan a sensible route onto the street. There was nothing for it. I would simply have to jump from where I was – a drop of what looked like about twelve feet.

So I jumped, landing hard on the stubbly grass below the tree, and felt a searing pain shoot up both legs. But there was very little time to sit yelping and rubbing them. Assuming they weren't snapped, I had to move them, and quickly, because along the street I just knew that the convent gates were opening. I could hear the familiar sound of the big plank behind the convent door being lifted up.

I staggered up just as the convent gate began to open. Desperate to get away before any of the nuns saw me, I plunged into the road, causing cars and trucks to swerve around me and their drivers to swear at me – 'Estúpido gamina!' 'Estúpido!' 'Estúpido!' – before diving into some trees on the other side of the road and scrambling up them, panting hard.

The trees were known locally as Matarratones, which translates literally as 'rat killer', because the berries are poisonous, but for me, a little monkey, they were a lifesaver. Within seconds I was once again looking down on the street. I saw a few nuns come out, including Sister Elvira, but as none of them had seen me climb into the bushes, it obviously never occurred to them that that's where I might be. I would run away, surely? That's what they'd be thinking. And even though the convent security man looked around for a bit, it never occurred to him to look up. After several minutes, he swore, slapped his leg and walked away. The job was done. I had escaped. I was free again. And one step closer to my beloved Maruja.

29

It took several hours to find my way back to Maruja. I stayed in the Matarratones for a good half an hour. I wanted to be sure I could get away without anybody seeing me, and I didn't put it past the nuns to have posted a watch by the convent entrance. It seemed ridiculous: surely they would have been glad to get rid of me? But from the way I'd seen Sister Elvira powering up the pavement, I was pretty sure they didn't see things like that. They'd been told to take care of me, and my escape meant they'd failed.

Once I felt safe, I slipped back down to the street and made my way, bit by bit, across the city. My route was uncertain. I didn't know this part of Cúcuta well, but, using lorries and buses to catch free rides when they were stopped at traffic lights, eventually, having zigzagged my way around several times, I saw places and landmarks I recognised.

By the time I reached the district where I'd lived with the Santoses, my weary feet hurt as much as my legs. I was also nervous. Supposing one of the family was out and about and spotted me? I decided it would be safer to keep my distance a little and find someone else to get a message to Maruja.

Happily, a likely candidate presented himself fairly quickly in the form of an innocent-looking little boy who was playing in the street. Stationing myself in the doorway of what looked like a derelict house, I whistled and then, once I had his attention, beckoned him over with my finger.

He looked a little nervous as he approached me, but he was obviously pretty streetwise. 'Hey,' he said. He was a good foot shorter than I was. Around ten? I wasn't sure. But a bold ten. 'What are you calling me for?' he wanted to know. 'I can knock you out in a second if you mess with me!' he added.

I waved a hand dismissively. 'I have a job for you. You want it?'

'What?'

'I need you to go to a house.' I told him which street it was. 'The first one,' I added, describing it to him as best I could. 'The other side of the bridge, OK? Ask for Maruja – you got that? Maruja. And whisper this message to her. It's very important that you whisper. Tell her Rosalba is waiting for her. Then bring her back here, to me.'

The boy pulled a face. 'And you expect me to do this for free?' He was obviously a true Colombian-raised child.

'I have many sweets in my pocket,' I said. 'And you can have them all as soon as you bring the lady to me.' I was lying, of course, but this would be a valuable lesson for the boy. Never trust a Colombian.

'So show me the sweets,' he said. He was learning pretty fast.

'I said only when you return with her. Didn't you hear me the last time? Tell her Rosalba is waiting. Go on. Hurry! Hurry, or I'll be gone before you're back. And then you'll get nothing. OK?'

I watched the boy run away and could feel my heart pounding. Would she be there? Would she come? Was she even still alive? I tried not to think what I'd do if the boy didn't return.

I was just beginning to think he had run away, sweets or no sweets, when Maruja appeared from around the corner. I felt joy and relief swell inside me as she approached, but she seemed markedly anxious about seeing me. She was dressed smartly, I noticed, and carrying a purse. I felt panic rise in me. Was she already planning to get a taxi and take me back?

'Rosalba!' she said, taking me by the shoulders and shaking me. 'What are you doing here? Why did you come? It's too dangerous for you here!'

I started to answer, but she was too cross to listen and carried on, 'Why did you run away? You were safe there! Oh, no . . .' She began looking around frantically in all directions. 'Rosalba, you have to understand, they are looking for you. They have their gang working to search for you and kill you. Don't you realise?'

I shook my head miserably. I hated that she was shouting at me. 'I came to find you,' I whimpered. 'I came to find you.'

Maruja's expression softened. 'Oh, Rosalba . . .' she said.

'I came to find you because you didn't come. You said you'd come every Saturday. But you didn't. I was so worried . . .'

'Oh, Rosalba,' she said again. 'Rosalba, I couldn't. It was too dangerous for me to go to you. They were after you. They were seriously out to find you and kill you. You have no idea how scared I was that they would. And I felt sure they had an idea that I was in some way connected, Rosalba. They were watching me too – that's why I couldn't come to you. I didn't dare to. They could have followed me. They probably would have followed me. And I would have led them straight to you. And they would have found a way . . .'

She fell silent, glancing up and down the street again. I saw that the little boy was lingering a few yards away, but apart from that the street was empty. For now, at least.

'Come on,' said Maruja, having obviously decided on a course of action. 'Come on, come with me. We have to take you straight back there.'

'But I don't want to go back! I want to stay with you!'

'Rosalba, you can't. You know that.'

'But I can't go back there! I won't! They beat me, Maruja! They beat all the orphans!' I yanked at the collar of my dress so she could glimpse my 'bruises'.

She gasped. 'They beat you?'

I nodded miserably.

'Oh, but that's terrible. I had no idea!'

I started to cry now, not because I was quite the actress I wished to be but because it mattered so much that Maruja didn't leave me. And she wasn't immune to my tears. She hugged me. 'Then you can't go back,' she said. 'How could I possibly send you back there? Oh, you poor child . . .'

'So can I stay with you now? Please?'

She shook her head. 'I can't let you. It's too dangerous – for both of us. For my family as well. And, Rosalba, my son Guillermo is going out with Consuela now. So they would find out so easily. I can't let you stay.'

I clutched at her dress, having nothing else left to hold on to. 'But where will I go?' I begged. 'What can I do? Please don't leave me.'

'Rosalba, you have to . . .' She seemed unable to speak now. Was she crying too? 'Rosalba . . .' She looked up at the sky, as if for answers. 'How can I do this?' she said to it. 'How can I?'

I held my breath. I realised how much she was risking to even be seen with me. And as I held it, she came to a decision. She looked at me again. 'Today,' she said, 'you can stay for today. I will contact my daughter Maria in Bogotá and see if perhaps she could take you in. Till then you must hide, though, and you must not leave the house. Not once. Not even to go into the garden. And you must be silent, as quiet as you can possibly be. Or they will hear you. I know they will hear you. And if anyone comes, you must hide in the pantry. That's the only way. Do you think you can do that?'

I nodded frantically. 'Yes, I can. Oh, Maruja, thank you, thank you.'

'So, come on. We need to get you indoors and out of sight. Round the back. That's what we'll do. That way, no one will see you.'

Seeing us moving, the little boy, who I had completely forgotten about, now followed, delivering a sharp kick to my shin.

'Oi,' he said. 'Sweets!' He thrust a hand out. 'Where are my sweets, *garrapata*?'

Garrapata was Spanish for a blood-sucking tick. A true Colombian boy if ever I saw one. I pulled a fierce face. 'Run away!' I said. 'Or I'll chase you and cut your tongue off!'

Maruja yanked on my arm. 'Rosalba!' she snapped. 'Behave!' She then gave the boy a few coins. 'Say nothing about this to anyone,' she commanded. 'Ayeee,' she muttered to me as he ran off. 'Oh, Rosalba. What am I doing?'

And Maruja hadn't yet done with me. Once I was safely inside her house, which was the closest place to heaven I had ever seen in my life, she rounded on me. 'If you steal anything – anything – from me or my children, I won't send you to my daughter, you hear?'

I nodded.

'I will throw you out. And then you'll be all on your own again, you hear me?'

Again I nodded, and I promised, trying hard to convince her. But why wouldn't she distrust me? I'd been a street kid for a long time – hardly better than an animal. I'd worked for the Santos family – all of them, except the girls, hardened cheats and crooks and killers. Why would she trust me to understand the difference between good and bad? I know if I'd been her I probably wouldn't have.

Yet she took me in and fed me, and I did my very best to be the person I knew lived inside me. A good person and most of all a grateful one. And I also learned a little more about Maruja and her family that day. She had been widowed young and was raising nine children single-handedly. Her husband had killed himself at the age of sixty-three after finding out he had Parkinson's disease.

'Which is why I cannot keep you here,' she explained. 'I have got to think about the children – think about my safety, for their sakes. But I am sure that Maria will take you in, if you can prove you're trustworthy'

'I can,' I promised. 'I can do it, I know I can.'

'And I believe you,' Maruja said. 'But that's not enough. I have to see it for myself, so I have had an idea. I'm going to take you to my good friend in San Luis. I trust her judgement, and I know she could use some help around the house at the moment – not to mention money – so I'm sure she'll agree to take you in for two weeks.' Maruja smiled. 'And that way everyone will be happy. You will be out of the way of the Santoses, my friend will get some much-needed help, and Maria will have a chance to see the proof of what I've told her. If my friend reports back favourably about you, then we will make arrangements to get you to Bogotá.'

*

San Luis is a tiny village hidden in the valley between two mountains, and at that time many poor people lived there. There was little prosperity or education, and little in the way of luxuries; teenage pregnancy and homelessness were both rife. Maruja's friend, who I think was called Isabel, lived there with her husband and three young children.

After an hour in a taxi, we eventually arrived. By now I was feeling nervous about meeting Isabel and her family. I felt sure I could do as I was told and behave well, but once again I was to be left on the doorstep of strangers and would have to adapt to a new set of rules.

Maruja, too, seemed nervous as we climbed out of the taxi,

checking I looked presentable, even if it was in my tatty convent dress, and wiping imaginary marks from my cheeks. I let her. This was perhaps my last hope to make a better life. If I failed this test, I knew I would be back on the streets.

Once the door was opened, I could see that they were close. Isabel's face broke into a wide smile of greeting, which only faded when she noticed how tense her friend was.

'Maruja,' she said, 'this is such a wonderful surprise. But why are you here? And why do you look so worried?'

She glanced at me now, as Maruja explained why we'd come. 'This is Rosalba,' she said. 'And she is in trouble with the Santoses.'

Isabel's eyes narrowed. 'Oh, to be in trouble with that family. Oh, dear. Oh, yes, I understand. But what can I do?'

'I need to get her away from Cúcuta,' Maruja told her. 'And I was wondering if she could stay here with you for a couple of weeks. I'd pay you, of course,' she quickly added. 'And also cover all her living costs as well.'

Isabel nodded. 'Well, I could certainly do with the money,' she admitted, smiling at me. 'But what will you do with her after that?'

Maruja explained her plan to send me to stay with Maria. 'But only on condition that you are satisfied she can behave herself. A sort of trial. Would you consider that?'

It seemed she would. I had crossed another threshold.

*

It wasn't the easiest two weeks. Isabel's family, like most of their neighbours, were extremely poor. Their house was falling apart and had no proper roof. It was single storey again – because of the ever-present risk of earthquakes – with a soil floor and a hole in the garden for a toilet. Inside it were just two rooms and a small kitchen, with a one-ring kerosene cooker. There was no running water, so Isabel's husband would have to fetch some from the nearby river, and little food. The family lived mostly on oats. Meat was sparse here, so what little I did see in that fortnight was in the form of bones with a few scraps of meat attached to them, normally sitting in bowls of thin soup.

But they were inventive. Sometimes the oats took the form

of porridge, other times they were used in a casserole, mixed with coriander leaves. There was also cabbage from the garden, and other green plants, and though the portions were meagre I couldn't have been happier. It was tasty and mealtimes were sociable, for this was a family – the first family I'd ever felt part of since I'd left my monkey troop in the jungle.

I didn't steal. The family had very few possessions anyway, but while the street kid was still in me, any possession was valuable, so that wasn't why I resisted. It was Maruja's voice, which I heard constantly in my mind, reminding me how I must be grateful for this opportunity that would decide my whole future.

I worked hard as well – something I was now good at and used to. I would cook the porridge, make the beds, clean the house and do the washing, and as the days passed I could tell that Isabel was pleased with me, which only served to encourage me more. At one point I was so grateful I even entertained the idea of getting them some meat. To steal some food for them would have been the easiest thing in the world for a teenage ragamuffin street kid like me. But it was my gratitude that stopped me from doing it. It would help them but at the same time harm some other poor person. This was the difference, I knew, between being good and being bad. And I desperately, desperately wanted to be good. So good that no one would look at me again and think I was just a bad kid from the gutter.

I had obviously not spoken to Maruja during my stay, but she was constantly on my mind, because she'd made it clear that my fate would be decided when she came to get me. Depending on what Isabel told her when she came back, she would either accompany me in a taxi to the airport, to board a plane to Bogotá, or – if the report was in any way negative – just give me some spare change to take back to the streets.

I found out later that she would never have done that, but I'm glad she lied, as it truly focused my mind. On the day she was due to return, I was so excited to see her that when she walked in I hugged her so hard that I nearly knocked her down. She didn't speak either. Instead, once I let go of her, she produced a ticket. A ticket to fly in a plane that would take me to Bogotá.

Still, today, I am awed by her generosity and kindness. She

wasn't a wealthy woman, far from it. She struggled financially and yet she did this thing for me. I will never be able to express quite how much that means to me.

But Maruja didn't have just a ticket for me that day. 'You have passed the test, Rosalba,' she told me. 'I'm so proud of you. And, to celebrate, I've bought you a present. Something special. Here,' she said, passing me a slim cardboard box.

I couldn't speak for a moment, I was so overwhelmed. I had achieved something for the first time in my life. I had actually achieved something good. So good that Maruja was proud enough of me to bring me a gift. Something I had earned. Something I hadn't stolen. I couldn't begin to explain how much those words alone meant to me – just hearing them was the best present ever – but she'd also brought a box, which was tied with a yellow ribbon. An actual present. The first I could remember receiving in my life. It was such a wonderful feeling that I wanted to savour it – having a treasure that I didn't have to steal from anywhere else. No guilt. Just given to me for free.

Isabel laughed. 'Go on, then,' she coaxed. 'Don't you want to open it?'

I nodded and put the box down. I did.

And if I'd been excited at being given a present of any kind, there were simply no words to describe my amazement at the beautiful thing I now saw before me. It was a dress made of pale-blue satin, with a big yellow bow at the front made from the same ribbon as had tied the box, and it felt like the most beautiful thing I'd ever seen. I'd seen pretty dresses, of course. Consuela and Estella had had several. But to see a dress of such beauty and know it was mine was a feeling I'll never forget.

'Come on, then,' urged Maruja. 'Let's see you wearing it. There's a clip for your hair, too, and some special white socks. Come on, I'll help you. I do hope it fits.'

And of course it did. It fitted perfectly, because Maruja had made it especially for me. She brushed out my hair and placed the clip – a little white bow – in my fringe. She had also bought a pair of white shiny shoes – my first ever – but only once I was dressed did she declare herself happy. 'You look beautiful, Rosalba,' she said.

And I did. I couldn't believe it. I had never felt so beautiful. I couldn't stop looking in the mirror, unable to quite believe the dainty, feminine girl I saw in front of me was actually me. But it wasn't just the dress that overwhelmed me; it was the love that had been stitched into it. The feeling that I was part of a family. I loved Maruja, I decided, more than I loved myself.

'Come on,' she chuckled, waving the plane ticket at me. 'Time to drag yourself away from that mirror, Rosalba. We're in a hurry. You have somewhere to be.'

30

'So now,' Maruja said, as we sped along in the taxi, 'we must be serious, Rosalba. You are still in great danger from the Santos mafia. You are still on their list. Do not look at anyone. Keep your eyes down. Don't be distracted by what's around you. They could have people at the airport. We don't know. So you must be on your guard at all times.'

I was trying hard to concentrate, but it was difficult. Everything seemed too unreal. Maruja had tried to explain what it would be like to travel on an aeroplane – 'not like a bus, or like a taxi, because it flies up in the air, like a bird does' – and it was hard to think of anything else. I couldn't stop trying to imagine it. About how it would feel to be so high up in the sky. Up with the birds, soaring through the air. I kept thinking back to my days in the jungle, when I would sit up in the canopy with the ground so far below. But on an aeroplane there would be nothing below me. It was scary and exciting all at once.

'Rosalba!' Maruja said, slightly more sharply. 'You are a witness. That's what you need to remember. You know things about the family . . .'

'But I don't know. Not really. I only know . . .'

'It doesn't matter. All that matters is what they think. And what they think is that you ran away knowing lots of their secrets. So they can't take the risk of letting you live. They never will. If they get the chance . . .' Maruja mimed a hand crossing her throat. 'Rosalba, I need to know you understand, because I won't be there to help you.'

'I understand,' I tried to reassure her. 'I understand.'

It was only when we'd actually arrived at the airport that I realised just how frightened Maruja really was. It would be years before I had any real sense of how readily the Santos family might have had me killed – just in case – but Maruja's fear now became infectious, transmitting itself to me through her trembling fingers as she straightened my hair clip and smoothed down my curls.

Camilo Daza Airport, looking back, was probably very small then, but to me, that day, it looked enormous. Everything seemed so big – the ranks of chairs, the swinging doors, the giant desks and counters. I felt dwarfed by it and also intimidated. It seemed so new and so grand, and so unlike anywhere I'd ever been.

'Now, here is a photograph,' Maruja told me, as we made our way to the sign that said 'Salidas'. 'This is Maria. She'll be waiting. She knows when to expect you and will be looking out for you. But this is so you can recognise her and don't end up going with the wrong person.'

It was a new thing to worry about. There seemed so much to worry about. And perhaps Maruja realised she had frightened me too much now. She leaned down. 'You can do this, Rosalba,' she told me firmly. 'You're tough, you're a survivor, you're smart and I believe in you.'

Hearing Maruja's words were like a shot of pure energy. I could almost feel myself growing taller and stronger and braver as she spoke. And she was right. I could do this. I was ready.

*

In those days you needed little in the way of documentation to fly anywhere internally. No passport, no identity papers, no birth certificate, nothing. Which was just as well, because I didn't own anything that proved I was alive.

No sooner had Maruja taken me up to the desk to get my ticket checked than I was heading through to the other side of the airport – the side she couldn't enter.

'Be careful,' she kept whispering to me. 'Be careful. Look at no one.' Her nervousness had completely transmitted itself to me now, and were it not for the fact that it was Maruja telling me to do this, I think I might have just turned around and run when she told me she had to leave me on my own. I had only the small case she had packed for me, my ticket and the little photo of the woman Maruja had told me was her daughter.

I studied the black-and-white photograph. The lady looked nice, with pale hair and pale eyes. Blue, I decided. They would probably be blue, like my dress.

I had been unable to find words that could ever match up to how I was feeling when I left Maruja. I could say thank you, and I had, but it felt too inadequate. I wanted to say so much, to tell her how grateful I was to her for giving me a chance, for trusting me, for believing I could make something of myself. But I couldn't. I could only tell her with my eyes and by my actions. I would show her my gratitude by making her and her family proud.

I tried very hard not to look back, because she had expressly told me not to. Keep your head down, look straight ahead, don't wave, don't draw attention to yourself. I was still staring straight ahead when I boarded the plane.

It was only then that I risked a quick backward glance, but I couldn't see her. There were just too many people, all milling around. And, given her anxiety about us being seen, perhaps she'd hurried away anyway. Now would I be safe from harm? I hoped so. I certainly couldn't imagine any mafia boarding the plane and felt myself relax a little bit. If they were going to get me, then surely they would have got me by now, wouldn't they?

Even so, as I was shown to my seat by the window, I couldn't help but try to scan the airport for her face, and when I couldn't see it, my heart sank. Now I really was on my own. As yet, anyway – there was still the question of the empty seat beside me. Who would fill it? Perhaps one of the mafia might come and get on the plane after all.

The cabin gradually filled and was soon bustling with people, and as each new person passed and my seat remained empty, I began to think – and to hope – that it would remain so. But then I saw a man – quite a young man – begin to approach. He was clutching a ticket stub, and as I watched him he seemed to count in his head and then fix his gaze on my row. I watched him carefully, as carefully as I used to observe things in the jungle. He was a tall man, fit-looking, and as he got nearer I began to focus. How would I escape if he turned out to have been sent by the Santoses? Where were the exits? How would I defend myself if he attacked?

Looking back, it sounds so foolish, but at the time I was deadly serious. Maruja's fear had got to me. My hands were clammy, and, as he finally took the seat beside me, I kept my face directed outward, towards the window.

The take-off itself transfixed me completely. I gripped the armrests of my seat as tightly as I had ever grabbed a tree trunk I was climbing, because it seemed a physical impossibility that something as heavy as an aeroplane could ever find the power to glide straight up into the sky. I could see how it was possible for birds: birds weighed almost nothing. But the weight of the plane and all its passengers was almost too scary a thing to contemplate. Yet here we were, up in the sky, the city of Cúcuta growing ever tinier beneath us, and finally I was able to unclasp my hands from the armrests and risk a glance towards my silent fellow passenger. He had a bible in his lap, but that meant nothing in Colombia. He could have half a dozen bibles in his lap and it would tell me nothing useful. Mr Santos had a bible. Everyone did. But even so, just seeing it there made me feel better.

He must have seen me looking at it. Must have been aware of my furtive glances, as he said, 'Hello.'

I mumbled some sort of response. He picked up the bible then. It was covered in blue leather and all the pages were edged with gold. The man smiled. 'I'm a priest,' he said, by way of explanation.

They were the very best words I could have heard.

We didn't speak again, the priest and me, for the rest of the two-hour flight. He read his bible and I spent the time staring out of the window, sipping the glass of juice the air hostess had given me and, once I'd calmed down enough to believe we wouldn't fall from the sky until we wanted to, marvelling at the rainforest carpet below me. The clouds, too – I couldn't believe how different they looked from our vantage point up here in the sky. But just before we landed, growing aware of the task ahead of me, I plucked up the courage to speak to him again.

'I have to meet this lady,' I explained to him, showing him Maria's picture. 'But I don't know where to go to find her. Can you show me?'

'Of course,' he reassured me. And though he was in a hurry to be somewhere, he got off the plane with me and led me to an important-looking lady in a suit, who promised she would make sure I found the person in the photograph. I sometimes think of that priest today and wonder where he is and what he's doing, and whether he might find it amusing to know that when I first saw him I thought he could be a mafia contract killer.

Bogotá airport seemed enormous; it was like an ocean of humanity. Everyone seemed to hurry here, not just the young priest, and I became more aware than ever of just how small and insignificant I really was. Without the help of the lady, who I think was some sort of airport security official, I could have got lost in an instant – I could have been swallowed up and no one would ever know or care. Except I realised that was no longer true. Someone would care. Maruja would. It was a wonderful feeling.

In the end, it didn't take long to find Maria. 'Is that her?' asked the lady, glancing at another woman in the distance, then back at the photo she now held for me.

I couldn't answer. I didn't know. But she looked like she might be. And then she waved, which answered the question. We had found her.

Maria wore three things on the day I first met her: a smart suit (she was so elegant, just like the lady who had brought me to her), a wide smile that immediately reminded me of Maruja, and something else – an impish-looking blond boy, who was wrapped around her leg. 'This is Edgar,' she told me. 'He's four, aren't you, Edgar? Don't be shy. Say hello to Rosalba.'

Edgar wouldn't. He was shy. And I didn't really blame him. I felt shy too, in my pretty dress, walking with this fine lady, a million miles from the street kid I never wanted to be again. 'Come on,' she said. 'Let's get you home to meet the family, shall we?'

I had to pinch myself to believe this was really happening. I felt such awe and respect for Maria. I still do. It was an incredible thing she and her husband Amadeo had done by taking in a stranger, a young girl with a less than commendable background, and accepting her into their lives so unselfishly. How many people would do that? They were very special, I decided.

On the way home, Maria told me a little more about her family. Amadeo was the manager of a hotel, and they had five children altogether, of whom little Edgar was the third. And though they weren't poor, there was not a lot of money to go round, as much of what they had went on paying for the children's education, which was apparently very expensive.

Maria also told me lots about her children – what they liked and what they didn't – and that though she couldn't afford to send me to school, she would do her best to teach me numbers and letters herself. To read and write! I couldn't wait to get started. She also told me I'd be sharing a room with Nancy, who, at seven or eight, was the closest to my age. Well, what passed for my age, anyway; I was still not entirely sure of it. I looked about nine, I was so tiny, but I knew that I couldn't be. So I'd been happy, at Maruja's suggestion, given everything we knew, to suppose I was now somewhere around thirteen or fourteen.

*

I settled in with the Forero family very quickly, the first few days passing in a blur of new experiences. But much as I relished my new life and family, the past kept on coming back to haunt me.

I began having terrible nightmares. Every time I closed my eyes I was transported back into the Santos house, being beaten, whipped and abused. It got so bad that I was too terrified to close my eyes and go to sleep, and when I did sleep, Nancy told me she could hear me crying and whimpering. Concerned for me, she told Maria.

'You know what?' Maria said to me one morning, a few days later. 'I've been thinking, and there's something that it seems to me might help you.'

'What?' I asked, wondering if she might give me some medicine.

'Your name,' she said. 'Who gave it to you?'

'Mr Santos,' I told her.

'And before that?'

'Before that I was known as Pony Malta.'

'The name of a drink! What a thing!' She laughed. 'And before that?'

'Before that, I was given the name Gloria.'

'And who named you that?' Maria wanted to know.

'A lady.' I frowned. 'She was horrible to me.' I didn't want to tell her anything about Ana-Karmen and the brothel. Now I knew what it had been, I was so ashamed of having lived there.

'You poor thing,' she said. 'What a life you have led. And before that?'

I shook my head. I didn't have an answer for that one. I shrugged. 'I didn't have a name,' I said.

Maria nodded. 'Uh-huh,' she said. 'Perhaps this is the problem. The only names you've ever known have been slave names.' She smiled again now, and it was the smile of a woman who had a plan. I knew that kind of smile. I'd often find myself wearing it. I liked plans. And Maria's was unquestionably a good one. 'What you need, my dear,' she said, 'is to have a name all of your own. A name that you've chosen for yourself.'

So it was that I thought about what might most suit me and after a few days finally decided on one that felt right. Maria then spoke to the priest, who baptised me as part of their family, and I came out of the church that day, aged fourteen or thereabouts, with my own name, Luz Marina, which translates as 'light' and 'sea'.

I loved that 'Luz'; loved the concept of finding the light after so many years in the darkness. But the choice of Marina was an interesting one. Would I have chosen it if I'd known that it referred to water? Perhaps not. But what I do know is that I chose it because I just loved the sound of it. It was a name that for some reason felt connected to me. I still wonder whether it came from a comforting past. Had it perhaps been my mother's name? My own?

I don't know. All I know is that I walked out of that church feeling like a human being, like an individual – no longer like an animal. *This is me. This is my identity. I belong to a family*, I remember thinking. *My name is Luz Marina, and I am not an orphan.*

With that knowledge came a sense that I was now a new person. And, more importantly, a someone – a free human being. I couldn't wait to start the rest of my life.

A note by Lynne Barrett-Lee

I first met Marina in the summer of 2011. Together with her daughter Vanessa, she had travelled down from Bradford to my agent's offices in London so that we could meet and decide if we 'fitted'.

For me, as a ghostwriter, that 'fit' is crucial. And I trust my instincts. If I don't click with the person I've been asked to work with, I know there is no point in moving forward. And I don't doubt the same applies in reverse. It's such an intense relationship, after all – such an intimate, frank and close one – that if trust isn't present, it cannot work.

And here was a poser. Of the many books I have been asked to consider ghosting, this one was singular – the story of a woman who'd been raised, in part, by monkeys. Or so they said. Did I believe it? I wasn't sure. I had read some of the material – there was a great deal of material – as well as glanced through two previous incarnations of the outline, both trying a different approach to make this vast and sprawling story work.

But the one thing that would clinch it was that face-to-face meeting, and, in the event, it was only the work of a few seconds for me to both trust in the truth of Marina's incredible story and to feel that magic – and non-negotiable – sense of 'fit'. Marina is very much the living embodiment of the little girl you have read about in this book. Now a petite Bradford housewife and indefatigable supergran, she still retains such an aura of mischief and wildness that it takes no leap of faith to marry up the two. Her beautiful daughter, Vanessa (the younger of her two children), has clearly inherited her mother's verve and lust for life. And since it was with Vanessa with whom I knew I would mostly be working (given her childhood,

Marina's written English is obviously shaky), it was delightful that we clicked in an instant.

Even so, having signed on the proverbial dotted line, I read the entire manuscript with a growing sense of anxiety, so much so that I almost pulled out. It's a huge, unwieldy story, and this was a huge, unwieldy document. No matter that it intrigued, appalled and excited me in equal measure, no matter that it was packed full of drama and pathos, it was still as wild a child as the subject at its heart. Painstakingly created by Vanessa, over several years of intense mother-and-daughter interviews, it was a labour of love, clearly, but what was also clear was that there was so much more to relate than could realistically be contained within a single, linear narrative. It was like the vastness of the rainforest, teeming with light and life and colour, and my job – once I fixed on the solution to the problem – was to weave a coherent path through it.

So my first task was to chop it in half. Brutal though that seemed, it felt an obvious solution: to focus more tightly on Marina's childhood journey, from the day she lost her home and loved ones – but most of all, her identity – to the day, at the age of fourteen or thereabouts, when she was once again a girl with a name.

After that – having consigned everything else to a box marked 'for the sequel' – the beast felt much easier to tame. And once I'd spoken to myself sternly about using so many wanton jungle metaphors, I decided on an approach that would take us back to the simplicity of how a small child relates to the world. Memories are tricky. As soon as you've made them, you instinctively tend to analyse them, overlay them with interpretation based on future knowledge, so it's all too easy, when describing events and images of early childhood, to do so with the benefit of hindsight. Where an adult might compare a particular shade of blue to a tanzanite, say, or sapphire, or the shallows of a tropical ocean, a tiny child – assuming they didn't live down a mine or on a Caribbean island, obviously – would have no such point of comparison, so the language had to be simple and unadorned by art for art's sake.

It was also important to establish such facts as were known. I needed no convincing, of course, but, for the reader to accept the veracity of the story, it was essential that the detail was correct. But how was this achievable, given that tiny Marina had no frame of reference? No convenient teacher bearing flashcards and new vocabulary? Here, too, Vanessa had done a brilliant job, spending many hours with Marina, homing in on specific memories, whittling down possibilities from many, many images, then cross-checking against known indigenous species. That the monkeys were probably weeper capuchins, that she ate guava and curuba, that the trees shed brazil nuts and lulo fruit and figs – all these facts are the result of painstaking research by Vanessa to give names to the images in Marina's memory.

But the biggest job Vanessa did was also the best one. To commit to paper, in a form that was instantly beguiling, what was for Marina no more than her stock of bedtime stories – the minutiae of a life that she'd thought was unremarkable to anyone save the family she'd finally created for herself.

How wrong she was. And what a privilege it's been for me to collaborate in turning such an incredible true story into what we sincerely hope is a riveting and moving book. I can't wait to get started on the next one . . .

Lynne Barrett-Lee

Organisations of interest

Below are details of two charities that do vital work both in primate conservation and for abandoned children everywhere. If Marina's story has moved you and you would like to know about what they do, we know they would be grateful to hear from you.

Substitute Families for Abandoned Children (SFAC)

Imagine you know a young girl who roams the streets with nobody to protect and care for her, or an eighteen year old now too old to stay in an orphanage and cast out to fend for themselves. Now think what trouble they could get into as prey for rapists, traffickers and drug-pushers. Now imagine that you could provide them with security, care and love. Well, maybe you can't do that – after all, it's a huge commitment – but you could help people that would.

Substitute Families for Abandoned Children hope for 'family-based care' over 'institutional care' for these children. Eighty per cent of orphaned or abandoned children have at least one parent alive or have extended family. In order to maintain the child's sense of 'roots', SFAC's first wish is to see children rehabilitated back into their families where possible and appropriate. Where that isn't an option, they are placed with responsible local 'substitute' families, trained and supported by SFAC through every step.

Thanks to a sympathetic neighbour, Marina found herself in a new family when she had none. As a result, her life was transformed and she became the woman you have read about. She may not have been alive today to tell her story had she not found a substitute family.

Please contact SFAC and you too could rescue girls like Marina all around the world. www.sfac.org.uk/

Neotropical Primate Conservation (NPC)

In far too many places around the world, our nearest biological relatives, the apes and monkeys, are suffering, losing their homes and their lives as a result of deforestation and wildlife trafficking.

In Colombia, as well as all Central and South America, NPC strives to protect monkeys and conserve their homes. In protecting the jungles and forests, the habitats are maintained not just for monkeys but also for the indigenous peoples, so that they too can maintain their traditional and cultural ways of life.

The battle against illegal wildlife traffic has become one of NPC's main activities. Wild animals are routinely hunted for meat or skins, as trophies or for the pet trade – a major threat to the survival of many species. With the help of rescue centres and the police, NPC are able to rescue, rehabilitate and reintroduce these trafficked animals back to their forests – the homes that Marina knew so well.

Please learn how you can be a part of their wonderful work at www.neoprimate.org

Thank you.